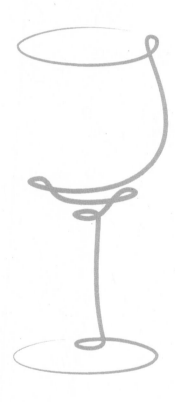

GOODGROG

A Life in Wine & Journalism

JOHN SCHREINER

 FriesenPress

One Printers Way
Altona, MB R0G 0B0
Canada

www.friesenpress.com

ISBN
978-1-03-916053-8 (Hardcover)
978-1-03-916052-1 (Paperback)
978-1-03-916054-5 (eBook)

1. BIOGRAPHY & AUTOBIOGRAPHY, EDITORS, JOURNALISTS, PUBLISHERS

Distributed to the trade by The Ingram Book Company

Dedication

This book is dedicated to my grandchildren: Adam and Sylvie Romanick; James, Rob, and Joey Cameron; and Alexandra, Michael, and Eva Schreiner.

Table of Contents

Why this book was written

During my sixty-five years as a journalist and wine writer (I was born in 1936), I recorded thousands of interviews. Inexplicably, I never once recorded interviews with my mother or my father or any other relatives. Only occasionally, I made notes of conversations with them in my diaries. Now, I wish I had shown as much curiosity about my family's history as I did about the many other people I wrote about. The intent of this book is to leave a more substantial record of my life for my family and for any friends who might be interested. Perhaps it will encourage them to do the same.

Most of us do not appreciate the historical significance of our actions and deeds. Most of us are fortunate to live ordinary lives. I would include myself in that group. I enjoy reading biographies—but they need not always be of Winston Churchill. Many of the biographies deal with comparatively obscure figures whose lives add detail and colour to the period in which they lived.

Often, these books are done only because the authors kept diaries and saved other documents during their lives. I lament the apparent decline in the practice of keeping diaries. This book was possible only because I began keeping a diary in 1956 and because I have scrapbooks of my clippings beginning in 1971.

The historical importance of diaries, however modest, came home to me when I was researching *The Refiners*, my history of BC Sugar Refinery Ltd. The company had an excellent and well-organized archive but, during one interview while researching the book, I stumbled across a diary of which neither I nor the company were aware. I had made an appointment to interview Beatrice Wood in her West End apartment in Vancouver. She was the daughter of J.W. Fordham Johnson, the executive who had been sent in 1905 to manage a sugar plantation in Fiji that the company had just purchased. He was not on site very long before becoming severely ill with some tropical disease. Over a few cups of tea, Beatrice Wood filled in some details of the family's Fiji experience. I was just packing away my notebook and my tape recorder when she asked: "Would you like to see my mother's diary?" And she let me borrow it.

It turned out to be surprisingly powerful. Helen, her mother, was in the habit of jotting a few notes almost every day. But there was a period of several months when she made no entries in the diary because she was at the bedside of her husband while he was being treated for amoebic dysentery, which affected his liver and required surgery. The diary's poignant silence told me how desperately ill Fordham Johnson was. (After his recovery, he ran the company in Vancouver for several years in the 1930s and then was appointed Lieutenant Governor of British Columbia.) The diary was not in the collection in the BC Sugar archive because there had been a falling out between the family of Fordham Johnson and that of the Rogers family who owned the sugar company.

Writing this memoir allowed me to reflect on how fortunate I was to be involved in journalism and also the wine industry at a time when both were flourishing. The *Financial Post* sent me on numerous international assignments in the 1960s and 1970s because the newspaper had strong advertising support for the supplements we published. The rise of the internet has long since deprived the print media of the revenues that once supported it. I also did a great deal of freelance writing for magazines and community newspapers, most of which ceased publishing when they were deserted by advertisers. When I was asked a few years ago whether I would recommend a career in journalism, I hesitated a long time before giving a qualified yes.

The wine industry trajectory has been quite different. In the 1950s, Canadian consumers, including me, had little knowledge and often little interest in wine. Fortunately, postwar migrants from Europe brought their wine palates and their expertise with them. Paul Bosc, the founder of Chateau Des Charmes Estate Winery near Niagara Falls, is a vivid example. A French winemaker from Algeria, he arrived in Canada in 1963, working initially for the Quebec liquor board. He discovered quickly how mediocre Canadian wines were when he was given a bottle of domestic sparkling rosé for Christmas dinner. He found the foxy labrusca flavours unpalatable. He set out to do something about the state of Canadian wine, working first with a Niagara winery and then, in 1978, founding his own winery. I interviewed him in detail when I was writing my first wine book in 1983, and I have tasted continually improving wines from Chateau des Charmes and its peers ever since. The quality evolution of Canadian wines has made it an exciting industry to write about, and one that people want to read about today. That is why I have been able to write twenty wine books.

This memoir recounts my parallel careers in business journalism and wine writing. To paraphrase Charles Dickens, it was the best of times.

One:
Growing up poor
but not knowing it

I began keeping a diary in 1956 because it seemed to me what an aspiring writer should so. I have kept a diary ever since. Even if the entries sometimes were monthly rather than daily, it provided the foundation for this memoir. Unfortunately, my ancestors were too engaged in farming to keep diaries. The limited amount of family history I know came from quizzing my parents on occasion and noting the answers in my diary. Conversations with my younger brother, Joe, added more detail, as did a community history published in Indian Head, my home town. Later in my career as a business journalist and wine writer, I recorded hundreds of interviews with the subjects of my writing. I regret that I never taped interviews with my parents.

Stefan Schreiner, my grandfather, was born in 1867 in Bukowina, a province in the Austro-Hungarian Empire from 1775 to 1918, which later became part of Hungary and today is in Romania. He was part of the flood of Central European migrants settling in the Canadian Prairies around the turn of the twentieth century, likely attracted by the Canadian Pacific Railroad's recruitment efforts in Europe. The province of Bukowina generated many German-speaking immigrants to Southern Saskatchewan even before the Great War. The Germans originally came to Bukowina in the late eighteen century, responding to an appeal of the Austrian-Hungarian Empire, which wanted a Roman

Catholic and German-speaking population in this part of the empire. They succeeded in agriculture. According to a history of Edenwold (a German-speaking enclave in Saskatchewan, along with Odessa and Vibank), published in 1981: "The German farmer in Bukowina was an industrious, self-confident and peace-loving individual, helpful and tolerant of his fellow countrymen. He was tirelessly striving for better management and continuously improving existing farm methods. ... The main reason that many of the Germans left Bukowina was the scarcity of available new land. The government was not selling crown land, and the Romanians were hanging onto theirs."[1]

Stefan settled his family in Indian Head, a prosperous town that had sprung up in 1882 on the mainline of the CPR forty-five miles (seventy-two kilometres) east of Regina. A community history of Indian Head, published in 1984, implies that Stefan left Bukowina to avoid being drafted into the army at age twenty-one.[2] The exact date of his arrival is not documented. The family history in the Indian Head book says: "Stefan worked in Indian Head as a gardener and his mother did washing." There is an independent record of S. Schreiner being a member of the work crew that laid the water line in 1904 from the water source southwest of town to Indian Head. I never heard anything about my great-grandmother coming to Indian Head and taking in washing. I wonder whether that was meant to be a reference to Stefan's wife, Elisabeth, and an error slipped through the somewhat casual editing process for this 800-page volume. Stefan's family included two children, Michael and Katie, who were born back in Bukowina. The other sons were born in Indian Head: John in 1903 and Adam, my father, in 1909.

1   *Where Aspens Whisper: Edenwold Remembers* by Edenwold Anniversary Committee, 1981.

2   *Indian Head: History of Indian Head and District*, Brigdens Photo Graphics Ltd., Regina, 1984; edited by L.O.T. Peterson.

Nine months after Adam's birth, his parents took their family back to Bukowina in Austria-Hungary. They returned to Canada in 1912.[3] As a result, my father was educated in Indian Head, where he completed grade eight before dropping out to pursue his vocation of farming.

"They made many trips back and forth to the old country, returning there from 1909 to 1912 and again from 1924 to 1928," the Indian Head history recounts.[4] According to my mother, Stefan took his three sons back to Europe in 1924 to find wives for them. Michael, the eldest son who had been born there in 1900, was promptly jailed for not having registered for military service. My father subsequently told me that, since the family had recently lived in a British Dominion, Stefan threatened to complain to the British consul. Michael was released when he agreed to serve two years in the Romanian army. Then he married and settled there when his wife, who did not get along with her mother-in-law, refused to move to Canada with the rest of the family a few years later. I remember my father telling me in 1974, after he and my mother visited Romania, that Michael and his only son, Steve, were sent by the German army to work in Russian labour camps during World War II. Steve died there of pneumonia and was buried in a coffin that Michael built. The German government paid Michael and his wife a small pension after the war.

After John, the middle brother, also served two years in the Romanian army, Stefan brought the rest of his family back to Canada in 1927 so that my father could avoid being drafted. During his time there, my father learned the blacksmith's trade. I don't believe he pursued that commercially, but he had a forge on his farm later, using it for fashioning horse shoes, among other minor tasks. As he came of age in Romania, his moustache also grew. The village barber refused to shave

---

3   I have a copy of the relevant passenger manifest from the SS *Amerika*, which sailed from the port of Cuxhaven in northwestern Germany, arriving in New York on July 7, 1912. According to this, Stefan was 44 and Elisabeth, his wife, was 38. They had their four children with them: Kate, 18; Mihaly, 11; John, 8; Adam, 3. The SS *Amerika* was a two-year-old Hamburg-America line vessel that, at the time, was one of the largest and finest ocean liners in service. It was a sister ship to the *Titanic* which sank in April 1912.

4   Ibid, page 665.

the young man because moustaches were considered manly. My father was teased when he returned to Canada by a woman who suggested he shave it. Being famously stubborn, he simply refused and kept a moustache his entire life. (When I was at the University of Toronto in the summer of 1959, I also grew a moustache, but with less success. "I must admit it looks silly," I wrote to my then girlfriend Marlene, including a photograph of myself. Marlene replied on August 9: "Really it's not too bad, but I won't especially demand to see it. ...It's your moustache, and if you feel like keeping it, I doubt if I would shave it off for you... I haven't decided yet if it does anything for you or not. Actually you are a very handsome man *really.*" I shaved what I called "this strip of fuzz" before returning to Regina.)

My father told me that his family returned to Canada because they had become "fed up" with the old country. His parents and Uncle John (who may have been married by then) travelled on ahead. My father followed, taking a ship that docked in New York. According to my brother, my father and a friend travelling with him became friendly with two young women on their way to South America. (A significant German-speaking colony was developing in Brazil). My father's travelling companion proposed continuing on to South America with them. Happily for me, Adam Schreiner returned to Indian Head.

The second trip to Romania almost cost my father the right to vote. In 1939, he had turned down the opportunity to get Canadian citizenship papers because it would cost $5. When told he would not be allowed to vote, he wrote to Ottawa to inquire about his status. Ottawa assured him that, since he had been born in Canada, he was a British subject. Not long after World War II began, two Mounties came to inquire about my father's status. When he produced the letter from Ottawa, one of the police—as my father recalled later—said: "We have no business here." But when an election was called in 1940, the poll clerk tried to stop him. My father simply sat on the clerk's table, preventing anyone else from voting, until the clerk allowed him swear on the Bible that he was a citizen of Canada.

Karl Kattler, my mother's father was born in 1878 and came to Canada in March 1912 from the community of Satulmare in Bukowina.

His family was to follow shortly. "The family was to come over on the ship, *Titanic*," Alverta Laskey, one of my cousins, recounted in a 1994 history for the Kattler family reunion. "They were delayed because one of the daughters, Wilhelmina, came down with the flu and died from it in Bukowina."[5] Karl's wife and the remaining six children followed in 1920. The six, all born in Bukowina, were Herman, Karl, Jacob, Ernest, Gertrude, and Caroline (Lena), my mother. They had another son, Henry, who was born in Canada. My mother, Caroline, was born on November 10, 1912.

According to Jack Kattler, my mother's brother Karl had been a horse trader for a wealthy Austrian farmer. Karl rented a farm near the Saskatchewan village of Odessa and planned to bring his family to Canada. However, the Great War broke out in 1914. His wife, Wilhelmina (né Albus), and her children, did not have a pleasant time during the war. In one of my diaries, I recorded what Jack Kattler had told me. "Food was scarce, but the family had a cow. A neighbour with a herd had hidden some cows and given others to neighbours to guard them from confiscation. My grandmother's cow escaped the Russian mess tins because the children in the family hung on to the cow and cried when the soldiers came to take the animal. The commandant told his men he had children like that at home and would not want to leave them hungry."

I remember Ernest, my mother's brother, who had such severe epilepsy that he was sent to an asylum for the mentally ill in Weyburn. He died there in 1948. I was young, but still old enough to remember his funeral—because his open casket spent a day or so in his parents' farmhouse before burial. (This apparently was a tradition carried over from the Central European community from which the Kattlers had emigrated.) Gertrude, my mother's older sister, was married to Max Seibel. They farmed near Qu'Appelle. In my diary in 1959, I recounted helping him for two days during the harvest. They had two sons and an adopted daughter, and a lot of bad luck. Jack Seibel, the oldest son, was crushed to death in a trench in 1964 while working in Regina. Marlene and I happened to be visiting Regina from Toronto and attended the funeral.

5 *The Kattler Family Reunion*, 1994. Unpublished.

Jack, my mother's brother, ended up working for the White Pass & Yukon Route railway. In the conversation I had with Jack in 1959—I had given him a ride from Indian Head to Regina—he told me that, at the age of twelve, he had ran away from home in the old country. He spent six months as a blacksmith's assistant and then, for a reason not explained in my diary, went to a priest's house for shelter. The priest, not realizing that Jack understood Romanian as well as German, told his housekeeper he was going to the police. Jack escaped by hiding in a load of lumber headed for some Black Sea port. Finally, he decided to return to his family, and just in time. Wilhelmina had been preparing to take the rest of the family to Canada.

Karl Kattler, my maternal grandfather, died in October 1955 of a heart attack after going home early from a wedding of one of his nieces or nephews. My parents and I were still at the wedding when we got the news that he had died. Wilhelmina then went to live with her two daughters—Gertrude Seibel (my mother's oldest sister) and Lena Schreiner, my mother. Wilhelmina was a sweet and pleasant woman. She died at the age of seventy-seven in November 1958. (I was one of the pallbearers at her funeral.) While her husband had a plot in St. Paul's Roman Catholic Cemetery in Vibank, she was buried in Indian Head. The reason is that she was Lutheran and, in that era, could not be buried on Catholic ground. Indian Head is a non-denominational burial ground. Karl, however, was not interred in the Vibank plot that is still registered to his name in the cemetery. It occurred to his family that Wilhelmina could not be buried with him when the time came. At my father's suggestion, Karl was buried in Indian Head. That is why he shows up in the register at two cemeteries.[6]

My mother, who died in 2004, did not start school until she was ten; her schooling in Austria was delayed by an injury that damaged her sight. Her brother Jack told me that when she was three or four years old, lime splashed into her eyes while she was watching her mother paint the walls of the house with it. According to Jack, she spent almost a year in hospital in treatment. In Canada, she had the equivalent of a

6   This is Joe Schreiner's recollection.

fourth grade education even though she was intelligent and remarkably literate. She left school to work as a domestic in Regina.

I do not know how my parents met. I would speculate it was at a dance. My father played the button accordion well enough that he frequently entertained at rural dances. My mother, a spirited personality, loved dancing. My father's mother disapproved of Lena, as my mother came to be known. Of course, that would never have stopped my stubborn father. They married in 1934.

Adam and Lena Schreiner wedding picture

Adam and Lena, who loved each other deeply, spent the first year or two of their marriage as a hired couple on the farm of Carl Pearen. My father was one of the farm hands, and my mother did domestic chores.

Employment on the Pearen farm meant they had housing, food, and $25 a month, which was rather substantial in 1935.

My parents then rented a small farm about ten miles (16 kilometres) south of Indian Head before I was born (prematurely) on February 26, 1936. Stefan's widow lived with our family for several years. She and my mother never did learn to care for each other. My mother once told me that her mother-in-law said I was conceived by another man, a nasty untruth. Apparently, I also came to dislike her. When I was about two, and my grandmother was ill in bed, my mother came in from the barn to find me heaving lumps of coal at grandmother and muttering that she was getting her own back. I have no independent memory of that. My grandmother eventually went to live with her oldest daughter and son-in-law on a farm near North Battleford. That likely was also a difficult relationship since he was a Scot, and my aunt had eloped with him against the wishes of her parents. I don't recall seeing my grandmother again until 1959 or 1960, when Marlene and I visited the family. By then, she was bedridden and senile. She died in 1966 at the age of ninety-three.

My twin sisters, Katherine Wilhelmina and Gertrude Elizabeth, were born on March 24, 1937. They were even more premature than I was. I do not know why they were sent home from the hospital; perhaps it was because the hospital then lacked an incubator. The family legend is that my mother tried to keep them warm on the door of the oven in the farmhouse kitchen. Katherine died on the afternoon of April 14, and Gertrude died late on May 1. They are buried in the Indian Head Cemetery in the grave of my paternal grandparents.

We were still on the rented farm in 1943 when I enrolled in the Interlake School, my first one-room school house. It was so named because it was located in a district of small lakes—Deep Lake (the only one I remember), Dry Lake, Raspberry Lake, Strawberry Lake, and so on. A number of my Kattler cousins were enrolled as well; I shared a double desk with one until the seat collapsed and we both banged our chins on the desk top. My older cousins helped me learn to speak English since I only spoke German when I started school. My facility with German stopped there because my parents switched at home from German to English to accelerate my learning English.

I have pleasant memories of this farm, although one Christmas, when I was seven or eight, my only gifts were two Uncle Wiggly books.[7] I finished reading both before noon and complained that there was no other gift for me. In fact, that was all that my parents could afford. We were poor, but since there was always food on the table and a roof overhead, I never quite realized how my parents must have struggled in those years as Saskatchewan emerged from the Depression. Throughout my childhood and adolescence, I never had the sense of being deprived.

I remember my father acquired the family's first battery-powered radio by bartering two pigs for it. We may still have been there when I got my first bicycle, a used two-wheeler with wheels about ten or twelve inches across. I showed my natural ability as an athlete by not learning to ride it until I was twelve and had outgrown it.

I also have a vivid recollection of the annual threshing jamborees. In those days, my father, like most farmers, owned a horse-drawn machine called a binder, because it bound the grain it cut into bundles called sheaves. These dropped from the rear of the binder as it moved around the field. Farm workers, including my mother, spent long days stacking the sheaves into small pyramids called stooks, which dried in the sun for several days before threshing. As I got into my teens, I also had to do some stooking. A capable stooker would lean the sheaves against each other, tepee style, so that none of the stooks would fall over or be blown over.

There were only a few threshing machines in any farm community; these were towed behind tractors from farm to farm, followed by a crew of farm workers and their teams of horses. Each host farm provided food for the workers, which meant morning and afternoon lunches, as well as breakfast and meals at noon and at the end of the day. My mother, likely with help from a few other farm wives, spent the entire day cooking to satisfy the voracious appetites of the workers, many of whom spent the nights sleeping in the hay barn after feeding their teams of horses. I expect my father was among the itinerant work

---

7   These were among a series of 79 children's books by an American writer, Howard Garis. The main character was an elderly rabbit who walked with a candy-stripped cane because he was lame with rheumatism.

crews, either hauling loads of sheaves to the thresher or wagon loads of threshed grain to the granaries. It was hard, dirty work with very long days. Getting the threshing done was a matter of some urgency before the weather changed and the fall rains came. Not only can wet sheaves not be threshed; they will rot. Harvesting got easier and faster only in the 1950s with the advent of the combine harvester, so called because it cut the grain in the field and threshed it immediately. My father made do with a hired combine harvester until he could buy his own machine.

Either in 1944 or 1945, my father was able to buy a larger farm about five miles (eight kilometres) west of our first farm. (My brother recalled them living briefly in a nearby house, but I do not.) My parents may have had mortgage financing from Osler, Hammond & Nanton, a Toronto firm that began handling farm mortgages soon after the Canadian Pacific was built across the Prairies. It became the biggest mortgage lender in the West, and I recall my father talking about the firm. The Depression ended with the end of drought and the wartime demand for food products, and prosperity returned to farming. My parents acquired a car, an old Chevrolet sedan. Until winter closed the roads, they made slightly more frequent trips into Indian Head to shop and do business. My brother, Joe, recounted my father, who was very attached to horses, telling how he came to own this car. A neighbouring farmer's wife had eyes for one of my father's horses, and her husband offered to trade a 1926 Chevrolet for the horse. My father, a great horse lover, initially refused but finally agreed.

The farmhouse was a basic and poorly insulated (if at all) two-storey, wood-frame building. One entered through a reasonably large porch, which afforded space for farm clothes and boots and assorted other storage. This led to a kitchen where the family did most of its living. It was heated by a wood-burning kitchen stove. Each spring, when my parents purchased newly hatched chickens, these cute and cuddly balls of yellow spent their first several weeks penned under the stove before they were big enough to be moved to the chicken barn.

The kitchen led to a large living and dining room combined. We only ate here on special occasions, such as when guests were being entertained on Sundays or around the Christmas period. When a telephone was installed—a party line that enabled everyone to listen to all other subscribers—it was mounted near the alcove in the southeast corner accessing one of the two sets of stairs to the second floor, which had three or four bedrooms. This floor was heated by the stove pipes that passed from the wood stoves below to the chimney. In winter, when it was just too cold to go to the outhouse across the yard, there was a chamber pot up there. During one Christmas season, my cousins and I were playing upstairs and someone knocked a pot over against a hot stove pipe. The nose-burning acrid odour is unforgettable. The house had no basement. For much of the summer, cool storage was provided by an ice house—a modest building over a pit which was filled every winter with ice blocks harvested from our dug-out pond. These were covered with insulating layers of straw. The ice lasted well into summer before melting. The other farm buildings were the barn, a few granaries, and a machine shed. My father had his blacksmith's forge there.

Of course, there was also an outhouse perched over a pit. It was a redolent building with two holes in the seat—God knows why, since it was unlikely that two persons would use the outhouse simultaneously. It was a common Halloween night prank that teenagers or youths would tip over outhouses. There were also accounts that some farmers deliberately moved the building off its pit so that, in the dark, pranksters would fall into the excrement. I never witnessed this nor did I get involved in tipping one. The outhouse had its own place in rural culture, the object of jokes and humorous books. In an era before toilet paper, outhouse users made do with old newspapers or mail-order catalogues. There likely was not enough light inside to read (not that anyone would spend much time in there). What light there was came from small windows high on the sides or, if the builder was artistic, from a half-moon-shaped window in the door.

For a number of years, we had a boarder, Ludwig (Louis) Wessner, a friend of the family who had also come from Satulmare, the same Austrian community my father's family had come from. (He died in 1974, aged eighty-two.[8]) He also had a car, a coupe; I caused him no

---

8   He was buried in Indian Head, as noted by the Saskatchewan Cemeteries Project on the Internet.

end of grief once, as a child, by stuffing chicken feathers into his gas tank. I would have thought that such mischief was out of character when I look at childhood photographs of me as a blue-eyed, curly-haired cherub. It is in a boy's nature, I suppose, to find out what would happen if…. This was about the same time that I discovered matches, burned my fingers lighting a fire in the yard, and hid on the roof of a building until my mother found me. There was no punishment then, but later, when I almost started a Prairie fire in a neighbour's field, my father dealt with me much more sternly. Lena's punishments seldom were fearful, but Adam meted out justice swiftly, either with a calloused hand or with the leather strap he kept for sharpening his straight razor. I was not punished often because I was not in trouble often.

My new school was Sunny South, another one-room school. It had been built in 1891 of stone, which is why the building survived about one hundred years, long after classes ceased there in 1961.[9] I began studying there in the fall of 1944, before the end of the European war. There was an RCAF recruiting poster on the wall. I got into controversy with some fellow students for drawing aircraft attacking a ship flying the Union Jack, an innocent and thoughtless action by an eight-year-old child. Indian Head was thoroughly loyal to the British Empire, having sent many men to Europe in both wars and, as the names on the cenotaph reveal, having lost many on the battle fields. The small German-speaking community kept its head down.[10]

Like most students and the teacher at Sunny South, I went to school with a horse (although occasionally I walked the two and a half miles or four kilometres). My father bought me a mare called Mabel, a rotund and generally amiable chestnut. I did not have a saddle, and because I never mastered pulling myself on her back, I always had to position the pony next to a fence or a wagon in order to climb on. Mabel, as I learned one spring day, liked to roll in shallow sloughs whether or not I was on her back. On one such occasion, she decided to roll when I was taking

---

9   *Indian Head: History of Indian Head and District,* Brigdens Photo Graphics Ltd., Regina, 1984; edited by L.O.T. Peterson, p 101.

10   Grandchildren Alexandra and Michael, who grew up in Moscow, were once called Nazis by a class bully, due to their Germanic surname, Schreiner.

a shortcut through a spring slough. The only casualty was a crushed lunch pail—the first commercial one my parents had purchased for me. I went back to taking lunch to school in a Rogers Golden Syrup pail, a ubiquitous lunch pail at the time across Western Canada. In winter, Mabel was hitched onto a caboose, a sleigh that was enclosed to protect passengers from the bitter cold. The reigns passed through a slit below the caboose's small window. All the horses spent the winter days in the school barn. In summer, they were tethered outside to graze.

There is something to be said for the one-room school house (although probably not much). The students spanned grades one through eight, with some grade-nine students taking correspondence courses. The teacher moved from one grade to another, keeping everybody working. I took forever to do mathematics, which I disliked, because it was more stimulating to listen to lessons being given to older students. I did not get into the multi-room school in Indian Head until 1949 or 1950, when my parents moved to their third and final farm two miles (3.2 kilometres) south of town.

Our circumstances improved with each move. The more fertile soils on that third farm produced better yields. The proximity to town enabled my parents to build a small dairy herd, selling milk to a new pasteurizing plant. We sold eggs, meat, and other farm produce directly to customers in town. As well, the family had steady income for many years from the gravel pit and the sand pit on either side of the farm yard. The farmhouse had been sited years earlier on the highest point of land before it was realized that an extensive esker of sand and gravel had been laid down by a retreating glacier. The income from those pits paid for many extra "luxuries" over the years, like the first freezer and the first television. These appliances were installed soon after electricity came to the farm in 1956, as part of a massive rural electrification scheme in Saskatchewan.[11] My parents lived there another twenty years before moving to town.

They retired from the farm in the 1970s to a new, but modest house, built in 1966 in Indian Head. The last year of farming was 1974.

---

11 T.C. Douglas, the premier of Saskatchewan from 1944 to 1960, was once asked what he regarded his finest achievement. "Rural electrification," he replied.

According to some Dominion Bureau of Statistics forms found in my father's files after he died, he planted 250 acres of wheat, 10 acres of oats, and 35 acres of barley in 1974. They retired comfortably enough to support a lifestyle that was not lavish. My father's 1983 tax return, for example, reported a net income of $38,854.90.

The move into town deprived my mother of the pin money she had earned for years by selling eggs and cream to residents in town. When my father's replacement pin money was not generous enough, my mother found a job at a restaurant in town. My father's pride was bent, but he had to adjust to her spirited independence.

My father's health began to decline in 1990 with what a doctor diagnosed as a mini-stroke. On a Saturday evening in March, he was to pick up my mother and her sister after their card game with friends in Indian Head. To everyone's alarm, he never showed up. He was found the following morning on a road north of town, walking away from town and toward the Qu'Appelle Valley. It was believed that he became disoriented while driving as far as the valley (about ten miles or ten kilometres) and back toward Indian Head, ending up stuck in a snowdrift north of town. After trying to shovel the car from the snow, he struck out on foot. In 1994, when my mother no longer could look after him, the family put him in the Golden Prairie care home in Indian Head. He gradually lapsed into senility and died in August 1998. I had visited him the week before, but I doubt he was aware of that.

After the funeral, I discovered that my father's will was one page long and written by hand, a type of will which, fortunately, was legal in Saskatchewan. The estate, which was modest, was left to my mother, with my brother and I to share it equally after her death.

By the time of my father's funeral, my mother also was showing signs of mental decline, such as forgetting where some of her pots and pans were. She lived alone in the house briefly before she also ended up in the Golden Prairie care home late in 1998.

Two:
Indian Head gets a history

Indian Head grain elevator

In 1955, Saskatchewan's Jubilee year, an essay competition was sponsored in our high school, with a prize of $100. I won it with a twenty-one-page history of the town of Indian Head.[12] Second prize was won by Glennys Obleman, who happened to be my girlfriend during my last year in high school. We drifted apart after I went to university. She was a very spirited woman who pursued a career in the air force.

That history essay was one of my first serious pieces of writing. I began writing not long after I learned to read. What I learned in high school soon fired the imagination to write poems and stories. My first published work was a short poem which was printed in a farm paper published by the *Winnipeg Free Press*. My father was mortified; not because it was mediocre doggerel, but because he never imagined his son doing something as effete as writing poetry.

As an aside, this was not to be the last piece of my poetry to be published. In 1960, when I was struggling for some extra money, I sold a bit of doggerel under a nom-de-plume to the *Regina Leader-Post*— the Regina daily newspaper that I joined in 1957 —and was paid one dollar. The verse was called "It's about time" for no obvious reason, and read as follows:

> The family car is the shiny result
> Of research and invention;
> A thousand draftsmen work five years
> On styling and suspension
> And build precision motors –
> But the price gets no attention.

Over the years, my father became reconciled to my choice of a career. He would have preferred that his sons both be farmers, which was his vocation. I never was interested in farming. My brother, Joe, who was born in 1944, did work on the farm briefly, but it was not his métier either.

Joe once told me of a remarkable handwritten will by my father, which had been tucked away in an old wood filing cabinet. It only came

---

12 An entertaining source of Indian Head history is this walking tour on www. townofindianhead.com/images/stories/PDF_files/heritage%20walking%20tour.pdf

to light when Joe sold the cabinet to an antique dealer, who found the document and returned it. My father had left the farm "to the boys" while my mother was to get the cash in the bank. However, if she remarried, the cash also went to the boys. Father apparently believed the new husband could provide for Mom. Fortunately, she never saw that will. My father's subsequent will was not so primitive.

After leaving the farm, Joe ran a lumber yard in a small town elsewhere in Southern Saskatchewan. When that did not work out, he returned to Indian Head and worked in a lumber yard there until leaving that to manage the McLeod's franchise in Indian Head, taking over the business in June 1995. A few years later, a shopping centre with big box stores opened east of Regina. Many of Joe's customers took their major business there, and the McLeod's store failed. Then Joe took over Shell Oil's franchise to distribute farm fuel and chemicals. His exposure to petroleum products may have led to the liver cancer that killed him in 2012.

He very nearly died in October 1995, when he had a heart attack. He was at work in the store when the attack began. He tried to ignore it, pretending it was a cold, but eventually decided to drive himself to the Indian Head hospital. There, he walked up to the reception desk, said he needed help, and then collapsed. He actually stopped breathing. After being revived, he spent several days in a Regina hospital, where a blockage in an artery was dealt with. When he recovered, he stopped smoking.

Joe's real avocation might have been either public service or the ministry. His two most active freelance jobs over several decades were as justice of the peace and marriage commissioner. He was very disappointed when, at 65, he was required to resign as a justice of the peace. The provincial government subsequently raised the retirement age, but he was not re-engaged. It became moot when he fell seriously ill with cancer in 2010.

His personal life also was unsettled. Carol Hulm, his first wife, was pregnant when they married in 1964. They finally parted in the summer of 1972. In my diary, I wrote: "She had fallen for Joe's deer-hunting friend, and Joe had fallen for the friend's sister." A few years later, Joe

remarried to Sandra Knoblauch. It was a much more stable relationship. Sandra happened to be a Lutheran; Joe converted to his grandmother's religion and, subsequently, became quite an active member of
that church.

By contrast, I had it easy: I knew I wanted to write and seized the
opportunities to do so when they came along. At Indian Head High
School, I was allowed to manage the tiny library, a task which appealed
because I could use the library's typewriter. I began working with the
annual yearbook committee in my first year, becoming the yearbook
editor in grade twelve. I also wrote fiction and poems and other text
for each yearbook. I would be embarrassed to read the fiction today,
but I don't regret strapping on the training wheels early. I even began
to do some freelance news reporting for a Saskatoon radio station. I
don't recall covering anything of consequence, supposing that anything
consequential happened in Indian Head, but it generated experience
and perhaps a few dollars.

In my final year or two at high school, I also wrote a weekly column
for the *Indian Head News* about school events. There was no compensation for that, but it allowed me to hang around the newspaper and
pick up some tips from Phil Flude, the editor and owner of the paper
from 1946 to 1968. I remember him as a classic country editor—a lean,
laconic cigarette smoker who wore an eye shade and who could set hot
metal type. The smell of hot metal and ink is a memory that still excites
my romantic imagination. Perhaps that is why I thought of becoming
a weekly newspaper editor myself a few times. At university, I worked
on the campus newspaper a few years with, among others, a student
from Meadow Lake called John Stack, whose father edited that town's
newspaper. As we got close to graduation, John mused that the two of
us should take over his father's paper. It never happened. He became a
successful Saskatoon lawyer, an art collector, and a director of the Bank
of Canada before cancer took him in his early fifties.

Unfortunately, I did not know enough to footnote my sources when
I was doing the town's history, a very grave failing for an historian. I
still have a carbon copy of the text but nothing at all to tell me where I
found all of the information. My primary source would have been the

back copies of the *Indian Head News*, supported by a few books and interviews with such individuals as Carl Pearen, one of the movers and shakers in Indian Head. In my files, I have a privately published and undated pamphlet by Tom Petty, a retired Indian Head school teacher, which may have been one of my sources. He did footnote some of his sources.[13]

Indian Head today is a bedroom suburb of Regina; its retail and service sectors largely hollowed out after the four-lane highway reduced the travel time between the town and the city (and its strip malls) to about thirty-five minutes. When I was growing up, that highway was gravel, and it took almost half a day to drive to the city (especially in my father's Willys-Overland sedan with its anaemic forty-horsepower motor). Many of the buildings along Indian Head's main street have been demolished, giving Grand Boulevard an appearance that is no longer grand. In the summers of 2008 and 2009, three or four blocks of Grand Boulevard were turned into the set for a television situation comedy called *Little Mosque on the Prairie*. The premise of the story involves an imam arranging to use the local Anglican church as a mosque. Episode after episode revolved around the generally harmless culture clash between the imam's family and the local yokels. Indian Head's fictional name was Mercy, which was plastered on many of the Grand Boulevard's remaining shops during filming.

The town was established in 1882 or 1883 after the Canadian Pacific Railroad laid tracks through this spot on the prairie, on its way west. In my history, I speculate on the origin of the name. It may have been inspired by a nearby range of hills called the Indianhead Hills because the hills apparently were littered with the skulls of individuals who may have perished during the several small pox epidemics of the 1800s. When the railroad station was being built, a skull was unearthed and given to Doctor J.W. Kemp, a local physician. Legend has it that, when the naming committee was stuck for a town name, the doctor put the skull on a cane that he jammed into the street. That was said to be the origin of Indian Head. There were few Indigenous residents in

---

13   Petty, T., *Echoes of the Qu'Appelle Lakes District,* privately published, 58 pages.

town—most were Métis—when I was growing up, but one could easily find arrowheads in the hills and valleys around the town.

When the railroad came through, an English syndicate established a fifty-three-thousand-acre farm under the management of a Major William R. Bell. It was one of the largest farms on the Prairies; so large that the major installed a primitive telephone system to connect outpost buildings on the farm. Bell also built a round stone barn, perhaps as a fortress against attack (which never came) from the Indians. The building was dismantled stone by stone in 2008 and was re-constructed not far from the original site by a historical society. The Bell Farm was not successful and most of the land was taken over by another English syndicate headed by Sir Thomas Brassey. He was not much more successful but was respected as an employer and a community leader. In my history, I quoted an earlier historian's view that he was "downright fine."[14]

Much of the subsequent prosperity of Indian Head arose from agriculture. The Dominion Experimental Farm, established in 1887, and the forest nursery station, established in 1901,[15] attracted agricultural professionals to live in the town and generated steady salaries through good times and bad. The federal government finally withdrew its funding for the nursery station in 2014. When I was in high school, I had a summer job one year at the nursery station, running errands for the scientists. One of my daily assignments was setting the light trap each evening for moths and emptying it each morning. The trap included a bag of potassium cyanide dangled inside a jar. This was positioned on the roof of one of our buildings, below a light bulb. The moths would be drawn to the light. If they flew into one of the glass vanes on either side of the light, they would fall into the jar and be gassed. In the morning, I would pin the best specimens onto specialized boards and leave them for the entomologists. I also assembled a small collection for myself because I was in awe at the beauty of the moths. Because

14　Georgina Binnie-Clark, *Wheat and Woman*, 1914; re-issued by University of Toronto Press. Binnie-Clark was an English woman who bought a quarter section near Fort Qu'Appelle. The book recounts her farming experiences between 1905 and 1908.

15　*Century-old nursery rundown 'mess'*, Regina Leader-Post, July 28, 2014, section D.

they are nocturnal, few people are aware of how beautiful they are. My little collection stayed with my parents when I went to university and ultimately was disposed of because I never pursued the hobby.

The fertile soils around the town yielded, in good years, such prodigious crops that in 1902, the elevators at Indian Head shipped 1.4 million bushels of wheat, making the town the largest shipping point in the world (according to my history). In a few years, the town had several banks, hotels, livery stables, and elevators. The theatre, built in 1906 and still in use as a cinema in 2022, was considered one of the best between Winnipeg and Calgary.

The town's current water system, a pipeline to the Squirrel Hills about eight miles (12.8 kilometres) southwest of town, was built in 1906. My nephew Conrad Schreiner, who had become the town's current foreman, found an old town ledger in 2009 that named one of the workers on that project as my grandfather, Stefan Schreiner.

In my history of Indian Head, I barely touch on the Depression, other than to note that the Bank of Montreal closed its branch in 1931 (there was a near total crop failure that year) and that many farmers were sustained by so-called "relief" payments from the government. The community history was not much more forthcoming: "It was a decade of coping with relief, seed and feed shortages, and unpaid taxes. The grant for the ladies' restroom was not forthcoming, and even the bounty on gopher tails was discontinued."[16] The bounty was restored in the better times after the war. When I was in elementary school, I was able to collect five cents for each gopher tail or for each set of crow or magpie legs turned in to our long-suffering teachers or to the municipal office. (Those animals and birds were targeted because they ate the grain the farmers were growing.)

The dire economic conditions were felt personally. I was born with a congenital cataract in my left eye. The disability was not discovered until my grandmother noticed that I had no sight in that eye. However, it was not until I was eight years old that my parents could pay for the surgery to stop the cataract from growing, long after the optic nerve

16   *Wheat and Woman*, page 12.

ceased to function. The surgeon, Emmett McCusker, discounted his fee so that my parents could afford the procedure. (The doctor also entered politics, gaining election as a Liberal Member of Parliament for Regina for one term.)

A more experienced researcher of history would have delved much more deeply into this and other events in the town's history. One of the great stories involves the Indian Head Rockets, a baseball team of Black American and Cuban players based in Indian Head in the 1950s. I got to see them play when my father, a great baseball fan, took me to some games. Along with the other young boys in town, I also took up the yo-yo, copying a favourite pastime of ball players.

During this time, a number of Black baseball teams from the United States found communities on the Canadian Prairies to sponsor them. The mayor of Indian Head at the time was Jim Robison, the sports-mad operator of a general store on Main Street.[17] In 1950, he arranged the purchase of the Jacksonville Eagles of the Negro American League. The team was called the Indian Head Rockets, taking its name from a service club that had been formed in 1946. Indian Head became the summer home of the team, with most of the players bunking on the second floor of the Dominion Café, a Chinese restaurant on Main Street operated by Charlie Koo. According to an article published by the *Regina Leader-Post* in 2012, they played eighty games that summer, including tournaments with money prizes. Indian Head had begun hosting a tournament in 1947, with $5,000 in prize money. The tournaments grew into three-day weekends that drew up to ten thousand people from all over Southern Saskatchewan. The Rockets team, which was not financially successful, folded after the 1954 season. It was high-calibre baseball, however, and some of the Rockets ended up on major league teams as the colour barrier came down. I recall another team at a tournament, which had the legendary Satchell Paige pitching in a game against a pick-up team of farmers from Kronau. I believe the game was called, mercifully, after five innings.

17 *Rockets once ruled Indian Head,* by Bob Florence, *Regina Leader-Post*, June 16, 2012, pp G3-G4.

Of course, my history essay did not compare to the previously mentioned *Indian Head: History of Indian Head and District* published in 1984. I can only envy the resources they had that were not available to me thirty years earlier. The most surprising thing that I discovered when leafing through the book was that a Ku Klux Klan chapter had been established in 1928. There is no indication of when it closed. But if Indian Head was able to sponsor a Black baseball team, the Klan clearly had no traction by the 1950s.

Three:
Geoffrey Chaucer confirms the love of my life

In the summer of 1959, I took a leave of absence from the *Regina Leader-Post*, where I had been working since the summer of 1957, to enrol in two English courses at the University of Toronto: Anglo Saxon English and Chaucer. I had two objectives: to decide whether I wanted to get a master's degree in English and to see whether a two-month absence from Regina would fracture the romance that was developing between Marlene and me. I learned that I was not that interested in further studies of English, as much as I enjoyed studying *Canterbury Tales*. But Geoffrey Chaucer did confirm the love of my life.

The relationship with my first girlfriend, Glennys Obleman, had ebbed not long after I enrolled at the University of Saskatchewan in 1955. She was a grade behind me in high school and, as one would expect, was soon dating someone else. Some years later, when she looked me up in Toronto, I learned that she had joined the Canadian Forces and then married. I carried a torch for her for several years while I was in university but eventually turned my attention to another university student—a sweet woman whose nickname was Bunny. She eventually married an engineer. As an arts student and a rival of the engineers, I considered I had let my side down.

At university, I did not spend much time dating girls. First of all, I could not afford it. Secondly, after nearly failing first year, I focussed on my studies and on a few extra-curricular activities (including *The Sheaf*, the campus newspaper, and the drama club at St. Thomas More College). There was no time for girls. Bunny came along only in the final month or so of university.

In my four years of high school, I was either the top student each year at Indian Head High or the second behind Jack Wilkinson. Jack was a skinny nerd who, after a degree in agriculture, succeeded as a farmer. In the final year in high school, I worked hard enough to be the top student and the class valedictorian. I passed all my final exams by recommendation although, at the suggestion of the French teacher, I wrote the French exam voluntarily. French was mandatory in first year university, and she thought I would do better having studied hard for the grade twelve examination. She was right. I earned a second-class standing in only two of the five subjects—English and French. I earned only third place standings in history and in physical sciences, and I barely passed philosophy, with a fourth place (50%–59%).

I was not well prepared for what awaited me in first-year university. First-year students had to take English, French, and physical sciences, along with physical education. The science course involved units of chemistry (basically a repeat of grade 12 chemistry), physics, and biology. There were about three hundred students taking the class in a vast auditorium and from professors sometimes no more interested in us than we were in the subjects. I disliked physics, not much of which I understood. Fortunately, biology was taught by an able teacher and engaged me once I got over the shock that the Adam and Eve story of creation was not true. That had been taught during the catechism courses I took as a child and, since I had never taken biology in high school, I had no inkling about evolution. This encounter with evolution occasioned my first, brief crisis of faith. I don't remember whether I discussed this with any of the Basilian fathers or whether I figured it out on my own. I was a student at the Basilian College, St. Thomas More, but we took some of our courses from other colleges and from secular professors. In that first year, three of my professors were priests.

No grades were given for physical education, which was just as well. Again, there were three modules. The first was swimming, a sport I have never liked or been good at. This was an activity we shared with students from other colleges on campus, including at least one of the Protestant colleges. A student at one of these colleges was from North Ireland, and he made it a point to bait the Catholics. I had not experienced comparable bigotry, having grown up an uncritical Catholic who accepted the fiction that ours was the One True Church. One day, this Irish student came up to me with a clipping about a Catholic missionary in Africa who had been struck dead by lightening in the door of his church. That was proof, I was told, that God considered Roman Catholicism an erroneous religion.

The second physical education module was badminton, a sport at which I was hopeless because I have sight only in one eye. One needs depth perception to play racket sports effectively. The third module was wrestling. As the second biggest student, I was paired with the biggest. I spent every class pinned under him; in the final class, he actually broke one of my ribs, but in such a way that the pain did not start for several days and left me with a lump of healed breastbone.

If I had taken any counselling—I don't know whether that was even available—I would never have taken philosophy. I took philosophy, an optional course, because I thought a writer needed it to think critically. I came away with only a tenuous grasp of Plato and Aristotle, in part because one of the texts was written by a Jesuit with a penchant for concluding his arguments with a Latin or, even worse, a Greek phrase. My intellectual shortcomings were aggravated by my inefficient study habits: I tried to work on every subject all the time. In my second and third years at university, I made it a point to take one easy course each year (art in second year, creative writing in third year) and to focus my time on the other four courses. It worked. I came within a whisker of graduating with honours in 1958. That gave me the idea that I should take more college courses, either with an eye to an academic career or to improve my writing.

I appear to have dated a few women in Regina before I met Marlene. In my diary on September 10, 1958, I refer to someone called Kathy who had been annoyed at me when I dated another woman on a blind date. For the life of me, I cannot remember who Kathy was, although I had a positive pen portrait of her. There were several more dates with her, but I also dated other women. I never had the courage to ask for dates with two fellow *Regina Leader-Post* reporters—Maryanne Fitzgerald and Donna Dilschneider—perhaps because I was intimidated by their comparative seniority in the newsroom.

I met Marlene in late 1958 and was immediately impressed. "She is made of two components largely, heart and brains," I wrote in my diary on January 5, 1959. Seven days later, I wrote that I had "passed the point of no return" and loved her. The catalyst was Conrad Rodney who, after graduating from university in commerce, was working in Regina as an accountant and rented the basement room next to mine at an apartment block. He talked me into going with him to the public dances that were held once a week at the Trianon Ballroom, an establishment with a rotating mirror ball and a live orchestra. At the second dance, I spotted Marlene across the room, with a group of her girlfriends. She agreed to dance with me, let me treat her to a Coke and, if memory serves, accepted a ride home (Con had a car and also a girlfriend.) I was attracted to her from the beginning. By the end of January 1959, I was admitting thoughts of marriage in my diary. By the end of April, I write of trying on a ring. It sounds like a whirlwind courtship. Or perhaps not: a diary entry on June 8 admits: "...finally I had the courage to kiss Marlene."

At the time, she was teaching accordion lessons, having taken up the piano accordion when her father brought one home and presented it to her. Accordions were everyday life in the communities in which we had grown up. My father, who played by ear, always had a button accordion and often entertained at country dances. Marlene's father, Ferdinand Dietrich, did not play the instrument, but he certainly enjoyed the music. Marlene and her older sister, Olympia, had already taken piano lessons. The piano accordion seemed a natural progression for Marlene, and she accommodated her father.

Ferd was a very large and gregarious man. His curiosity was insatiable. Throughout his life, he peppered me with questions about a surprising range of topics. He was a lifelong supporter of both the co-operative movement and the Co-operative Commonwealth Federation (CCF) political party because he believed in those principles. He always managed to earn a living, starting with taking over the family farm and then running a general store in a village (now gone) called Cano in Eastern Saskatchewan. In 1952, he moved his family to Regina so that Marlene and her siblings could go to high school. Ferd and Apollonia, Marlene's mother, ran a modest rooming house. He also travelled about rural Saskatchewan as a salesman. Then he qualified as a stationary engineer. That got him a career looking after the steam plant and furnaces at the provincial jail in Regina. He retired in 1973 and died in May 1996, at the age of eighty-eight. His wife, slight in stature, was a sweet-natured woman with a high-strung personality. When dementia crept up on her toward the end of her life, Ferd arranged to have her housed in a private care home and then in the Santa Maria Home, a much better facility in Regina run by nuns. Apollonia died in February 1997.

Ferdinand and Apollonia Dietrich wedding photo

The opportunity to invite Marlene on a first date fell into my lap. A Kentucky Fried Chicken (KFC) franchise opened in Regina in the spring of 1958. I was assigned to interview Colonel Harland Sanders, the founder of KFC and later its brand ambassador when it became a chain of franchises. After the interview, he gave me two vouchers for meals at the restaurant. The irony is that I had developed a dislike for chicken from eating too much of it while growing up on the farm. Even so, I was not about to turn down a free meal if it enabled me to have a date with Marlene. I invited her to lunch, and the romance took off. I found her quite attractive, both physically and for the essential goodness of her personality. (I still feel the same way about her seventy years later.) What did she see in me? I was conceited enough to assume that, as a newspaper reporter, I was just a lot more interesting than her other male friends. Of course, we had shared a common ethnic and religious background. The youth clubs we belonged to in our respective parishes formed a comfortable social set for both of us.

Neither of us let the flame of romance go out during our two-month separation when I was at the University of Toronto. We wrote each other at least twice a week—chatty and affectionate letters, not steamy letters. Marlene's letters also were filled with news, for she also had a momentous summer. Early in summer, she resigned from Ray Hunker's accordion studio, where she had taught accordion music for three years.[18] "Saturday will be my last day at Hunkers," she wrote on July 19. "I can't say it scares me. I begin my holidays on the 19th and will probably spend most of them job-hunting."

Her letter gave me the opening to reply that I would also have to consider my job options the following year. "I cannot stay with *Regina Leader-Post* forever because a one-newspaper journalist is not a well-trained journalist."

Marlene took a three-week course at a secretarial school to refresh her typing skills and learn how to operate a Dictaphone. She applied at a number of places and began work in early August at the Saskatchewan Government's Public Service Commission. However, she did not put

18   Ray Hunker, who died in 2020 at the age of eighty-nine, had a long career as an accordion teacher with a studio in Regina.

music aside. Having joined the Musicians Union earlier in the year, she formed a duo with Joe Lichtenstein, a violinist, and they performed occasional concerts.

Marlene jamming on accordion

In my diary on August 23, 1959, the day I boarded the night train to return to Regina, I commented on writing a lot of letters that summer. "I must have written one-third more than I received," I begin this puffed-up note, "and certainly, there are two dozen in my trunk. Most are from Marlene, who regularly wrote twice a week. Her constancy extended beyond her letters; she is really more than I am worth." By my September 9 diary entry, I had concluded that she would "make a wonderful wife... This winter, I face two major decisions which will shape my future: am I to remain a journalist; and should I marry Marlene?" By September 25: "I cannot be without her."

We had, in fact, carried on an extensive correspondence with each other that summer, and many of the letters have survived. Marlene had packed a lunch for my first few days on the train. "The food was fit for a prince," I said in my first letter. "That lunch convinced me that you are beyond a doubt the most thoughtful and valuable woman I know." All of my letters that summer, while never steamy, ended with the romantic assertion of how much I missed Marlene. And she responded similarly. By July 21, I was gushing: "And will it be wonderful to see you! All the time when my mind is not on my work, and sometimes when it should be on my work, it is creating dream castles and crowning you queen."

My letters were a blend of sensible and nonsense. I fancied that I was a good poet, adding the occasional doggerel. The poem included in my letter of July 15 is embarrassingly typical:

I'll Be A Squirrel's Uncle!

There was a little black squirrel
Sitting on a bench.
And he was begging salted nuts
From a pretty wench.

And I was walking in the park
On my evening jaunt
When I espied the lucky squirrel
Perched beside the blonde.

I said, "I'd love to take the place
Of your pet, if I may."
So she fed her last nut to me
And laughing, walked away.

I have never regretted that summer, which cost me a little over $400—a lot of money at the time. I can't tell from my diary whether that figure includes the tuition or just the living expenses. I stayed in residence on campus, in a pleasant second-floor room with a single bed and a desk. My biggest shock was Toronto's incredibly hot and humid summer. I showered several times a day, often had difficulty sleeping at night, and sometimes rose very early in the morning to go to church, because it was cool there. I did not socialize much with other students, in part because I was conserving my funds and in part because I was studying hard. Anglo-Saxon English was so difficult that I had probably forgotten most of it within a week of finishing the course. I graded B in both my exams, which probably ended my notions of doing postgraduate work. I still remember the *Canterbury Tales* with great fondness. I also read many other books that summer, most notably Boris Pasternak's *Dr. Zhivago*, the first book by a Nobel laureate that I read.

I never followed through on taking another course from the university by correspondence, although I did get a list of the books I would need to read. "This morning I obtained a description of the winter course and felt weak in the knees after reading the eighteen-page summary," I wrote Marlene on August 6. "I think at least two dozen books are listed to be read, and generally, it is a course of philosophy and politics rather than English." Once I returned to my job at the *Regina Leader-Post*, I soon was too busy to take on a course—especially since I had been burned once by philosophy.

On a few occasions, I was entertained in the homes of Torontonians who belonged to Moral Re-Armament, a movement that had been started in Britain in 1938. After World War II, it spread internationally as a spiritual peace movement and one that was opposed to socialism and communism. The MRA members in Regina were suspicious of the CCF, if not downright opposed, and made an effort to recruit opinion leaders including young reporters. They made quite an effort to involve me in MRA. I became uneasy both of their right-wing views and of the nascent anti-Catholicism of MRA and eventually got free of their attentions. I had become a member of the Third Order of St. Francis a few years earlier, and I asked Father Sebastian, who ran the Franciscan Monastery in Regina, about MRA. He advised me to stay away from MRA, and I took his advice. Subsequently, I became assistant novice master of the Third Order chapter and edited a monthly newsletter.

I had become heavily involved in trying to master journalism and courting Marlene. If I can believe the anguished prose in my diary, I was not confident in my ability as a journalist. But I was confident in my personal life and in love with Marlene. We did a lot of things together: for example, we went to the opening of a new civic centre in Moose Jaw on September 19, 1959, where the main attraction was a concert by Louis Armstrong and his band. We became engaged on January 17, 1960 and were married on September 17 the same year.

John and Marlene Schreiner wedding portrait

Incredibly, I neglected my diary for months, writing nothing about the wedding, the honeymoon or our first home. We did not have much of a plan, if any, for our honeymoon week in North Dakota. The highlight, aside from getting to know each other intimately, was that we saw John Kennedy give a speech. The American election campaign was on. He had a brief stop at the Fargo airport about 5:00 p.m. one day. I had read about it in a newspaper the day before, and we joined the crowd at the airport when *Caroline*, his airplane, arrived. A set of stairs was pushed against the plane. Kennedy came out and, from the top of the stairs, delivered a twenty-minute speech on agriculture policy. Then he went back into the plane, and *Caroline* took off for the next campaign stop. He defeated Richard Nixon to become president.

Back in Regina, we moved into a small three-room flat on the second floor of a house not far from the cathedral, and we resumed our jobs. Marlene, by this time, was working at the legislature, and I was still writing politics for the *Regina Leader-Post*. This was an interesting period. Nationally, the CCF had been transformed into the New Democratic Party. Tommy Douglas resigned as premier to go into federal politics. Meanwhile, Woodrow Lloyd, his successor, had begun to launch the province's—and Canada's—first medical insurance program. I did an enormous amount of work covering the public hearings. I was no longer around for the 1962 doctors strike because the *Financial Post* had hired me, and we moved to Toronto in mid-1961.

Our finances were so tight during the early years of our marriage that Marlene itemized food and other purchases in little notebooks. By the end of our first decade, my salary had risen to the point where we were comfortable and could afford luxuries. At Christmas, in 1970, I spent $40 to buy a soapstone carving of a walrus that, for no obvious reason, we chose to call Angus. For Christmas 1972, I bought her an Elna sewing machine for $292.95; it was overhauled in 2018 and still is serviceable.

Four:
What if my first car
had been a Studebaker?

When reflecting on my life, there are more themes than just wine and journalism. This chapter recounts my taste for foreign automobiles while the next chapter deals with my affection for cycling once I had learned how to ride a bicycle.

I learned to drive when my father put me to work on the farm's Cockshutt 60 row crop tractor, one of many brands that are now history. Based in Brantford, Ontario, Cockshutt Farm Equipment Ltd. was founded in 1877 as the Brantford Plow Works by James G. Cockshutt, an implement inventor. In the 1930s, the company began manufacturing tractors under licence from American firms, including Allis-Chalmers and Oliver. The Brantford plant switched to military production during World War II but, starting with the Cockshutt 30 model in 1946, began making the first production tractors designed in Canada. Production of the Cockshutt 30 model ceased in 1956. After the company was involved in a hostile takeover, the farm equipment division was sold in 1962 to the Oliver Corp. of the US, which retired the Cockshutt name. Cockshutt lore is preserved by an international club, a website, and collectors of the restored reddish-orange tractors.

My father was a dedicated horse lover, but he eventually saw the need for tractors, first owning a hulking brute with steel wheels. The Cockshutt 60, bought used, was either his second or third tractor. It was small compared with subsequent generations of machines, but it had rubber tires, a power take-off to drive farm equipment, and was easy to manoeuvre. It was a three-cornered machine because the two front wheels were close together (hence, the row crop designation). It steered easily between rows and had a tight turning circle. My biggest surprise on that tractor occurred one morning when I was driving it home from town after a repair. The garage had not reconnected the steering properly and, when I tried to make a ninety-degree turn from the road into our farm, those front wheels would only move about twenty degrees. Fortunately, I had the presence of mind to stop the tractor before ending up in the ditch. After my father died, I looked through some of his papers and discovered that the Cockshutt 60 was sold in 1950 (along with a tiller) to Henry Kattler, my mother's youngest brother.

My driving skills were learned at the wheel of my father's Fargo truck. Fargo was one of three American manufacturers that merged in 1928 to form Chrysler Corp. In the United States, the Fargo brand was soon overtaken by Dodge, Chrysler's other truck brand. The Fargo brand, essentially rebadged Dodge trucks, survived in certain export markets. Because Chrysler had separate chains of dealers in Canada for Dodge and for Plymouth, the Fargo truck line was introduced in 1936 and manufactured in Windsor for Plymouth dealers. The company continued to make parallel truck lines in Canada until 1972.

My father's truck, also purchased used, was a pickup manufactured around 1948 or 1950. According to one website, the manual shift lever was on the steering column. My memory is of a floor-mounted shift. The cab of a Fargo was famous for being so capacious that four people could sit side by side on the bench seat. More than once, there were foursomes in my truck—two high-school aged males and their dates—as hard as it is to imagine anything romantic about a farm truck. Eventually, I was allowed the use of my father's sedans, a succession of Chrysler products that were more comfortable and more pleasant for spooning at the drive-in. He had owned a few interesting cars before settling on Chrysler; the most peculiar was his 1940 Willys-Overland, a low-powered sedan not much larger than a Volkswagen. My mother used to drive it quite briskly until one morning, while on the way into town with eggs, cream, and me, she was caught in some loose gravel, which whipped the car into the ditch. Some eggs broke, some cream spilled, and her pride was hurt.

I was seventeen when I got my first driver's licence, in a rather casual manner. My father and I went into the Indian Head RCMP detachment, and my father waited while I wrote the test. The corporal then asked my father how well I could drive and, on being assured that I had plenty of experience with farm vehicles, he give me a licence without a road test. I don't believe I had to take a road test until applying for a licence in Montreal in 1967, a city then with some of Canada's worst drivers.

It was in 1958, after I graduated from university, that I bought my first car, financing it with a personal loan from my university classmate Conrad Rodney. When he decided he did not care to be my banker, I replaced him with a finance company.

I could only afford a used car, of course. At a used car lot on Albert Street in Regina, I found two vehicles that interested me. One was a Studebaker Hawk that was just a little too expensive for me. However, it had racy lines and, for its day, a powerful engine. Studebaker, which was to go out of business in 1966, began producing the stylish Hawk models in 1956. I only came close to buying a North American car again in 1969 when I took a test drive in a new Plymouth Valiant. The boring base model was quite affordable, but the moment that desirable options were added, the price went through the roof. However, if I had started with that racy Studebaker Hawk, I might have purchased other North American cars. As it is, I have never owned one.

The car I bought, which cost me $550, was a 1952 Hillman Minx, an underpowered British-built sedan from a company that Chrysler took over in the 1970s. Aside from the fact that I could afford this car, its attractions included leather upholstery that still had an appealing aroma after years of use. The shift control was on the steering column, leaving an unobstructed bench seat that was, as Marlene would attest, ideal for courting. The car was not in the best of mechanical shape. Once, we drove to Swift Current from Regina (I don't remember why), and the car did not have the power to climb back up from the modest basin in which the community nestles. I actually had to back up the hill. When I went to the University of Toronto in the summer of 1959 for two months, my father had a mechanic in Indian Head rebuild the engine. The car still did not have much power. After driving around Saskatchewan for a week during the 1960 election campaign, I traded it for a black 1957 Volkswagen with 28,500 miles on the odometer. It cost $1,000 plus my Hillman.

Volkswagen had earned a reputation for building cheap and reliable cars. My experience after owning two VWs was that the reputation for reliability was undeserved. I had endless fuel pump problems with my second one, a 1960 model purchased new for $1,648. The repair involved a minor part, but until I found a German-trained mechanic who diagnosed the problem accurately—the car would stall when it got warm—it cost me a fortune in needless repairs. Likely because we were watching our finances, I did not have a radio installed in the car. On November 22, 1963, Marlene and I were in Niagara Falls with my mother. We heard the initial bulletins about President John F. Kennedy's assassination from a television set in a gift shop. We drove all the way back to Toronto and did not know he had died until we got home.

The 1957 model had its quirks. The rear window was a two-paned design too small for effective rearward vision. It was not until 1960 that the VW engineers made the roof strong enough to accommodate a large window. That is quite surprising, considering that by then the design was a quarter century old.

The 1957 also had a gasoline heater under the front hood, since the rear-mounted engine was air-cooled. When running, the heater consumed almost as much fuel as the engine. The heater in my car cleaned its injectors when they became clogged with an explosive backfire in the left front wheel well, where the heater exhaust was. One cold November in 1960, Marlene and I, and my brother, drove to Rabbit Lake to visit my Schreiner grandmother. The backfiring gas heater was so frightening that we turned it off and endured the cold. I seldom used the heater, no matter how cold Regina was in winter. Happily, the 1960 model dispensed with the gas heater, affording more room under the hood as well as some peace of mind. The engineers had figured out how to channel the engine heat through the car, which was now comfortable in winter. And it was certainly economical to drive, if one did not include the servicing costs. Volkswagen's service protocols, it seems to me now, were mischievously padded for such a comparatively simple vehicle.

By the winter of 1968, the salt on the streets in Toronto and Montreal had eaten right through the floor boards of our Volkswagen. Temporary repairs were made while we looked at other vehicles. The choice was narrowing down to Volkswagen's station wagon—since we needed to accommodate Maureen, Alison and John, our three children—until we went to the Montreal auto show one Sunday afternoon. Just as we were leaving, we walked by display of a Peugeot 404 station wagon. The external design was rather angular and less than eye-catching, but the interior was superbly finished with leather-like plastic upholstery. The rear floor had four or five long rubber ribs to prevent cargo from sliding. The roof rack was a sturdy steel frame attached with six screws, a design more appropriate for the Dakar to Senegal Rally (which Peugeot frequently won) than to life in urban Canada. I always needed help to lift the heavy rack and position it on the roof, but once screwed in place, it was very secure.

We had never heard of Peugeot. (I was aware of Renault, having tested a Renault Dauphine—a terrible car—before buying my 1960 VW.) The day after the auto show, I mentioned the car to Jack Whelan, a colleague who was one of the advertising salesmen in the Montreal office of McLean-Hunter. He remarked that another of his colleagues, then selling *Chatelaine* magazine advertising, had once worked for Peugeot Canada. When I asked Jacques (I no longer recall his surname name) about the cars, he assured me that it was (and remains) a major French car company. (Peugeot began building bicycles in 1882, later expanding to cars; my first ten-speed bike, purchased in 1970, also was made in France.) Jacques said that if I was really interested, he would see what deal he could negotiate with his former employer. The next day, he said I could have a 404 wagon for about $2,750, just $65 above list price. The deal, much cheaper than a new VW wagon, was too good to pass up. With taxes, the first of our three Peugeots cost $3,024, and the subsequent inflation flowed considerable value through onto trade-ins to the next two. Our first Peugeot was robin-egg blue because we had no choice of colour, given the deal! We broke it in that summer by driving to Prince Edward Island on vacation, with most of our luggage secure on that industrial roof rack. With a sturdy four-cylinder engine, probably displacing 98.7 cubic inches, its eighty horsepower was adequate as long as one worked the column-mounted four-speed manual shift.

When we moved to Vancouver in 1973, we had the car shipped by rail from Toronto to Saskatoon. Marlene and our children were spending July in Regina while we waited to get into our house. She retrieved the car from Saskatoon; I flew to Regina, and we all drove to British Columbia. By then, the Ontario road salt had started to rot the body-work even though I had paid for Ziebart undercoating. We traded it in on a new green 504 station wagon in 1975. It was Marlene's favourite of our three, with more adequate power (ninety-six horsepower from a 1.7 litre engine), decent cargo space, and good drivability in snow, but—alas—without a rally roof rack. Later, I read that the vehicle had one of the worst ratings in US government crash tests. We got a generous trade-in allowance on the 404, having bought it cheaply. That residual benefit even made our final Peugeot more affordable when, in 1982, we bought a brown 505 sedan. Still with a manual transmission, this had more power (2.2 litre engine with 120 horsepower) and the usual great Peugeot suspension and handling. But like all of these cars, it could have used a bit more power.

In 1986, we also bought a new Subaru station wagon. This was the vehicle that our son, John, drove when he went to the University of British Columbia. While his sister, Alison, had commuted to the campus by bus (a long commute from the North Shore), John said he had had enough of long commutes by bus after previously attending Vancouver College. Once in 1988, he crashed the Subaru against a curb. The damage looked slight, but the repairs cost $1,200. When John graduated from UBC and went to Taiwan in 1992, I sold the Subaru and we went back to being a one-car family.

By 1988 Peugeot was exiting the North American car market. The brand we had been driving for nineteen years now had become a dead end. In fact, when I advertised the car in the *Vancouver Sun*, there was just one response—from a professor of French at the University of British Columbia who, happily, took the car off our hands for $4,100—more than I had paid for my first Peugeot.

We switched now to a 1989 Toyota Camry and, for the first time, bought one with an automatic gearbox. Marlene said she had had enough with shifting gears in city traffic. Toyota by this time had achieved its envious reputation for reliability, quality, and efficiency. In buying this car, I was able to avoid car dealers. Phil Charland, a fellow member of the winemaking club I had joined in 1975, was working in car leasing and agreed to source a car for me. My son, John, and I test drove several imported cars (he was flattered that I wanted his input), and we decided that the Camry was the nicest of the lot. I told Phil what I wanted, he quoted me a price, and I wrote him a cheque. I had a much less pleasant experience in dealing with a Jim Pattison salesman when we bought our second Camry, a 1997 model, and I vowed never to buy another car from a Pattison dealership.

The Camry cars were as solidly reliable as all the car critics reported, but neither was especially interesting to drive. I finally tired of the Camry in 2007, although I am sure the car would have functioned well for many more years. This time, I considered a Nissan Altima, having almost bought a used Maxima a few years earlier, and a Honda Accord. We settled on the Accord as the better looking and better handling sedan. The Accord was still running well in 2022, with more than 180,000 kilometres on the odometer. If there is one more car in our lives, I would bet it would be another Honda.

Why have I owned just imported cars? At first, that was all I could afford. Later, it fit my counter-culture attitude towards the Detroit car companies; I loathed their continual production of big, heavy, inefficient vehicles. I preferred the smaller imported cars, not just for their size but also because, in the case of Peugeot, they were somewhat distinctive in Canada. I preferred not to drive what everyone else was driving. Lately, the ubiquitous Japanese cars have won me with their reliability.

But what would have happened if my first car had been the Studebaker Hawk?

As a sequel to this reflection, I actually spent a year or so on the automobile beat at *The Financial Post* in 1970 and 1971. I was really not a very good automotive journalist and was glad to move on, but I did get to drive a few interesting cars. One was an Opel sports two-seater so low to the ground that one saw hub caps of other cars in the rear-view mirror. In May, 1990, years after I had left the beat, a publicist for Jaguar insisted I drive one of their cars for a week: a $70,000 red coupe with a voracious appetite for fuel. It had a 5.3-litre, twelve-cylinder engine. We drove to Pemberton and back on a fine Sunday. I was trusting enough to let John drive it on Saturday evening when he was out with a friend and their girlfriends. Many years later, John disclosed that he got the car well above the speed limit on the Upper Levels Highway. My week with the Jaguar inspired an article on the luxury car market; the publicist had succeeded in getting the desired publicity.

The most fun I had as an auto journalist was the year that General Motors took a contingent of journalists out to Mosport race track near Oshawa and let us put two laps on each of their new models. It took me most of the afternoon to figure out how to attack the track, which hosted the Canadian Formula 1 race in the 1960s. I could not get a Corvette going above eighty-five miles per hour. I might have done better in the Corvair, but the car had broken down by the time my turn came. However, in a Camaro, I managed to touch one hundred on the back straight by forcibly holding the shifter in a lower gear until the revs almost red-lined, and then shifting—only to begin braking sharply for the curves before the pit straight. It was a blast. I can still drive Mosport in my mind. I also developed an interest in Formula 1 motor racing. I saw Stirling Moss drive a Lotus (which broke down) at my first Canadian Grand Prix at Mosport. He was a legendary driver in his day. He was knighted, but he never managed to win the world championship, primarily because his cars always had reliability issues. After Canadian television sports channels began carrying the races live in the early 1990s, I became an avid fan of the sport.

Five:
Bicycle adventures

I was about six years old when my parents bought me my first bicycle, a second-hand machine with twelve- or fourteen-inch wheels. In spite of being seated low to the ground, I spent most of the next six years falling off before mastering the art of balancing on two wheels. To my embarrassment, several cousins borrowed the bicycle and learned to ride before I did.

Once I learned how to ride, I asked for a full-sized bicycle—and not just any machine but a new balloon-tired Schwinn that was advertised on the back covers of my favourite comic books (*Roy Rogers, Superman*). Schwinn Bicycle, founded in Chicago in 1885 by Ignaz Schwinn, was then an iconic manufacturer of two-wheelers that were much more advanced, or so it seemed, than those from CCM—Canada Cycle & Motor Co, the major Canadian manufacturer. Schwinn went bankrupt in 1992; the brand was bought by new owners, went bankrupt again, and was revived a second time in 2001. CCM also went bankrupt. Both were victims of the tidal wave of imports from Asian bike manufacturers.

My Schwinn was by far the most glamorous bicycle in Indian Head at the time with its gleaming paint job and the fat tires on twenty-four-inch or twenty-six-inch rims. I got it when I was in grade eight or nine. For a time, many of my envious classmates borrowed it during recess and lunch breaks for fast-paced spins on Indian Head's recently paved Main Street. Some who took it for a ride bullied me to get access to the bicycle.

Balloon tires were great on pavement, but we lived about two miles (3.2 kilometres) south of town. The bicycle, which had a heavy steel frame, was something of a chore on dirt roads because of the rolling resistance of balloon tires. That was resolved partially one morning when I was riding to school beside my friend Ron Jackson, who was on his horse. As I often did, I hung onto the stirrup. On this morning, his pony kicked out the front wheel. The only available replacement was a twenty-seven-inch rim and tire, probably from a CCM bicycle. My formerly glamorous bike now looked ridiculous but rode a little easier in dirt. I used the bike until I left home for university in 1955.

A few years after Marlene and I moved to Toronto, I bought a single-speed clunker from the T. Eaton & Co. warehouse store for just $35. I did not want to gamble more until I was sure that my love of cycling was rekindled. Cycling was then becoming fashionable with the arrival on the market of three-speed and ten-speed machines. In June 1971, I spent $85 for a French-made Jeunet ten-speed bicycle. About the same time, I bought a three-speed woman's model Jeunet for Marlene. Both had steel frames and were heavy, although not as clumsy as my old clunker. My bicycle had a mileage counter. By the end of year, I had put on 302.4 miles (484 kilometres). That would have included commuting to work that summer. The two summer months, when traffic was significantly lighter, were the only months of the year when I thought it safe to mix it with cars. There were no bicycle lanes in Toronto in those days.

When I moved to Vancouver in the spring of 1973, I shipped my Jeunet out so that I could do recreational cycling on the weekends. It was a major adjustment to cycle on the hilly terrain of Vancouver and the North Shore. I had my only significant accident on two wheels on August 26, 1973, when on a Sunday ride, I came around a corner too fast not far from home. My front wheel skidded on a strip of gravel across the road, still unpaved after sewer line work. I came down hard, broke my collarbone, and spent much of Sunday afternoon and evening in the emergency ward. I was recovered by October 14 because I logged a twenty-four-mile (38.4 kilometre) ride that Sunday. Cycling got easier in June 1975, when I replaced the Jeunet with a much lighter

Dawes Galaxy bicycle. In 1987, I upgraded to the bicycle I rode until 2016, an alloy-framed, fifteen-speed Allegro that cost me $700.

By the end of 1973, I had ridden another 500 miles (800 kilometres). Regrettably, I stopped logging mileage. The total would have been impressive. Aside from recreational rides on many weekends, I began to commute to work when the weather was favourable, generally from April to October. The ride into the city in the morning took about fifty minutes, and the return trip, when I had hills to climb, took about fifteen minutes longer.

Vancouver in those days had very few bicycle lanes. I worked out a route that was comparatively safe, except when a stiff wind was blowing across Lions Gate Bridge. The bridge was the most hazardous part of the journey because bikes and pedestrians shared a meter-wide sidewalk with no barrier to keep a cyclist or a pedestrian from falling into the traffic. When there were strong crosswinds, one had no option but to get off and walk the bike over the crest. The bridge had other hazards, including debris that caused flat tires. On October 6, 1981, I was cycling to work and listening to news reports about the assignation of Anwar Sadat, the President of Egypt. The date is fixed in my mind because I got one flat at the south end of the bridge. I pulled off into Stanley Park to repair the tire and, in my rush, I pinched the tube and caused a second flat. I arrived at work late and greasy but well informed on Egypt's tragedy.

Ultimately, my whole family was outfitted with bikes. Marlene's heavy Jeunet was ditched for a lighter ten-speed Norco. I can't recall what the children rode. One summer, we spent a week bicycle camping on the St. Juan Islands. (Maureen did not come because she was working.) The major park on one of the islands involved a long uphill ride, which was difficult for Alison and especially for John. He kept stopping until Marlene talked him into proceeding again; there was no other choice because our car was on the mainland.

On several May long weekends, one or other of my children came along to cycle in the Skagit Valley, from Sedro Woolley to a campground in a Washington State park about twenty miles (32 kilometres) to the east. The most memorable was the 1980 weekend with John when the

Mount St. Helen's volcano exploded violently. The eruption happened about 8:30 a.m. on Sunday morning. Even though we were camping about two hundred miles (320 kilometres) north of the volcano, we heard several explosions. I told John it must be the American military. We climbed on our bikes and cycled seven miles (11 kilometres) into Rockport, where we went to church, shopped for groceries, and had lunch. Then we went back to the campground and loafed away the afternoon. I had a radio, but there was no radio reception, so we remained ignorant of what had happened. It was only when I went to the local store for milk before dinner that I saw television pictures of Spokane enveloped in volcanic ash. Had the wind been more northerly, the Skagit Valley would have been full of ash and cycling might have been impossible. As it was, the eruption killed fifty-seven people—scientists and hikers on the mountain and residents on its slopes. Forty years later, a *New York Times* article concluded: "Mount St. Helens *remains a profoundly hazardous volcano*...."[19]

The last bicycle camping trip to the Skagit Valley was with Maureen in May 1982. It was a weekend dedicated to repairing father and daughter relations. Late in 1981, she had acquired a boyfriend. He was not an admirable character (he once was arrested for pulling a knife in a bar), but it took Maureen some time to see through him. She was coming around by that spring.

Neither Marlene nor our three children developed into cycling enthusiasts (at least until Maureen and her husband, David Romanick, discovered electric bicycles in 2022). I suppose they never had as much fun on two wheels as I did. Or perhaps they were just put off by some of the family cycle tours I led.

I finally stopped cycling recreationally in 2015 or 2016. I needed a new bicycle because the drop handle bars had become uncomfortable; I was getting a sore neck. My bicycle was too old to be fitted with handle bars that would have allowed me to ride upright, without the aching back. A new bicycle likely would have cost me $1,000 or more and that was too much to spend for the diminishing riding I was doing.

19 *New York Times*, May 18, 2020: "The Mount St. Helens Eruption Was the Volcanic Warning We Needed."

Besides, I thought the risk of falling and breaking a hip was not worth taking at the age of eighty. Had electric bicycles come onto the market earlier, I might have purchased one to help me conquer the hills of North Vancouver.

Six:
Was I really meant for journalism?

On June 10, 1957, John Diefenbaker led the Progressive Conservatives to a federal election victory for the first time in a generation, winning enough seats to form a minority government. The result surprised many, including the editors at the *Regina Leader-Post* newspaper in Regina, where I had begun my journalism career that year with a summer job. Considering the inauspicious way I handled my assignment that election night, it is remarkable that I spent the next forty-four years in journalism.

I had applied for a summer job at the newspaper sometime around the beginning of the year. Bill Thomson, the managing editor, replied, asking for my clippings. I had no clippings. I had never thought to keep a scrapbook when I was writing my high-school column, nor did I clip the few articles I did for *The Sheaf*, the university newspaper, so I did not reply to his letter. Looking elsewhere for a summer job, I signed up to plant trees in British Columbia. It was a common student summer job at the time and paid well. Of course, growing up on the Prairies, I had no concept of tree planting in the mountains and likely would not have lasted very long in that extremely taxing job. However, a few weeks before I was due to go to British Columbia, I received a second letter from Thomson, asking why I had never sent clippings. Since I was already home from school and relaxing in Indian Head, I went into Regina for an interview and, even without clippings, I was hired.

Either he saw latent talent or he just needed some sober bodies in the newsroom of a paper that experienced a fair amount of turnover and alcoholic journalists. I abandoned the tree planting because the newspaper offered what I wanted—the chance to learn the craft of writing. Journalism was not an end in itself.

Like all green reporters at the *Regina Leader-Post*, I started with the training-wheels assignment of writing obituaries. Every morning, I would get the galleys of the paid obituaries we were running in our classified section, and then I would call in at the two Regina funeral homes to see if there was any more detail on the deceased. Finally, I telephoned relatives of the more interesting persons. I did not get much guidance from the editors in writing these, so I just stumbled along for a few weeks. One day, however, I submitted one with a lede that the deceased had come to the West in a Red River wagon. The city editor congratulated me on this touch of colour and gave me my first byline. Now I grasped how to start a story. Perhaps I should have figured it out by reading the more experienced writers, but I have always learned best by doing. I don't read instructions well.

From obituaries, I graduated to covering speakers at the Rotary and Lions Club luncheons, held on alternate weeks in the Hotel Saskatchewan. The attraction was the free lunch until I came to detest the food (there was a particularly indigestible cold meat salad liberally seasoned with vinegar) and ate my sandwiches at the office before arriving to cover the speakers. The speakers were seldom very newsworthy. The exception was Father Athol Murray, who was principal of Notre Dame College in Wilcox. He was a larger than life figure and had turned Notre Dame into a powerhouse in sports as well as a school where delinquent boys were set straight. Father Murray, who died in 1975, also was quite politically conservative. At the service club that day, he delivered an intemperate critique of the provincial government's proposed "socialized" medical care plan. The story practically wrote itself. Socialized medicine became so contentious that, as I recall, the Archbishop sent Father Murray away from the province until matters cooled down.

The *Regina Leader-Post* was a thoroughly Liberal newspaper. It was owned then by the Sifton family, one of whose ancestors, Sir Clifford

Sifton, had been a major Liberal cabinet minister and a promoter of western settlement. The editor was D.B. Rogers, whose brother Norman had been Mackenzie King's defence minister in 1939 (and was killed in a 1940 plane crash). It never occurred to my employers that the Liberals would not win the 1957 election and, on election night, they deployed newsroom resources accordingly. The best reporter covered the Liberals. Other reporters, in declining order of experience, were assigned to cover the CCF, the Social Credit and, finally, the Progressive Conservatives. I was sent to the Conservative committee room. Having voted Liberal myself earlier that day (my first vote), I watched the results with the same amazement as everyone else. John Diefenbaker flew into Regina that evening and swept through the jubilant committee room about 10:00 p.m. After he left, I joined a group at a party at the home of Sandy MacPherson, a lawyer who was the city's leading Conservative. When I got back to the newsroom about two in the morning, I was sufficiently inebriated that Bill Thomson sent me home. Fortunately, a more seasoned reporter had been travelling with Diefenbaker and did file a story. This had been a big story, and I had not recognized it.

Undoubtedly, I learned from such mistakes, although I was surprised by how much self-doubt I harboured during my early years at the paper as I progressed through several beats. For some months I worked the night shift, a scary experience because the night editor was a serious alcoholic. I learned some journalism from him when he was sober, but it was not unusual for him to arrive about seven in the evening and fall asleep slumped over his desk for the next three or four or five hours. That forced me to learn how to lay out the morning edition as well as reporting on various nightly occurrences. I once covered a stabbing and, in the story, wrote flatly that A had been stabbed by B, based on what the police told me. The night editor was too inebriated to tell me that a crime was "alleged" until the police had a conviction. Had B been proven innocent, the *Regina Leader-Post* would have been in trouble. That was another mistake I never repeated.

The staff at the *Regina Leader-Post* certainly were a mixed bag. One writer was an alcoholic defrocked Anglican priest. He was a beautiful writer when he was sober and wrote a column on religion that was well regarded in the community. It was another matter when he was into the bottle. He may have lasted a year. He was not the only alcoholic. There was a reporter who kept a book on his desk by Søren Kierkegaard, a Danish philosopher, likely to create the impression that he was intellectual. This reporter's breath always smelled of mint because he sucked cough drops to cover up his drinking. Yet another reporter was fired after he got drunk in a Hotel Saskatchewan suite while he was naked and had the door open. The suite across the hall was then the residence of the Lieutenant-Governor of Saskatchewan. Even those who got through most days without alcohol could imbibe heavily. Many of the males left Friday afternoon after work to go to a nearby beer parlour and drink. (Women were not yet permitted to drink in the beer parlours.) Soon after I joined the paper, I went to two Friday afternoon sessions, expecting an hour or two of stimulating conversation. When I discovered that most of the talk consisted of dirty jokes, I stopped going. I have never been big on trading dirty jokes, but in the late 1950s, I was especially prudish.

Duncan, the night editor, was well read and interesting to talk to—when he was sober. One September evening in 1958, I diarized a conversation in which he forecast the rise of China as a power. On another night, each of us drank two beers while we worked. These were strange evenings. He had a girlfriend who also drank. At times she showed up in the newsroom with her pet wolfhound. I do not recall the circumstances, but Duncan left the paper in late September, to be replaced by Murray Masterton, a hard working New Zealander.

In January 1959, I was made one of the paper's political reporters, a promotion that astonishes me now since I did not cover myself with glory at first. In my diary for September 25, I wrote: "Twice during the Liberal convention [this week], I was disciplined for not reporting sufficiently, and the second reprimand carried an ultimatum to produce or lose my treasured beat. I believe I can try, but I am lazy and my political savvy is not nearly as sharp as it ought to be. Perhaps I am not meant to be a reporter." And I speculated that I was "not intelligent enough for my ambitions and not dumb enough to be easily contented."

Obviously, I worked harder because I kept the beat. A few weeks later, I was interviewing M.J. Coldwell, the avuncular national leader of the CCF. In early November, I appeared in two political panel shows on television. My first experience, a panel discussion with Solon Low, the national Social Credit leader, was traumatic. I was so spooked by the television lights in my face that I barely heard a word of Low's reply to my questions. That was the first and last time that I had such disabling stage fright in a broadcast studio, and a good thing, because I did a lot of radio and a little bit of television during my career. During that same month, I was in hot water over how I reported the Saskatchewan Federation of Labour's position on the CCF being folded into the labour-supported New Democratic Party. That left me unhappy with the *Regina Leader-Post*. I applied for the news editor's job at the *Swift Current Sun,* and they actually offered it to me at $95 a week. Even though it was more than the $335 a month I was getting at the *Regina Leader-Post*, I decided to stay in Regina since I had proposed marriage to Marlene on January 17, 1960. That in itself was amazing because, as I noted in my diary, I had no savings to speak of, given what I was earning. (When we married, Marlene had $1,000 and a television set.)

However, opportunity came my way as I began covering my first session of the Saskatchewan legislature. The members of the legislative press gallery included an independent freelance writer and broadcaster named Chris Higginbotham. An avuncular Yorkshireman with a rich broadcasting voice, he had been writing about Saskatchewan for many years for outlets including *Time* magazine and the Canadian Broadcasting Corporation. Chris took me under his wing and engineered freelance opportunities that I would never have secured on my own at the time. In 1960, I earned $287.50 from *Time*, $123 from the *Toronto Star*, $12.50 from the *New York Times,* and $60 from the CBC, along with $170 doing now-forgotten writing jobs for the provincial government. I am certain these were all jobs that Chris, who was quite busy, turned over to me. I wrote for many of these outlets in 1961 and, on my own, added the *Financial Post*.

I had obviously decided that I wanted to remain in journalism. In June 1960, the director of the provincial government's Bureau on

Alcoholism offered me a public relations job at $426 a month, and I turned it down. By then, I had decided that I did not want to spend the rest of my days in Regina (even though I was aware that Marlene might not want to move). I had spent a week at the *Calgary Herald* in April 1960, during the one-week break the *Regina Leader-Post* always gave its legislative reporters when the session ended, in lieu of overtime. At end of the week, I was offered a full-time job at the *Herald* but turned it down because I wanted to cover the 1960 election campaign in Saskatchewan in May. "The important thing," I wrote to Marlene from Calgary, "is that I have established a contact here and will be welcome back when they need reporters. You will like Calgary." My recollection is that I covered Tommy Douglas' speeches for a week at campaign events in towns such as Biggar, Shaunavon, and Swift Currant. In September 1960, I even flew to Minneapolis for a job interview with *Time*. Nothing came of it, but with the expense money, I bought a new pair of slacks.

The *Financial Post's* western bureau chief in Winnipeg at the time was Jean Edmonds, a remarkable woman who later became an associate deputy minister in the federal government and had an Ottawa office tower named for her. Before joining the civil service in 1964, she spent twenty years with the *Financial Post*. We met when I began doing some freelance pieces for her. In June or July of 1961, the *Financial Post* flew me to Toronto for an interview with R.A.M. McEachern, the paper's brilliant and curmudgeonly editor.[20] Like the *Time* interview, I saw this as another chance for a flight. (I was infatuated with aircraft.) I booked an overnight Trans-Canada Airlines flight to Toronto, spent the day there, and flew back to Regina on another overnight flight. I was so tired at work that I fell asleep in my chair at the Saskatchewan Hotel, where James Gray, then an oil industry lobbyist, was interviewing me after lunch about Saskatchewan politics.

As I learned later, McEachern was intimidating, but I was too naïve to pick up on that. He quizzed me for an hour or so and was interested in what I was reading. I replied that I read *Harpers* and *Atlantic Monthly*

20 A good pen portrait can be found in Peter Newman's memoir, *Here Be Dragons: Telling Tales of People, Passion and Power*, McClelland & Stewart, Toronto, 2005.

regularly and *Maclean's* occasionally. Considering that *FP* and *Maclean's* were the same family, that was a stupid thing to say. Someone later told me that the remark would have appealed to his iconoclastic view of Maclean-Hunter. He took the afternoon to think about his decision and then offered me $500 a month.

"That much?" I blurted.

"I can always pay you less," he replied. He must have wondered just what sort of country bumpkin he was hiring.

I started there in September 1961. Marlene, who had been a secretary in the Public Service Commission in Regina, found a similar job with a public health nurse in Toronto (until our first child came along).

I was unprepared to be a business writer. How I survived my first five months at the *Financial Post* is a mystery because I was in the dark most of the time. I recall being sent to the Canadian Chamber of Commerce meeting in Halifax that October (another airplane ride!), where I spent most of one night writing a report on the meeting. The story was so poor it was never published. And no one said anything to me about it, probably because the Chamber meetings were rarely newsworthy. We always sent reporters (I went to several more of the annual meetings) because the *Financial Post* had to be seen mingling with business leaders.

Early in 1962, I was given the labour beat and that saved my career in journalism. During my two years covering Saskatchewan politics, I had become familiar with, and sympathetic to, left-wing politicians and labour leaders. Here was a beat I could engage with, and I did. I believe that by the time I left the beat to transfer to the paper's Montreal bureau in 1967, I was a capable and well-regarded labour reporter.

I was not entirely settled into my career as a journalist. I considered a number of career changes in 1968, including teaching. I do not recall being that unhappy with the Montreal bureau, since we had just moved there in the fall of 1967, a month before Expo '67 closed. I turned down the first of several offers from the Canada Department of Labour's public relations department in January 1968. The director of the department, David R. Monk, had contacted me in September 1967. "The records indicate that last fall you were exhibiting some interest in employment with the Department," he wrote. I could hardly consider that after just moving to Montreal.

I was more interested in a career change a year later. In September 1968, I had applied for three different positions, including assistant to the President at Humber College—for which I was turned down politely. In November of that year, I turned down an offer for a senior writer post at Ontario Hydro, which paid $232 a week. I did not think I could turn it "into the satisfying career it should be." In early 1969, I turned down an offer from Petlock, Ruder & Finn, a public relations firm in Toronto.

I spent two years, 1967 to 1969, in the paper's Montreal bureau before returning to Toronto and becoming General Business Editor. I continued to write a lot about labour. My clippings in 1971 included a number tagged "Report on Labour." Early that year, I reported on an interview with Charles Levinson, a Canadian who was the general secretary of the International Federation of Chemical and General Workers' Unions. He was promoting world-wide unions as a counter-point to the rising number of multi-national companies. In February, I did a column on a confrontation between the Steelworkers and the building trades. In March, I wrote about the Canadian Labor Congress' $1 million campaign to organize white collar workers. I also had a column, Labor Today, in a Maclean-Hunter trade magazine called *Plant Administration/Engineering*. At the time, Maclean-Hunter had a stable of these magazines, several of which, such as *Canadian Hotel and Restaurants*, provided outlets for my freelancing.

A year after we returned to Toronto from Montreal, I was offered a another job with the Canada Department of Labour as a "senior interpretative writer." In a letter I wrote October 25, 1970, I turned the offer down because I had recently had a promotion at the *Financial Post*. "I have almost gone to the Canada Department of Labour twice in the past," I told the department's director of public relations. "Perhaps it will yet come about." In 1974, I turned down a $25,000 public relations position with Imperial Oil Ltd. "I'm not sure I want to be involved in such a large organization," I wrote in my diary. "I am having too much fun with this open-ended job of mine." I most certainly left money on the table. My salary only rose to $21,000 in January 1975.

I learned many techniques of business writing through the labour beat as well as from the numerous feature reports that the *Financial Post* published in that era. These reports enabled me to develop specialties. For example, I wrote several packaging industry reports. The transportation reports I handled led to the commission to write my first book, a school resource book called *Transportation*. One of a series of five such trade paperbacks, it was published in 1972 by McGraw-Hill Ryerson Ltd. and Maclean-Hunter. By that time, my title at the newspaper was General Business Editor, and I was managing a group of six writers as well as reporting.

As I look over my clippings, I am astonished at the breadth of subjects I wrote about, given how little I had known about business writing a decade earlier. There was, for example, an amusing piece in April 1971 about Fiat, the Italian car maker, doing winter testing of its vehicles at Wawa in Ontario. Since I have never been in Wawa, I think the story was set up by a Fiat publicist. In May, I wrote a feature on the competition in the ballpoint pen market and another on Budd Automotive Co. of Canada doubling its Kitchener plant. I cannot find the clipping, but I recall writing about potato chip history and production. Chips still were a relative novelty. My recollection is that chips had been produced first in 1853 by Cornelius Vanderbilt's chef at Saratoga Springs, New York.

In June, I wrote a long analysis of the rising opposition in Canadian cities to expressways. The hook was the decision of the Ontario government to cancel the William R. Allen Expressway in Toronto after $79 million has been spent on it. To illustrate it, I took Alison, my younger daughter, to the site of the proposed expressway and photographed her standing on what would have been a foundation. The photograph was published with my *Financial Post* article. I also made predictions about the growth both of rapid transit and of cycling. It was about this time that I also bought my first ten-speed bicycle, as noted in the previous chapter.[21]

21 *Financial Post*, June 12, 1971: "The city does not belong to the automobile."

In June, I was in Winnipeg where I interviewed a businessman named Albert D. Cohen for feature on his company, General Distributors of Canada, which was the Canadian distributor of Sony consumer products. At the time, Sony had emerged as the Apple of its day when it came to consumer electronics. My first tape recorders and radios were all made by Sony. Cohen had forged a friendship and business relationship with Akio Morita, the founder of Sony. Cohen was in on the ground floor: He and his wife honeymooned in Tokyo in 1954, and he was so impressed with Japan that he opened a buying office there in 1956. His first order: Sony transistor radios. The article still reads well today.[22]

In July, I did a long analysis of new federal labour law; another long article on trucking magnate Don Reimer buying his company back from Jimmy Pattison; a profile of Roy Atkinson, the president of the National Farmers Union; and another long profile of Trimac Ltd., a Calgary trucking firm. In September, I wrote a review of a book on the Canadian welfare system by a Regina lawyer called Morris Schumiatcher. In his day, he was the most contentious lawyer in Saskatchewan. He had been an advisor to Tommy Douglas' CCF government in 1944 but then became rabidly right wing. I did not like his book, which was entitled *Welfare: Hidden Backlash.* I said it was "rhetoric of the Old Right."[23] In September, I wrote a very long piece about the woes of the pulp and paper industry, with sidebars on industry research, labour relations, and on a Russian pulp and paper mission to Canada. In October, I had a lengthy profile of A.E. McKenzie & Co., a major Winnipeg flower and vegetable seed producer.

In the same month, I wrote a long profile of tire producer Dunlap Canada Ltd. That may have led to my being a guest a year or two later when Dunlap sponsored a press trip to the Sebring race course in Florida. The company chartered a DC-3 to fly our group from Kitchener to Florida, a journey that took an entire day, given the speed of the aircraft and a stop in Pittsburgh to clear Immigration. There was an open bar, and one of the journalists drank so much that he urinated in his pants. On the

22 *Financial Post,* June 19, 1971: "General Distributors keeps its star hitched to Sony."

23 *Financial Post,* September 11, 1971: "Will welfare schemes reduce all Canadians to the status of Indians?"

return flight, he was seated deliberately next to a window of a foursome playing cards, rather than close to the bar. He remained sober. The point of the trip was to showcase the radial ply tires just launched by Dunlap. They were mounted on one of the cars in the race. Unfortunately for Dunlap, the car's gearbox broke down after just a few laps. But I levered the experience into a feature on radial ply tires.

My willingness and/or ability to tackle a wide variety of topics continued the next year. I began 1972 with a long feature on the commercial calendar business. There had been a suggestion in some quarters that calendars as an advertising vehicle had had their day. My article showed otherwise. I quoted someone from W.H. Smith & Sons who said: "It's quite a big business." The article was a comprehensive survey of the many calendar types that companies were giving away. That is no longer the case today when few, with the exception of real-estate salespeople and funeral homes, give away calendars. In any event, it is easy to make one's own calendar. I began doing a calendar for our family in 2008, usually with photographs I took on annual travels. In 2020, when the pandemic killed travelling, I took a lot of photographs portraying the pandemic lockdown we endured and that became the calendar's theme. The 2021 calendar used images of flowers, with all the photos taken with the remarkable camera on my new iPhone. Images of the Okanagan wine country in the 2022 calendar celebrated my visits there after COVID- 19 kept me from visiting wineries for two summers.

In March 1972, I wrote a lovely and long feature about Toronto's Park Plaza Hotel, then one of the city's best hotels (a recent guest had been Prince Bernhard of the Netherlands). The focus was on a delightful man named Ed Shaunessy, the Park Plaza's elegant general manager. He was such a veteran hotel manager that he served as an advisor to writer Arthur Hailey in writing a thriller called *Hotel*. Reading my article today, I am astounded how freely the hotel's VIP guests were discussed. How did I get to write a piece like this? I suspect I was led to the opportunity by a good publicist. The *Financial Post* in those days was not hostile to public relations practitioners.[24]

24   *Financial Post*, March 4, 1972: "To fill 85% of the rooms, just pamper the guests."

In March, I wrote a comprehensive article on the struggle of Canada's 88 FM radio stations to make money. The consensus was that an FM station succeeded best when allied to an AM station because the older AM format could steer some advertisers to the FM sister stations. In 1972, FM broadcasting was relatively new. Despite the superior quality of the FM sound, the content was largely limited to music—even though the world was not awash in FM-ready receivers. I ended the story predicting FM would take off because car makers had begun installing radios with FM bands as well as AM. How did I become an expert on FM radio? Simple: I just interviewed a lot of industry executives. That was how I became an "expert" in so many diverse topics.[25]

One of the stranger topics I tackled was the game of squash. Because I have sight just in one eye, and therefore lack good depth perception, I rarely played racquet sports, and never well. I had to endure a unit of badminton during my first year at university. I have no idea why I did the article, which was at least 1,500 words long. On reading it today, I obviously applied the usual technique—extensive interviews with experts associated with the game. When I mentioned my handicap to one of them, I was advised to interview Ted Tilden, the president of Tilden Rent-A-Car, who also had sight just in one eye, the result of a skiing accident. He competed in squash by outrunning his opponents. And he loved the sport. "To me, it's got the effect of three martinis after work," he told me.[26]

From time to time, I even wrote about symphony orchestras. That flowed from my interest in classical music acquired during my first year at university and nurtured whenever the opportunity came along. When I was living in the basement room in Regina, I borrowed a record player from the public library, along with a few vinyl discs. One was a recording of *The Nutcracker Suite*, excellent entry-level classical music. I attended my first concert in January 1959, to hear the Regina Symphony play Beethoven's Second Symphony and Sibelius' *Finlandia*.

25   *Financial Post*, March 18, 1972: "FM radio—waiting to become a bride."

26   *Financial Post*, December 19, 1972: "This game is better than three martinis after work."

After we moved to Toronto, we bought a Blauplunkt radio with good audio reproduction. I may even have connected a turntable to it. I got serious in Montreal, after assembling a stereo amplifier from a kit. I started buying recordings of Beethoven and other classical composers. Either when I was in the Montreal bureau, or shortly thereafter, I wrote a big feature on the health of Canadian symphony orchestras.

In the spring of 1974 (there is no date on the clipping), I was in Winnipeg for an interview with Leonard Stone, the general manager of the Winnipeg Symphony. Then thirty-nine years old, he had been general manager for four years and had the orchestra in good financial health due to his edgy marketing of the product. "I've been accused of merchandising the orchestra like soap," he told me. "Well, you can't do without soap." I managed to dig out some entertaining anecdotes: a bass player lost three teeth when punched by a drunk in Flin Flon—and the drunk had not even been at the concert. And I took in the rehearsal that morning and stayed for that evening's concert in Winnipeg—the Bruckner Fourth Symphony.

In March 1975, I wrote a long feature on the Vancouver Opera Association, which had just hired a superstar conductor, Richard Bonynge.[27] The article sounds like I knew something about opera, which was not entirely so. I have never been much of an opera lover (despite my love of other classical music). I find most operas to be tedious renditions of fatuous stories, even if I have taken the occasional opportunity to attend an opera. Once, when I was doing the Germany report, I went to Nurnberg for a weekend that included the performance of Beethoven's *Fidelio*. I had a complimentary ticket to the evening. It was black tie; I managed to rent the appropriate garb, but I had overlooked that I was wearing brown shoes. I wonder how many other opera attendees even noticed.

The Vancouver Opera, like many arts companies, was running a deficit, but the administration clearly counted on the celebrity of the new artistic director to attract patrons and contributions. Because of his schedule, Bonynge did not conduct the Vancouver Opera until 1976.

27 *Financial Post*, March 29, 1975: "When you've got superstars, angels are in high demand."

I believe Marlene and I attended a performance of *The Merry Widow*, with Joan Sutherland—the conductor's wife—in the lead role. She had a beautiful voice, but her large frame did not flatter the role theatrically. I also wrote a long article on Bonynge and the Vancouver Opera for a magazine called *AudioScene Canada*.[28] Bonynge, who was to have his contract extended by five years, had taken an aggressive and ambitious approach, even talking about having a new opera house built. It never happened.

"Bonynge precipitated a crisis in the relationship between the Vancouver Symphony Orchestra (VSO) and the Vancouver Opera Association (VOA)," my friend, Alex Nichol, told me later. Alex, who later became the founder of Nichol Vineyard in the Okanagan, had been a double bass player with the Vancouver Symphony Orchestra before he got into winemaking. "I was personnel manager of the VSO when this crisis was coming to a head." The two organizations had been sharing musicians. That would not work when Bonynge proposed compressing the opera season so that he and Sutherland could look after their many international opportunities. It would have left a big hole right in the VSO's season. "I think it was this stalemate that was the backdrop behind Bonynge's departure," Alex says.

In April 1977, I wrote an article, once again for *AudioScene Canada*, on the Vancouver Symphony as it moved into the Orpheum. The VSO had previously performed in the Queen Elizabeth Theatre (as the VOA still does), which had appalling acoustics. "It was as though a wool blanket had been wrapped around them," the VSO's publicist told me. The Orpheum was built in 1927 as a vaudeville theatre and was later converted to a movie theatre. In the early 1970s, Famous Players wanted to turn it into a five-screen theatre but, in the face of a community campaign to save the Orpheum, sold it to the city. It was then renovated to become an excellent venue for the VSO. Marlene and I were season ticket holders until 2020.[29]

28 *AudioScene Canada*, March, 1976, pp 24-25: "Richard Bonynge and the Vancouver Opera."

29 *AudioScene Canada*, April, 1977, pp 59-62: "VSO."

General Business Editor was not my favourite job at the *Financial Post*. I did not enjoy the administration and personnel relations that the job required: I much preferred to write. An opportunity came early in 1973 when the *Financial Post* decided to open a bureau in Washington, DC. It was offered to me, but I turned it down, as did another of the reporters. However, the paper had opened its Vancouver bureau in 1972. Hyman Solomon, who had been posted to Vancouver, was quite interested in Washington. (By coincidence, Hyman Solomon had come to *Regina Leader-Post* when I was there and was immediately one of that newspaper's best reporters. After several years in our Washington bureau, he transferred to the *Financial Post's* Ottawa bureau where he had a distinguished career until he died of cancer. In 1992, after his death, the Public Policy Forum in Ottawa established a prestigious journalism award that bears his name.)

Neville Nankivell, then the *Financial Post* editor, agreed to move Hyman to Washington asked me to recommend one of my group for Vancouver. I recommended myself. Neville was surprised, but he agreed to the transfer, which happened in May 1973. It proved to be the best career decision I ever made. As western bureau chief, I got to report on all of Western Canada and also to develop the other Post bureaus and a network of stringers across the West. At the same time, I began writing about wine, leading to a second career as a wine writer. I doubt that career would have flourished if I had remained in Toronto.

Seven:
Airplanes—
An Unrequited Love Affair

Carl Kattler, one of my mother's brothers, worked for many years with the White Pass & Yukon Route Railway and lived in Carcross in the Yukon. I was about six years old when he visited us in Saskatchewan. He must have sprinkled his conversation with exotic references to bush pilots in the Yukon because I asked him to send me an airplane. In the manner of adults, he promised to do so and then put it out of his mind. I pestered my parents about that airplane, which never arrived. Finally, they bought me a metal airplane, a model of a twin-engine commercial aircraft with a double tail. It became one of my favourite toys. It also engendered a lifelong interest in aviation. Had I had sight in both eyes, I would undoubtedly have learned to fly.

I remember my first flight vividly. I was then a very junior reporter at the *Regina Leader-Post*, assigned to the two beats—hotels and obituary writing—that were used to teach the craft to young reporters. On the hotel beat, I went every morning to the three major hotels in the city, as well as to the Canadian Pacific ticket office in the railroad station, to ask if anyone of interest had arrived in the city that morning. In the days before privacy laws, the desk clerks would actually tell you if they had interesting guests.

One morning, the clerk at the King's Hotel said that a Texan flying for Ducks Unlimited had checked in the day before. At that time,

Ducks Unlimited chartered small aircraft to fly grids over the Prairies in the summer. The pilot, from 100 to 200 feet altitude, counted the ducks swimming on the sloughs below. An extrapolation of that count estimated that year's duck population and, thus, the bag limits for the hunt that fall. I suppose that it is done by satellite today.

I rang the pilot's room. Not only did I get an interview, he invited me to fly with him the next morning and experience the count. We took off about 8:00 a.m. on a fine, sunny morning, in his single-engine canvass-covered Piper Cub. The seats were line astern, which was a good thing. The little plane was buffeted so much in the rising air currents that I left my breakfast in an airsick bag, the only time that has ever happened to me. But the flight was still an exhilarating experience, and I was proud of the article I wrote (although I might cringe at it now). Since then, I have enjoyed almost every flight I have taken, even recording annually the number of hours spent in the air.

My first commercial flights were on Air Canada Viscounts and Vanguards, pressurized turboprops made by the British Vickers firm. When I was being interviewed by the *Financial Post*, I took red-eye flights from Regina to Toronto and back. Marlene and I had another Vanguard experience flying back to Regina for Christmas 1960. Once again, I took the red-eye back to Toronto on Christmas night so I could go to work on Boxing Day. I stayed awake in the office even if I did no useful work.

My first trans-Atlantic flight was to Scandinavia when I was assigned to write a report on Sweden. For some reason, I flew via New York, catching an SAS (Scandinavian Airlines) flight to Copenhagen where I stayed for several nights. I had not made a hotel booking but, inspired by some guidebook, went to a downtown tourist information center where one could book small hotels and or bed and breakfast accommodations. I spent an hour or two milling around with mostly backpacking students until I had a booking. It was in a charming small hotel with a dining room where, because of exhaustion, I feel asleep briefly at the dinner table.

It was the first of a lengthy series of punishing jet-lag experiences, especially during my several trips to Japan. Invariably, it took me three or four days before I stopped waking up at 4:00 a.m. I dealt with that by going for walks with my camera if there was daylight. One morning in Tokyo, I found myself watching teenagers playing baseball at 5:00 a.m., a commentary on how crowded a city Tokyo is. The downside was the need to get to bed right after dinner. I was dragged to a rather dull dinner one evening early during one trip where there were several speeches in Japanese. At one point, I snapped awake with my nose just inches from my plate. Then when I got back to my hotel, I could not get to sleep.

The longest flights were to Australia and New Zealand, especially in an era when the aircraft lacked the range to do so without a fuel stop. I recall arriving in Sydney at 8:00 a.m. after about eighteen hours of travel. I was on a wine tour, and there was just time to get to the hotel to shower and shave before we had to be at a restaurant run by the late Len Evans, then Australia's best known wine writer. It was a loud and bibulous lunch, leading to a very sound sleep that night.

In 1973, I was among a group of ten travel and wine writers invited on the inaugural Qantas flight from Vancouver to Sydney. The outbound flight stopped in Fiji where our group spent a fairly pointless overnight stay at a resort before completing the final leg of the flight. The return flight from Australia stopped in Tahiti, this time for three days, with time for snorkelling above a spectacular coral reef. The Gauguin museum, we discovered, had none of his canvasses. Somewhere, I also picked up food poisoning which struck hard—hot and cold chills, trips to the bathroom—at 35,000 feet en route to Los Angeles. Even in those days, the immigration line at Los Angeles seemed infinite, especially to someone with diarrhoea. We had been routed through Los Angeles on a Pan American flight because a strike in Australia had grounded Qantas.

Before the current generation of long-range passenger jets, fuelling stops were routine over the Pacific. Once Marlene and I returned from Australia with a stop in Honolulu. Three Boeing 747s filled with Asian passengers landed just before our plane. There was another infinite immigration line. The customs officers soon were processing the hordes with cursory looks at passports before stamping them. When Marlene and I presented our passports, the official's head snapped up, and he looked at us. "You don't look Japanese," he said.

On another occasion, I was returning to Asia with a Honolulu stop and was lucky enough to be in first class. Beside me was a deadheading pilot. Of course, we talked about aircraft for some time. Then he arranged for me to sit on the jump seat behind the pilots and watch the landing, which was at night. It was almost magical. I wore a headset and listened to the laconic conversation between our pilot and the control tower. The privilege of sitting in the cockpit with pilots ended when airlines began to lock the flight deck after terrorists highjacked passenger jets and crashed them into the World Trade Centre in New York on September 11, 2001.

Most commercial flights, at least until the twenty-first century, were comfortable experiences—luxurious even, if you happened to be in business class or first class. The 747 has an upper deck that, on some carriers, is used for first class, with seats big enough for comfortable sleeping. I don't recall the carrier, but I do remember being in one of those seats, slipping off to sleep with a snifter of cognac—which was still there when I awoke. It had been a smooth flight.

Being interested in wine, I always enjoyed wine with meals at 35,000 feet, even if one is told that the taste buds are not sharp at altitude. Mine worked well enough. Wine service in economy class was usually mediocre, although Canadian Pacific and Wardair tended to have better wine than Air Canada, which had cheap Bordeaux wines in small bottles. The Canadian wine industry was perennially annoyed that the national airline refused to serve Canadian wine in economy. The reason was that Canadian wines in the 1970s and 1980s were mediocre, even worse that cheap Bordeaux wines. When Canadian wines were offered on flights, passengers refused them so often that flight attendants called the wines "million milers"—because, as someone explained to me, "they never left the aircraft."

In 1976, the Canadian government sent a trade mission to Southeast Asia led by Don Jamieson, then the minister of industry. He liked his wines. I was attached to the mission as a journalist. We were flying in a Boeing 707 operated by Canadian Forces rather than in a commercial aircraft. The food served by our military crew was the same basic fare they might have served to a plane full of servicemen: sandwiches. But thanks to Jamieson, we had a bottomless supply of Chablis and red Burgundy. Also thanks to the minister, our flight, on its return, stopped overnight in Honolulu.

The wine service was always better in business and first class. In May 1990, I was invited to a winery tour in Spain. To get there, I flew KLM from Vancouver to Amsterdam, changing planes there for Madrid. On the flight to Amsterdam in business class, a good dinner was served, and wines were poured generously. That was followed by a movie; undoubtedly, I had a cognac at hand and was totally relaxed and comfortable. Just as the movie was ending, I decided to be first in line for the washroom. I jumped up abruptly and promptly fainted; I had been too relaxed, and there was not quite enough blood flowing to my head when I stood up. A nurse on board sat beside me for the remaining hour or two of the flight; then I was wheeled off the plane and to a doctor, who found nothing wrong when he examined me. Finally, he asked how much wine and cognac I had consumed. When I told him, he snorted and advised me not to have any more that day. I only had a beer on the flight to Madrid.

The quality of the beer was the only good thing I could say about my 1985 flights from Montreal to Prague and back on the Czechoslovakian national airline. I had been invited to attend a trade fair in Brno, as a journalist. There was no option but to fly the Czech national airline, which was then still using elderly Russian-made Ilyushin jets. The plane creaked and rattled. The seats were not very comfortable, and I doubt there was much of an entertainment system on board. The cabin was laid out so that the smoking section was on the left and the non-smoking section was across the aisle. This was certainly the worst national airline I have ever flown with.

While I continued to log my flight time annually, the novelty of flying gradually faded. That is mostly because airport security has become more and more onerous; service on board has become more and more mundane; and some cabins have become less comfortable.

My fascination in aviation took an unusual turn in 1986, when I took an interest in blimps, spurred by attending a conference that fall in Vancouver on lighter-than-air (LTA) ships. Either that summer or the summer before, I had arranged a visit to a large hangar in Tillamook, Oregon. It housed four different LTA vehicles including the so-called Cyclo-Crane developed by Aerolift Corp., listed on the Vancouver Stock Exchange. Four British Columbia forest companies had invested about $4 million in the project in search of a vehicle that could be used in logging. The Cyclo-Crane was a Rube Goldberg design that completed test flights but never was used commercially in the coastal forest industry. I did a substantial feature in the *Financial Post* and became somewhat knowledgeable on LTA. The only tangible benefit was that I got a ride on a Goodyear blimp that cruised around Vancouver during Expo 86.

Eight:
Our household missed the Cuban Missile Crisis

The Soviet Union and the United States were on the brink of war in October 1962 over the (ultimately successful) American demand that the Russians withdraw the missiles they had placed in Cuba. In some quarters, October 20 is remembered as Black Saturday. Not in our household: Maureen, the first of our three children, was born that weekend. Potential Armageddon was not on our minds. There were, thankfully, no comparable global crises competing for our attention when Alison was born on May 6, 1964, and when John was born on March 27, 1969.

I used to blame the pitter-patter of Maureen's feet on the wooden floor of our Toronto apartment for causing us to be evicted about a month before Alison's birth. It turned out our landlords decided we were using too much hot water, among other irritants.

Initially, we had rented the top floor of a two-storey house, and our landlords were an immigrant couple from Eastern Europe. We had found the place quite by chance when we arrived in Toronto in 1961. We were driving west of St. Clair Avenue, not at all sure of where we were headed, when I needed a bathroom break and spotted a service station at St. Clair and Bathurst. We pulled off onto a side street and spotted a "for rent" sign in the window. The apartment was bigger than the one we had rented in Regina. We could afford the rent, and the location was convenient to public transit. The landlords were pleasant, although they cooked with a great deal of garlic, the odor of which permeated our suite and probably our clothes. We lived there for a year, and because they did not want children in the suite, we moved to a suite nearby in North Toronto until Maureen's pitter-patter eventually forced us to move on.

Staying in the neighbourhood that was now familiar to us, we found a rental house at 545 Cranbrook Avenue in North Toronto. The entire neighbourhood then was populated by plain, cookie-cutter bungalows built after World War II on surprisingly large lots. Today, virtually all of these homes have been replaced by much larger houses.

The Cranbrook bungalow was in a quiet neighbourhood but within walking distance of a small shopping plaza and an excellent Jewish bakery on Bathurst from which we acquired the taste for fresh bagels. Robert and Renata Herz, who became our closest friends in Toronto, lived in a similar bungalow a few blocks away. Marlene and Renata became acquainted after meeting in the maternity ward when Alison and Liza Herz, Renata's daughter, were born. Renata was an older mother and Liza was her first, and only, child. The two mothers provided mutual support over copious quantities of tea in each other's kitchens.

Robert and Renata were ferociously intelligent. She had grown up in a prosperous merchant family in Czechoslovakia and had been well educated at a school, probably a convent school, that turned out elegant and well-mannered ladies. As the Communists were taking control in 1948, she acquired an exit visa by arranging a marriage of convenience to a Dane; it was never consummated. Once out of Czechoslovakia, she joined relatives already living in Ontario. Robert was also Czech but was otherwise an unlikely choice for a husband to Renata. She was a devout Roman Catholic, while Robert was an agnostic Jew who had survived a Nazi concentration camp. I don't recall him ever discussing the experience; Renata alluded to the nightmares that Robert endured. Instead, our always lively conversations focussed on literature, business, our children, and their travels, all of it more positive than the Holocaust. It was Robert who warned me that I risked missing out on promotions by transferring myself to Vancouver from the newspaper's head office in Toronto. That was strange, coming from him; he was not obviously ambitious and worked most of his career as an office manager with a plastics manufacturer. We remained friends, exchanging letters, telephone calls, and visits, until they died—Renata first and then Robert, who had had heart problems.

We lived in the Cranbrook house for two years until we were able to buy our first house. This happened in 1966, when we purchased 200 Old Orchard Grove, also in North Toronto. We found this house by identifying the neighbourhood in which we wanted to live and then driving up and down the streets to search out houses for sale. We had looked in other neighbourhoods. I recall looking at a large duplex north of Highway 401. I believe we decided against it because it was too far from public transit (the subway then stopped at St. Clair). As well, we were comfortable with North Toronto, a neighbourhood convenient to all the services we required.

We bought our home at 200 Old Orchard Grove for $22,000 and sold it eight years later for $44,000. Built in the 1920s, it was a two-storey brick house with leaded windows. The lot was 33 feet wide and 110 feet deep. There were two covenants on the property: we were not allowed to operate a gravel pit or an abattoir, which suggests that North Toronto was once quite rural. The house shared a driveway (wide enough for a European compact but not for a full-size American sedan) with its architectural twin, on a similar narrow lot. Our neighbours were an elderly brother and sister who had lived there since the home was built. They did not have a car, but they were firm that we were not to park on the driveway because it also served as the sidewalk to the side doors of our houses. A reclusive couple with curious hobbies—he once built a clavichord and had a partially completed harpsichord in their front room—they warmed to us slowly over time. For him, the epiphany came when he saw me torching and scraping old paint from the house in a laborious preparation for repainting the wood trim and the garage. That generated the first of our few conversations.

It was a charming house with three small bedrooms on the second floor. When John needed a room of his own, I built a bunk bed to accommodate Alison and Maureen in the other bedroom. Alison recorded this in a 1971 reference in her diary: "My father made a bunk bed. We had to stay up until 10 o'clock." I am not sure why they stayed up; perhaps it had something to do with the fact that I used soft wood for the first mattress frame, and the slats cracked when the girls climbed into the beds. I had to replace the slats with hard wood.

On the main floor of the house, there was a compact kitchen, a dining room, and a cozy living room with a fire place. (A pigeon once fell down the ivy-covered chimney and was trapped for several days before being rescued). The porch at the back, which I insulated, became my study. The low, unfinished basement was, when we moved in, dominated by a hulking furnace that originally burned coal but had been converted to oil. A few years later, the burner began backfiring dangerously one cold winter night. The plumber that we summoned recommended against rebuilding the burner and pointed out that the house was connected to the outside gas line, something we did not know. So we activated gas service. The new gas furnace, on which the gas company gave us a rebate, was no larger than a suitcase, including the seven-gallon (32-liter) tank of hot water that heated the radiators in the house. It gave us much more room in the basement.

Old Orchard Grove was a pleasant, tree-lined street that ran from Avenue Road, a couple of blocks to the west, almost to Yonge Street, perhaps six blocks to the east. Two sets of neighbours with children about the same age as ours became good friends. Marlene played tennis with David Lilienstein, a pudgy university professor. His wife, Lois, was a singer with the successful folk trio, Sharon, Lois and Bram, that specialized in music for children. Joyce and Ralph Scane lived further down the block. He was a lawyer and law professor, and she was an educator. We kept in touch for decades after we eventually moved.

When I was transferred to Montreal in 1967, we chose to rent our house rather than to sell it. We were happy to return to Old Orchard Grove in the fall of 1969. Judging from diary entries the girls made, they were also happy. In 1971, Alison kept various little books in school called *News of the Day*, or simply *Work Book*.

May 5, 1971: "Yesterday, I got a new bike. It was red and shiny. The bell and kickstand were a present from the man at the store. My dad told the man that it was my birthday on Thursday. I am happy I got a bike. Now I can ride with my sister and have fun."

May 16, 1971: "In the summer holidays we might go to Cape Cod, and after that we might go to Boston. My sister and I will have to sleep in the back [of the station wagon].

November 22, 1971: "On Saturday my family and I went to the Royal Winter Fair. We saw cows, bulls, sheep, and goats. We ate some beans and cheese. We saw a big squash and we saw tobacco."

December 9, 1971: "Yesterday [Sunday] my dad, my sister, and I went to cut our Christmas tree."

* * *

From Alison's Work Books in 1972:

February 14, 1972: "Yesterday my brother gave me a black eye. He threw something at me."

April 12, 1972: "On Friday next week my grandma and grandpa are arriving by train."

May 15, 1972: "My father is in Asia. He went there a few weeks ago. We send him letters.

May 17, 1972: "Today, my grandparents are leaving. I am very very very very sad."

June 7, 1972: "Last night my dad came home from Asia. He brought us lots of things."

Alison's first so-called "diary", begun in school in September 1972, provides glimpses of the family life, from art lessons and skating lessons to shopping trips (popular) and birthday parties (even more so), and whiffs of discipline.

September 7, 1972: "My grand-parents are coming [referring to Marlene's parents]. We will go to Niagara Falls."

September 27, 1972: "On Saturday my father, my sister, and my brother and I went to a toy party. There was a fairy godmother and a clown. I really enjoyed it all." The reference was to a Toronto toy company that invited journalists once a year to bring their families and let the children play with the toys. It was a clever promotion for the toy company.

September 29, 1972: "Two of my teeth are loose. I hope they fall out. I will be very very happy."

October 10, 1972: "On Friday I went to the orthodontist ... I might get braces." In fact both she and John did. In 1974, we committed to $1,700 worth of dental work for Alison. I believe John's dental work was even more expensive. Maureen complained for years how unfair it was that we had spent so much on dental work on her siblings and not spent a compensating amount on her. The complaints ended after I finally lost my temper and reminded her that she had no dental issues.

October 30, 1972: "On Halloween I am going out. I am going to be a fairy. I will wear a long gown with polka dots on it. I will have a wand and a crown. I will look pretty."

November 20, 1972: "A couple of days ago my mother put my Halloween candies with my brother's. I will get them back. I like them. I was mad. I had a lot."

December 8, 1972: "Today after school I might go shopping. I will get my Christmas presents. I will get my sister some nail polish and a book. She likes nail polish."

January 3, 1973: "For Christmas I got a radio. I like it."

January 17, 1973: "My dad is going to Vancouver today. He is going to visit my grandparents. He will come home on January 24. I am excited."

January 26, 1973: "On Wednesday my dad came home from Vancouver. He brought us a book [Peter Pan]. He also brought hats [toques] for us and a record [Burl Ives]." That was the end of her first diary.

The modest diaries that Maureen and Alison kept were encouraged by their teachers. The glimpses of our lives at the time underline my belief in the value of such records, however modest. Parents are always trying to pass on values and tastes. In 1968, Marlene scrapped together the money to buy our Mason & Risch[30] upright piano by saving the monthly family allowance cheques sent by the federal government at the time. One of our tastes is classical music.

"I am going to a symphony next Friday because my sister went yesterday night," Maureen recorded on June 2, 1970. "This is the second time I've been to a symphony." Her journal covers only June, the last month in the school year, notable for a field trip to Centre Island in Toronto, trips to the local swimming pool. and one to the library. Maureen already had her own library card, but she had forgotten it at home. Both girls were enrolled, briefly, in Brownies. In Maureen's papers, there is a two-page essay on Brownies in the Netherlands.

Maureen's school books show her ability for creative writing. And in the period prior to the family move to Vancouver, she occasionally wrote a brief letter to me and included it with Marlene's letters. "You won't believe what Kathy and I did in school today!" she wrote on June 1, 1973. "We challenged two boys in our class to a cake-baking contest.

---

30   Mason & Risch, established in 1871, grew to be a major Canadian piano maker, based in Toronto, through to the 1980s.

We are baking chocolate cakes. We are not allowed to get help." I do not know whether she and her friend won, but Maureen did become quite adept at cooking (as did Alison and John).

Alison's school books indicate she was quite social. Cleveland School in North Vancouver in the early 1970s had the students write regular self-evaluations that now seem brutally frank. "I finished my math and observation," Alison wrote on March 11, 1974. "I could have been quiet, because I talked too much, and I could have done more, but I tried very hard and I couldn't help talking." She made similar admissions several times. "I could have been quieter, and I could have concentrated more," she wrote April 30. I wonder what the teachers did with this self-criticism.

At various times, Marlene's letters to me added details about the children. "John had his first swimming lesson Monday & it wasn't that successful," Marlene wrote to me in Vancouver on May 29, 1973. "I expected him to jump in as always, splashing away. Not so—he stood in the water up to his knees—finger in his mouth, & the last 15 minutes hanging onto his penis. He informed me later that he had to go to the bathroom. And except for when the instructor had him, that's where he stood—very close to tears... I just never thought it would bother him. So I hope tomorrow will be more successful. He goes 3 times a week." In fact, she stopped taking him to swimming lessons because he was afraid of swimming—a fear he overcame later in life.

We did not know North Vancouver when we moved there in 1973. The Vancouver housing market was tight at the time, and I did not have much time to look at housing because I did a lot of travelling between May and July, when Marlene and the children followed me to Vancouver. One realtor tried to talk me into buying in Richmond, but I had no desire to live in a community that is actually below sea level. I was interested in southeast Vancouver, but real estate agents kept discouraging me because of the rising East Indian population in the neighbourhood. I did find an appealing home in Shaughnessy, but it was slightly beyond what I thought we could afford. Meanwhile, Marlene had sold Old Orchard Grove, and she came to Vancouver for a week in May to help me find a home. Someone recommended a realtor on the North

Shore who showed us half a dozen houses in North Vancouver that we could afford. After I got over my aversion to dealing with the bridges to get to work, we bought a home on a delightful cul-de-sac called Lodge Road. Aside from the fact that the house, barely three years old, had a leaky roof that we replaced in 1982, it was a good choice on a large lot with mature conifers. Not long after we arrived, a neighbour's tree fell into our backyard during a wind storm—fortunately not onto our roof. There have been many wind storms since, but no more trees came down; we did have one cut down that would have become a problem if it had remained.

Lodge Road was convenient to public transit and, more importantly, to schools, both a ten-minute walk for our children. They were enrolled at Cleveland Elementary School and went on to Handsworth Secondary School (with the exception of John). Established in 1961, Handsworth went on to become a major school. Judging from some of its illustrious graduates, it excelled in athletics and music. Maureen and Alison both took piano lessons privately and achieved a fairly high level, but they did not have the interest to pursue musical careers. Patricia Hoebig, their tough but highly competent teacher, had a son and a daughter, Desmond and Gwen, who both went on to major careers as professional musicians.

We had a significant medical fright in September 1979, when Marlene was diagnosed with a tumour behind one of her ovaries. We did not know whether it was benign or cancerous until she had surgery a week after the diagnosis. Fortunately, it proved to be benign. A few decades later, a polyp in her lower intestine did prove to be cancerous, and the surgeon removed some of the intestine to ensure no cancer had been left behind.

Our proximity to three mountains on the North Shore, all with ski hills, gave the children the opportunity to take skiing lessons. John got his first set of skis in early December 1980. "He's been phoning the ski report for the past month," I wrote in my diary on December 3. John and Maureen became quite adept at downhill skiing. Alison, Marlene, and I preferred cross-country skiing. They took lessons. I would have benefitted from lessons but never took any.

Ours was a workaholic household. The children all had part-time jobs while going to school. Maureen began working in a McDonald's franchise. After high school, she attended Capilano College for a semester before deciding the academic life did not appeal to her.

Alison first worked as a chamber maid in a local motel. She lasted a month before finding a much better job as a cashier at Canadian Tire. Her earnings helped her with expenses at the University of British Columbia (although we paid tuition). She also was able to finance a French-language course in the summer of 1985 at McGill University in Montreal. (I was visiting wineries in Quebec that summer and arranged to meet her at the end of the course, where we took in a Montreal Expos baseball game in the Olympic Stadium.)

After graduating from the University of British Columbia with an arts degree (psychology major), she spent six months in 1987 in French immersion at a university in Montpellier. She returned home bilingual but broke and went to work as a receptionist with Pemberton Securities, one of Vancouver's oldest brokerage firms. The job soon became permanent, and she transitioned to a broker's assistant. By the following March, she had scored 90 in the Canadian Securities Course. This was to set her on a career in the financial industry despite her university degree in psychology. It also replenished her bank account: in July 1988, she bought a new Honda Civic. In December, she accepted a job offer from money managers VanBrit Investment Management and found herself making $20,000 a year. Early in 1992, she moved to Connor Clark & Lunn, another investment firm, at a salary that was $6,000 higher. We had a celebratory dinner with a bottle of Chassagne Montrachet 1987. She did well there (with a $3,000 bonus six months after joining them). And the bonuses kept rolling in. At the end of 1993, when my bonus was $650, Alison's bonus was $4,700, and Maureen's was about half that.

On Easter, 1995, Alison brought her new boyfriend, Rodney Cameron, around for dinner. We liked him a lot better than her previous boyfriend, a young man from New Zealand. "Neat beard, good manners," I told my diary about Rodney. They married in April 1997. Raising three boys took her out of the work force for a time. In 2007, she began working one day a week at Blueshore Financial. Three years later, she began working full-time, expanding her financial acumen in the investment and estate services department. In 2018, she moved into another department, dealing with the institution's software applications. She has shown remarkable versatility for a psychology major.

John showed little musical aptitude. His sports were soccer and baseball. To his disappointment, we did not enrol him for hockey, in part because of the inconvenient practice times. He also did not attend Handsworth. Marlene and I thought the school's flexible class hours might tempt him to waste time with the other boys in the "smoke hole"—as the students called the ravine just east of the school where they congregated with cigarettes. Instead, we enrolled John at Vancouver College where the Christian Brothers taught a much more structured program. The Brothers subsequently were notorious for abusing students at the Newfoundland orphanage they ran. There also was abuse at Vancouver College. (One abused student later committed suicide). John, who was not abused, did well enough at the college to get into UBC, where he graduated in 1991 with a major in Asian studies.

I had some influence on the careers of John and Maureen. When Maureen dropped out of Capilano College even before completing her first year, she was a bit adrift. I telephoned a friend, Marnie Huckvale, who had a small advertising agency, and asked if she knew of anyone who needed a receptionist. She and her partner did. Maureen started there, which was the beginning of a long career with various advertising and marketing companies, including McKim and then J. Walter Thompson. Her great strength is her ability to organize projects and see they are completed on time and well. In 1992, she moved to the Vancouver-based creative firm named Ken Foo, for the owner, and subsequently to Tree Top Marketing, another creative firm, until she retired in 2022.

Maureen completed scuba diving lessons in January 1988, presumably because a new man had come into her life: David Romanick, who enjoyed scuba diving. At one point in his work life, he even became a commercial geoduck diver on the West Coast, a dangerous way to earn a living. He was also an ironworker, a trade that also has plenty of risky jobs. But the trade eventually led him to a series of jobs with Canada Post, the riskiest of which was being a letter carrier.

Maureen has a strong interest in travel. She was still a teenager when she and a girlfriend booked a vacation in Hawaii. The arrangements were made while Marlene and I were in New Zealand. She had not sought our permission, which would have been a difficult conversation. In retrospect, I am glad it did not happen and that she got to enjoy the trip. She and David began their travels with a three-month trip early in 1994 to the Orient, Australia, and New Zealand. Subsequently, when their son and daughter matured, the children went along on various trips.

When John was trying to decide his major at university, we had a long conversation one evening about the courses he liked. It turned out he liked Asian history. I did not exactly suggest that he major in this, but I did point out that Asia would be increasingly important in the years ahead. He majored in Asian studies and graduated in 1991.

Like all of our children, John had a summer job throughout university. He earned his first paycheque, $248.00, after starting as a clerk at Mark's Work Wearhouse in August 1985. In his last four months there, ending April 1988, he earned $2,673. In May 1988, he moved to a better-paying sales job at T. Eaton & Co., earning $3,434.14 that year. I could never understand how all of our children juggled school work and part-time jobs. John failed his first-year economics course at UBC, perhaps proving he had too much on his plate. But he continued with part-time jobs while improving his university marks. He was certainly successful at Eaton's. His income in 1990 from the retailer was $7,455.28; and it was $6,758.04 in 1991, according to his T-4 tax slips. By the time he left in 1991, he had received seven letters of commendation from his manager; these all had been triggered by customer praise for his service.

He ended up with enough money in the bank on graduation that he could go to Taiwan in 1991. However, in the weeks before he left for Taiwan, he began having such severe headaches that he ended up having a CAT scan and an overnight hospital stay for medical tests. It was an extreme case of stress, but once he settled in there, he did well. He spent two years there and learned to read, write, and speak Mandarin. It took courage to do that. He earned a six-month bursary at $400 a month and then found a part-time job with Trade International, a local trading company. John also took up dragon boat racing one summer. As well, he found time to teach English. "I teach about eight hours a week, and I plan to expand that to about fifteen," he wrote in a card one Christmas. That income and his savings meant we did not need to finance his studies in Taiwan.

Elizabeth Smart, his high-school sweetheart, followed him to Taiwan and also studied Mandarin. Elizabeth taught English at a school called the Taipei Language Institute. On completing their Mandarin studies, they moved to Hong Kong in mid-1993 to find jobs. We loaned them $6,000 to help get established.

John's departure for Hong Kong in September 1993 occasioned an emotional entry in my diary. "I have a bit of an empty feeling," I wrote. "This time, this is not a student going off to school—this is the last of our children leaving home for good. I am also a bit apprehensive and will be until he gets a job. But I believe he has done the right thing to return to the Orient. I'm proud of what he has accomplished so far—not just learning Mandarin but also developing some business skills." He finally got a job in late November with Executive Access, an executive search firm. It did not take him long to get established. His annual salary in 1995 was $43,000—and that in a city with a 15% income tax rate. He got on his feet quickly, because by December 1994, he participated in a family gift to set up my first internet account. In his first email to me, John wrote: "I used Grampa's money to buy a pair of pants, and I will look for some studs for my tuxedo shirt to spend Granny's money. I did mention to you that I bought a tuxedo, didn't I? (I can already picture the expression on Mom's face.) I am using my bonus money, and I figured that I would use one in HK. I have already needed one once, and I will need one again for New Year." The money here must refer to money we sent as gifts.

Elizabeth worked at a variety of jobs, including executive search at Executive Access, before joining Fidelity Investments (because she had worked in banking in Canada). Several years later, Elizabeth's British citizenship led Fidelity to transfer her to London in 1999. They had married in 1996, and John was able to move to London by virtue of her passport. There, he found employment with IMAX in 2000 that led to an exceptional sales career in theatre development. He also became a British citizen, then an advantageous passport for travelling in Europe.

In July 2001, Elizabeth and John parted. John was surprised and hurt. It took several months, with a lot of counselling from his family, before he came to grips with the loss of a woman he had loved for sixteen years. They divorced in September. To my surprise, she wrote us a quite civil letter early in September. "You both have been fantastic parents-in-law," she wrote. "I couldn't have asked for anyone better."

I replied in a similar spirit, for I had always liked her. "We are grateful to know that you have good memories of this household," I wrote. "We also have warm memories, whether it be of travels in Asia and Britain or Sunday dinners at home. I don't suppose I will ever squirt whipped cream on my pie without remembering you." That referred to an occasion at our dinner table when I squirted whipped cream all over her by accident. I had been quite fond of Elizabeth.

John had been assigned Russia for IMAX. He negotiated the opening of the first IMAX theatre in Russia (in Moscow) in September 2002. He also met and eventually married a Russian employee of IMAX, Olga Pilnikova. After living in London for a few years, they moved to Moscow in October 2011. In 2020, it was déjà vu all over again for John, leading to divorce from Olga.

A very good salesperson, John developed Russia into the third largest IMAX territory, with fifty-one theatres. (China and the United States are larger territories.) Unfortunately, John had to move back to London in the spring of 2022. The sanctions imposed on Russia for its invasion of Ukraine that spring made it impossible for IMAX to continue its Russian operations because the theatre franchisees no longer could get Hollywood films or remit fees. John was reassigned IMAX territories in Western Europe and the Middle East and, in 2022, he relocated to the IMAX subsidiary in Dublin.

There is something to be said for being workaholics. When John went off to Vancouver College—the last out of the nest, so to speak—Marlene decided to return to the work force early in 1977. She worked at several jobs, including a secretarial job at Vancouver City Hall and then at Vancouver General Hospital. Then she took a medical terminology course, which led to becoming a medical office assistant. In May 1988, she went to work for Curtis Latham, a family practice doctor in North Vancouver. Six years later, she moved to the office of Suzanne Montemuro, another general practitioner. She quite enjoyed her career in the health sciences field.

Our approach as parents and our apparent success has been to support our children when they needed it, including financial support at crucial moments. For example, Maureen and David decided to buy a condominium in the spring of 1991. The money they needed for a down payment was locked up in term deposits. We gave them a $20,000 second mortgage, which they repaid when the term deposits matured. Subsequently—this was primarily Marlene's initiative—we established registered education savings plans (or their equivalent) for each of our eight grandchildren. The grandchildren ended up with about $35,000 each to finance university education.

Nine:
The French lessons were endless

French was a required subject through high school and in first year at university, even in Saskatchewan. During the first three years of high school, French was taught by the English teacher who was not adept with French. On her retirement, a much better teacher took over grade twelve at Indian Head High. This was a good thing as the first-year of French in university, taught by a priest called Father Mallon, would have been a lot more difficult without the extra preparation in high school. Even so, five years of study left me able to read a little in French but not able to converse in it. Yet in 1967, the *Financial Post* transferred me to the Montreal bureau. Of course, I took evening French lessons, first at McGill and then in the Montreal Catholic School system. I passed McGill's evening extension course for intermediate French with only 63%. I improved my ability to read French but did not make much progress in speaking it. Perhaps I could have applied myself harder. I should have immersed myself in a fully French-speaking community for six months or so, but I could not afford to do it, and the newspaper would not have paid for it.

We arrived in Montreal a month before the end of the 1967 World's Fair. Naturally, we found a limited availability of rental accommodation. We ended up in the lower half of a four-plex in Montreal West. It backed onto the Canadian Pacific Railway's marshalling yards. Surprisingly, we quickly became accustomed to the sound of trains shunting back and forth in a steep cut just beyond our backyard. By ironic coincidence, our landlord was a railroad engineer. He lived in the basement, but we rarely saw him. That was an inconvenience when the furnace broke down one very cold New Year's Eve, and he was not around until the following day. We had to move in with friends until the heat came back on.

We enrolled Maureen and Alison in École St-Richard in Côtes Saint-Luc, a French school run by nuns. We were among a number of Anglophone parents doing that in spite of a stern warning from the principal that the school would be teaching the culture as well as the language. By the summer of 1969, when we vacationed in Prince Edward Island, I was surprised and delighted to hear the girls chatting in French with Francophone children on the beach one day. Alison went on to become fluent in French, taking a summer course in Montreal and, after university, a six-month course at the university in Montpellier, France.

I had two choices in public transit from Montreal West to my office downtown on Peel Street (almost directly across from the headquarters of Seagrams, then Canada's leading whisky maker). There was a slow and long bus ride or the quick commuter train that served Windsor Station in the morning and evening rush hours. I much preferred the comfort of the train, and it had the advantage of forcing me to walk about 45 minutes twice a day. In turn, that exercise allowed me to lunch often on the juicy smoked-meat sandwiches at Ben's De Luxe Delicatessen, a Montreal landmark from 1908 until its closing in 2006 after the employees formed a union and voted to strike.

The two years during which we lived in Montreal were at the end of the era when English speakers living there could get along without speaking French. The public relations director for General Motors Canada in Quebec, André Arnoldi, told me of a recent past when English was the dominant language in the major department stores, such as the T. Eaton Co. and the Montreal-headquartered Ogilvy's, which now operates as La Maison Ogilvy. The Quebec government and many French Canadians had become more assertive during the so-called Quiet Revolution when Jean Lesage was premier from 1960 to 1966. By 1968, Arnoldi told me, he was able to do business in French in these stores.

Earlier that year, I was on a Canadian National train to Montreal from Toronto and overhead a Francophone passenger ask a rail employee a question in French. When the employee replied that he spoke only English, the passenger heatedly asked why he should have to speak English when he and his ancestors had lived in Quebec and had spoken French for three hundred years. It was a fair question but also one fast becoming a moot point after federal law in 1968 made French one of Canada's two official languages, and Quebec law in 1974 made French that province's official language.

It was an interesting two years. To begin with, we moved to Montreal at the beginning of October 1967 so that we could take in the final month of Expo 67. As it happened, the site reopened in 1968 as Terre des Hommes with a number of the pavilions converted to new exhibition space. The British Pavilion, as an example, was used on weekends as a concert hall with recorded music. I heard Beethoven's *Missa Solemnis* there for the first time and hated it. It took me another twenty or so years of listening to classical music to appreciate the great Beethoven mass. Cash-strapped Montreal could not afford to continue Terre des Hommes in 1969, but ironically went on to host the Olympic Games in 1976 and to build a stadium that was not paid off for a generation.

Our interest in classical music flourished in Montreal. I had developed a taste for classical music in my first year at university. My landlady in Saskatoon, a robust Dutch lady named Blom, often sat down in the evenings by the family's large radio to listen to classical music loud enough that the second-floor tenants, of whom I was one, heard it. At first, it was an irritating distraction, but by Christmas, I had acquired a taste for this music. Several years later, I borrowed a small record player from the Regina Public Library and was enchanted by *The Nutcracker Suite*. Later in Montreal, a few months before John was born, Marlene and I attended a live performance of the ballet. I discovered that I needed glasses when Maureen and Alison commented on details on stage that I could not see clearly.

I had purchased a good turntable in 1967, plugging into our excellent German radio. Then in Montreal, I built a Dynaco stereo amplifier from a kit and bought decent speakers. I recall the weekend when I soldered the amplifier together, concentrating so intensely and working so late that I was unwell the next day. So was the amplifier. I took it to the store where I had purchased the kit, and I let their staff fix my inept soldering. It worked well then and gave us a great deal of listening pleasure—until 2013 (with one change of tubes), when it was replaced with a solid-state amplifier.

While I gradually began buying albums, I also borrowed some from the Fraser-Hickson Library, a private library serving the city's English language community in Westmount. The quality of the book collection was spotty. I once came across two volumes written in 1936 by a Toronto lawyer who was comparing Roosevelt's New Deal *unfavourably* to the policies of Benito Mussolini, the Italian fascist.

Quebec's nationalism erupted into both separatism and terrorism at this time. The Front de Libération du Québec, a radical sovereigntist group operating from 1963 to 1970, began terrorizing the city with bombs in mail boxes and elsewhere, including a massive explosion in the Montreal Stock Exchange on February 13, 1969, injuring twenty-seven. "This was the third bomb in three days and roughly number sixty over the past year," I noted to my diary that day. The other two bombs that week had been placed at federal military buildings. The violence escalated, with bombings of the Reform Club (the club for provincial Liberals), the Queen's Printer book store, and department stores. "There is a good deal of nervousness among the English-speaking element of the city, notably those who are newer arrivals," I wrote. That very likely included us. With the birth of John in March, we had three young children in a city with an atmosphere of political instability and random violence. In March, the police arrested a twenty-five-year-old FLQ member, Pierre Geoffroy, who confessed to having been involved in more than thirty terrorist bombings. The effusive confession suggested to me that he was taking the heat for his compatriots. Students at Université de Montréal took up a collection for his defence.

The posting to the bureau was only meant to last two years. In a diary note on May 11, 1969, I wrote: "We had decided to stay here an extra year, but have now changed our minds. The gut reason is a desire to get back to our [Toronto] house and back to developing roots and friends in the community." As Anglophones, we certainly had not put down roots in Montreal, nor even tried hard for that matter. And Quebec was becoming too hostile to Anglophones, with René Levesque, the separatist leader, predicting that Confederation had just five years to live.

Events came to a head in October 1970, a year after we had returned to Toronto, when a separatist terror cell kidnapped James Cross, the British trade commissioner, and Pierre Laporte, the provincial minister of labour. Cross was eventually released, but Laporte was murdered. The murderers fled to Cuba and, I believe, escaped prosecution when they returned to Quebec many years later. Pierre Trudeau, the prime minister, invoked the *War Measures Act* that October and more than four hundred individuals were swept up in arrests; charges proceeded against sixty-two. I agreed with Tommy Douglas and the NDP in opposing the *War Measures Act*, which inspired a lot of vigilante actions. I noted some in my diary. The British Columbia government passed an order-in-council to permit firing teachers who expressed support of the FLQ. The French Canadian Association of Alberta fired the editor of its newspaper after he published the FLQ manifesto. The CBC cancelled a documentary called *Lenin the Revolutionary*. Troops were on the streets in Montreal during a civic election, perhaps because Mayor Jean Drapeau and Premier Robert Bourassa both suggested a coup was being planned against the Quebec government. A Toronto rabbi suggested detaining any Arab sympathizers of the FLQ in Canada. The French CBC stopped broadcasting music written by pro-independentists. Singer Pauline Julien was arrested in a left-wing book store and kept in jail for a week. She was never charged, but several of her radio and television appearances were cancelled.

I called the whole *War Measures Act* episode "Chaplinesque". But it did deflate violent separatism. Since then, the Quebec nationalists tried twice to win referendums to break up Canada before the province gained substantial concessions and the separatism threat receded. The federal government subsequently replaced the *War Measures Act* with the *Emergency Act,* a far less open-ended legislation. It was not invoked until February, 2022, when Prime Minister Justin Trudeau—Pierre's son—decided he needed its powers to end a series of protests that had paralyzed Parliament Hill and central Ottawa with parked convoys of trucks, and closed several Canada-US border crossings. The protests initially sought the ending of restrictions arising from public health efforts to contain the spread of the COVID-19 pandemic. Some of the protest leaders proved to be dangerous extremists with financing, in part, from extremist groups in the United States. The *Emergency Act* enabled governments to mobilize the police resources needed to disband the protestors, tow away some of the trucks, and prevent some of the funds from getting into the hands of protest groups. On this occasion, it was the protest that was "Chaplinesque".

Ten:
The *Financial Post* was
a roller coaster ride

The editors I worked with in my career at the *Financial Post* were a mixed lot when it came to ability and talent. They were rarely dull. Ronald McEachern's successor in 1964 was Paul S. Deacon, who had been the newspaper's financial editor. He was a member of a well-known Toronto family prominent in the brokerage business. He was also a war hero, having survived many tours with 620 Squadron of the Royal Air Force during World War Two. Paul had a friendly personality but he was also a very proper person who always kept his suit jacket buttoned when in the office. On one occasion, he decided to banish bylines deemed too informal for the august *Financial Post*. One of our copy editors, Al Epp, hated his given name Alvin, but that became his byline. Mine had been Jack, and Paul decreed it would be J.A. I would not have objected if he had asked, but because he did not ask, I insisted my byline would be John—as it has been ever since.

Paul died in 1996 at age seventy-three. After he had retired, Neville Nankivell, a business journalist born in Australia, took over. His style was more informal, and he was more approachable. He also had the misfortune of taking over when competition from *The Globe & Mail's* "Report on Business" began to cut into our circulation and our profits. Seeing this, Neville in 1984 began proposing that the *Financial Post* should convert the weekly paper into a daily. It was 1988 before the company figured out how to do it. Because we lacked staff with daily newspaper experience, Maclean-Hunter sold the *Financial Post* paper to Sun Media in 1987. In time, that led to the appointment of other editors, with Neville being sent to London in 1991 as editor at large. He completed his career writing columns and think pieces from Ottawa, where he retired.

The daily *Financial Post* was really two papers: a tabloid during the week and broadsheet on weekends. Each had its own editor until they were merged. For the weekend *Financial Post*, an academic named John Godfrey was recruited from the University of King's College in Halifax. An Oxford graduate, he had been the university's president and also taught journalism. By coincidence, I had already met him. In March 1983, we were on the same Canadian Pacific Airlines flight from Halifax to Montreal. A severe winter blizzard swept across Eastern Canada after we were airborne. The pilot told us that the airports at Montreal, Toronto, Halifax, and Plattsburgh, New York, were all closed by weather. He just kept flying west, landing finally in North Bay in mid-afternoon. The airline bussed us to a hotel in town to wait out the storm overnight. I found myself lined up next to John to check in and get our dinner vouchers. He proposed we dine together and, since the airline was paying, he ordered chateaubriand for two with a good red wine. He was a charming and erudite companion. Those qualities were evident as he settled in at the *Financial Post*. That was not the Sun culture, however. John left in February 1992. The following year, he was elected as a Liberal to the House of Commons, eventually becoming a minister of state for infrastructure before retiring from politics in 2008.

His departure from the *Financial Post* was civilized, unlike the sacking at the same time of investment editor Carlyle Dunbar[31] and mining editor John Soganich. They were given one day to clear out their desks. In 1993, Sun Media offered voluntary early retirement buyouts to nineteen employees. After seeking advice from Macdonald Shymko & Co., a Vancouver financial planner, I turned it down. The planner's fee was $763.88, and I was able to get the company to pay since only

---

31 Carlyle Dunbar died in 2021 at the age of ninety. After leaving the newspaper, he was a successful private investor as well as a writer and blogger on business topics.

the Toronto employees had access to an advisor. It was money well spent. Not only did I have seven more years with a good salary and benefits, but I also had a chance to participate in options to buy Sun Media shares. When Conrad Black acquired the *Financial Post*, those options translated into about $100,000.

Maclean-Hunter had instituted a deferred profit-sharing plan in 1977 for permanent employees. I had also joined the employee share savings plan in 1971 and, including share splits, had accumulated 3,152 shares by 1993. By the time Rogers Communications Inc. took over the company in 1994, I had 4,708 shares for which I was paid $82,396.70. The company also had a stock participation plan allowing employees to purchase shares with interest-free loans. I began to participate in it in 1980, subscribing for four hundred shares. Due to the company's profitability and a number of share splits, I accumulated more shares. On my 1993 tax return, I reported the sales of 6,923 Maclean-Hunter shares for $83,101, with a capital gain of $72,716.02. There were also a small number of shares in an anniversary share plan. Under this plan, I was awarded each year the number of shares corresponding to my work anniversary—in other words, twenty-five shares on my twenty-fifth year with the company. By the end of 1993, I had 268 shares under this plan. With the sale of all of these shares, I reported another $41,064 capital gain in 1994. Fortunately, there was then a lifetime exemption of taxation on $100,000 of capital gains. I had accumulated a nest egg toward my retirement.

John Godfrey was replaced by Diane Francis in 1992. She had already been a *Post* columnist for three years and remained editor until 1998, after which she became editor at large. The *Post* really had two editors at that time. The executive editor hired by Sun Media to run the newsroom was Maryanne McNellis. Diane's turf included editorials and columnists. With her high profile, she accepted many speaking engagements which were meant to lift the image of the newspaper. She wrote columns that were deliberately provocative, occasionally racist, and sometimes just silly.

Diane and Maryanne—both Americans—were very different and, I suspect, did not like each other. Maryanne had a viperous way with staff which soon earned her the nickname, McNasty. When a colleague of mine in the Vancouver bureau asked for a pager, she refused. When he responded that I had had one for at least five years, I began to hear second-hand that Maryanne wanted me to cancel mine. For reasons I never understood, she may have come to dislike me but obviously could not get rid of me unless there was cause or a significant severance package.

About 1995, Maryanne began sending out weekly memos to the staff. I took to saving those in which I was named favourably. While I enjoyed the compliments, my motive was to accumulate ammunition in case I was terminated. I just never quite trusted Maryanne.

Perhaps I misinterpreted her attitude. In 1996, I had a particularly strong year as a reporter with a number of old-fashioned scoops that beat *The Globe and Mail*, our arch-rival. That led to being mentioned in dispatches, so to speak, in a memo Maryanne sent to staff on August 20, 1996. She wrote: "Gold stars to John Schreiner for his excellent work getting the Bema copper-gold story well ahead of the competition. We understand they went nuts after he scooped them. Just goes to show what a senior talented journalist can do with the right connections. John has had a number of fabulous scoops over the past year—great work." I also received a $500 bonus.

The year 1996 was one of my strongest. My string of scoops garnered a breaking news award, the Dalton Robertson Award, in February 1997, along with another $500 cheque. In October 1996, I won a Jack Webster Award for economic writing—for an article on the struggles of the Loewen Group, a major funeral home operator headquartered in Burnaby that was forced into bankruptcy by a rogue Mississippi jury. The former was one of several awards given by the *Financial Post* at annual staff meetings. The Webster awards recognizes top-flight journalism in British Columbia. It involves a trophy, a modest cheque and, at that time, a dinner at a large awards banquet every October at the Hyatt Regency Hotel. The menu the year I won was chicken accompanied by a wretched Brazilian Chardonnay. I ordered a British Columbia Chardonnay from the wine list, at my expense, because I was not going to celebrate with plonk.

I am not quite sure what got into me in 1996: I think I had decided to prove to myself and to everyone else that I had not lost my edge. Bema Gold was a Vancouver junior mining company, one of the many juniors I had covered as part of my regular coverage of the Vancouver Stock Exchange. The VSE had a chequered reputation because so many scams and fraudulent promotions occurred on the exchange. I believed that many of the listed companies had merit. Bema, to which I had given extensive coverage, was one of those. By this time the company had listed on senior exchanges. One afternoon, after the market had closed, Bema's chief executive briefed me on very positive drill results from a Peruvian project, which were to be released before trading resumed the next day. Indeed, the Bema CEO even posed for a photo that we ran with the story. Bema put out its press release after *The Globe and Mail* had gone to press. However, we had a later deadline, and I was able to write a front-page story for the *Post*—and the stock soared. This was typical of how aggressive I was in 1996. Two weeks later, I scooped *The Globe* again when I was the only reporter covering the annual meeting of Prime Resources Inc. on the day when Murray Pezim turned the presidency over to his son, Michael. Pezim was in declining health, dying in 1998 of a heart attack.

I was not the only one who disliked Maryanne's management style. In March 1997, *Frank,* a satirical gossip magazine, published a memo written by Glen Flanagan, a departing *Financial Post* employee. He had worked on the desk until he was demoted after privately complaining to the publisher about the newsroom's management. "I am the 48th employee to resign from the FP newsroom since [Maryanne McNellis] took over three years ago," he wrote. Number 49 quit a few days later to take a public relations job. In my diary, I observed that "Flanagan was a jerk, but it takes two to tango."

In October 1997, when I moved from reporting to writing editorials (which put me in Diane's orbit), Maryanne ordered that my relatively new Macintosh computer be given to a new reporter sent to the Vancouver bureau, to be replaced by one sent from Toronto for me. In a few days, I received an obsolete Macintosh II with virtually no internet capability, sticky keys, and a fuzzy monitor. It had actually been decommissioned, and Toronto did not want it back. I complained to Diane who arranged the purchase of a new computer for me. I was grateful to Diane even if I almost never agreed with her views. She was still writing columns for *National Post* in 2022.

For all her popularity, Diane could be antediluvian. One of her first columns for the *Financial Post* chastised the Progressive Conservative party for not passing a resolution deploring the RCMP for allowing its Sikh members to wear turbans. Another of her columns early in 1992 proposed controlling rising health care costs by shutting medical schools for four years to reduce the number of doctors. When Bob Rae was the NDP premier of Ontario, she waged an effective and damaging campaign against him, both in the paper and in her speeches.

There was another shakeup in the newspaper's management when Conrad Black bought the *Financial Post* in 1998 as the foundation for the *National Post*, his new daily. Having owned newspapers on Fleet Street, Black imported a number of British journalists, with a Canadian magazine editor, Ken Whyte, as editor. After having been a star two years earlier, I now I became invisible, perhaps because I had spent the previous year writing editorials (a job that bored me). The new management did not need an editorial writer in Vancouver—but I had no idea what was expected of me. On the morning of the first edition of the *National Post*, I actually had to phone one of the managing editors to ask what their plans were for me. I expected to be offered a severance package and would have taken it. Instead, I reverted back to reporting general news and, since I was never that busy, I began researching and writing a book on icewine, a style of wine with which Canada was getting an international reputation at the time. I became quite bored with the *National Post* during the final years before I retired. Looking back on those two years, I wish I taken early retirement to devote myself entirely to wine writing.

Eleven:
The Vancouver Stock Exchange

When the Vancouver Stock Exchange merged with the Alberta Stock Exchange in 1999, managers of the new exchange chose to headquarter it in Calgary. That did not last long before the exchange was absorbed by the Toronto Stock Exchange. At the time of the move to Calgary, I chastised the head of the Vancouver Board of Trade for not battling to have the unified exchange based in Vancouver where it would remain a significant part of the city's financial infrastructure. His lame response: the NDP government in Victoria was so unsympathetic to business that it was not worthwhile to go to bat for the exchange. Whether or not that was so, a campaign to keep the exchange would have been handicapped by the long-time hostility of the *Vancouver Sun* and one of its toughest investigative journalists, David Baines. He once remarked to me that the VSE was "a sewer" that needed to be shut. His writing was so contentious that, in the fall of 1992, he received a death threat.

I had a more generous view of the VSE. The exchange, which had begun operating in 1907, did spawn quite a remarkable number of questionable and dishonest promotions. But in the many years, beginning in 1984, in which I wrote a weekly column called *Western Markets,* I had no difficulty in finding listed companies that had merit as well as companies that lacked merit. In May 1986, I wrote about two such new listings on the VSE: Tree Island Steel Company and Mr. Jax Fashions Inc. The latter was run by Joseph Segal, a prominent businessman and a future member of the Order of Canada. Admittedly, quality listings like that were not as common as one would have hoped.

But the exchange already had a bad reputation when I began writing about it. In November 1974, the Co-ordinated Law Enforcement Unit—an agency of the provincial government—released a report suggesting some actors in the market had links to organized crime. Cyril White, then the VSE president, called the report "irresponsible." It may well have been since there was no effective government action following that report.[32] However, a few years later, the VSE members rebelled and installed new directors. White resigned and was replaced by Robert Scott. In the spring of 1977, the Canadian Broadcasting Corp. did a damaging exposé on national television that caused the shares of many listings to collapse. At the same time, Rafe Mair, the new provincial minister of Consumer Affairs, announced legislative changes designed to clean up the VSE, much to the outrage of the brokerage community. I am not sure how much he achieved. Rafe was an activist minister in a number of areas, including the reform of liquor laws. In any event, Scott made some progress, but I think the unsavoury promoters were always a step ahead of him.

Over the years, there were many attempts to clean up the VSE with limited degrees of success. Donald Hudson, president of the VSE from 1982 to 1995, was never quite able to get on top of the abuses. In October 1984, on an occasion that came to be called Black Friday, the share prices of six junior companies with interrelated directors collapsed suddenly, wiping out $40 million in value. That strange manipulation seriously undermined the work Hudson had been doing to clean up practices. "What we have not got credit for is that we do have quite an active compliance program," he told me.[33] The Black Friday debacle, which left several brokerage firms on the hook with margin accounts, triggered some reforms at the VSE as well as in BC securities legislation. Beauford Resources Ltd., which was suspended after its shares dropped from $11.25 to $1, was taken over in the spring

32 *Financial Post*, November 2, 1974: "VSE blasts market crime report."

33 *Financial Post*, December 29, 1984: "Criticism taking toll on VSE."

of 1985 by a group that included Nelson Skalbania. That should have been an indicator that fun and games would continue on the exchange, no matter how hard Hudson tried to turn it around.

The VSE had long been an exchange of junior mining companies, but in 1985, there was a strong flurry of junior technology companies. Often, mining juniors were just renamed and repurposed. For example, Baz Resources Ltd. re-emerged in the spring of 1985 as CHoPP Computers Corp., proposing to build super computers.[34] It proved to be a scam: the principals did not have the technology and probably not the intention to build such computers. The shares rocketed from 17 cents to $125 and then collapsed. The BC Securities Commission halted trading in 1987.

In 1986, Adnan Khashoggi, who was billed in the media as the world's richest man, managed to list three promotions on the VSE—a satellite launch business; a search for King Solomon's mines; and a company called Skyhigh Resources. The shares were run from 60 cents to $72 before the air went out of the company. Promotions like that were endemic on the VSE. The British Columbia government had commissioned a study of VSE trading in 1978. The conclusion was dismal: "The odds of losing, overall, are 84 per cent—about five times out of six."[35]

In March 1989, I wrote a piece about a two-pronged effort by the VSE to improve its image. One was a national advertising campaign on the virtues of a junior exchange. The other involved an upgrading of the listing policies so that the listed companies would have more substance. The previous year, the VSE had been the venue of the "Carter-Ward" stock manipulation in which a Texas mutual fund was sold shares of VSE listings at inflated prices. And in April 1989, a former broker named Dale Ciochetti and his wife, Linda Hazlett, received jail terms for a fraud involving International Tillex Enterprises Ltd., a listing for which Ciochetti had been lead underwriter. That spring, the VSE was savaged by critical articles in both *Forbes* (which called Vancouver "the

34 *Financial Post*, May 4, 1985: "Computer technology turns Baz into Chopp."

35 *The Greater Vancouver Book*, The Linkman Press, 1997: "The Vancouver Stock Exchange" by John Schreiner, pp 502–503.

scam capital of the world") and *Barron's*. Hudson called the Forbes article a "defamatory ... and libelous story."[36] However, the business embarrassments kept popping up. For example, the Kuwaiti Investment Office in 1988 paid $17.8 million for control of a listed company called C.E.L. Industries Ltd. A year later, after C.E.L. had incurred major losses in its Swiss research and development arm, the Kuwaiti investment was worth $3 million.[37] In May 1993, Hudson announced a series of reforms at the same time as James Matkin, who had been commissioned by the provincial government, completed a scathing report on the VSE early in 1994.

Another notorious promoter was Harry Moll and his Pineridge Capital Corp. In 1988, Moll had managed to take over Potter's Distilling Co. and then used that for a grander acquisition of Calona Wines. Harry had style. The Calona takeover was celebrated with a reception at Hy's to which I was invited. The wines and the canapes were served by spectacular young women with very long legs and very short skirts. Harry often lunched at a nearby restaurant where he and his associates drank a lot of Calona wines. It is believed that about $1.4 million was siphoned from Calona's treasury to Pineridge before the company got rid of Harry. Before the dust settled, Swiss investors that Harry had brought into Pineridge in 1990 had controlling interest in Calona Wines and kept control until 2005, when Andrew Peller Ltd. bought Calona.

In spite of all its problems, the VSE was rescued time and again when one of its junior listings actually succeeded. One of the more memorable successes was brought about by Murray Pezim, perhaps the most colourful promoter active on junior exchanges in Canada, especially on the VSE. Many of his promotions were simply outrageous— such as a public company that proposed marketing greeting cards from the stars of Las Vegas and Hollywood. Pezim talked it up and investors, including himself, actually drove up the value of the shares on the VSE. However, the promotion and the shares eventually collapsed, producing

36 *The Financial Post*, June 3–5, 1989: "VSE woes stir deep concerns about the future."

37 *Financial Post*, August 1, 1989: "Kuwaiti agency takes millions in losses on VSE-listed firm."

nothing more than highly entertaining news stories. But Pezim also had viable gold exploration projects, several of which succeeded and earned him a place in the Canadian Mining Hall of Fame. The one I covered extensively was the Eskay Creek gold discovery in northwestern British Columbia in 1988. Prospectors had been looking for the deposit since the 1920s. Pezim told me: "It's real ... It's a big world-class orebody."

It was, and trading in a number of VSE companies went wild. After the discovery, gold was produced here for at least a decade. However, Pezim later was accused (and acquitted) of insider trading. That reflected the expectation the regulators had of the VSE, and the promoters associated with it. In a column I wrote in September 1989, I said: "Listing speculative stocks is the VSE's oft-misunderstood *raison-d'etre*. It is a corner of the investment community fraught with risk, where investors are often lured to lose their money by hyperbole at best, and fraud at worst. Several bogus stock promotions that came to light in the last several years have given the VSE such a reputation that its less speculative listings have been scrambling to get onto other exchanges."[38]

Donald Hudson retired in 1995. His successor was Michael Johnson, the former Canadian head of Household Finance. The press conference at which he was announced was one of the more unpleasant ones that I ever attended. Johnson had come from Toronto and clearly was not fully up to speed on the VSE. David Baines asked a number of hostile questions that threw Johnson off balance. "I understand what's driving the reputation, but I don't know what's real," he told the news conference. "The exchange is a lightning rod for all the problems that occur in its sphere." Johnson's stern and disciplined approach went a long way to eliminating the excesses (for example, VSE employees were forbidden to trade in VSE-listed companies). He was so stern, in fact, that by late 1998, many in the Vancouver brokerage community were arguing that he had—as one broker told me—"thrown the baby out with the bath water." Some began to press for a merger with the Alberta Stock Exchange, which had been considered several times in the previous decade. It finally happened in 1999. Both were then

---

38 *Financial Post*, September 5, 1989: "Gold play may have saved the VSE's image."

taken over by the Toronto Stock Exchange in 2001 to become the TSE Venture Exchange.

David's associate in muckraking was a self-appointed stock market investigator named Adrian du Plessis, once a floor trader for the VSE. I once described him in print as a zealot who shared David's view of the VSE, not mine. I have forgotten the circumstances, but on one occasion, Adrian did something that embarrassed me. He had worked with Jim Matkin on his investigation of the VSE, likely providing him ammunition. I know he helped David in digging up mud. Sometime in the mid-1990s, the British Columbia Securities Commission hired him to be an investigator. When he started digging up presumed mud on other BCSC staff, he was terminated after four months. A retired judge, Lloyd McKenzie, was hired to examine Adrian's grievances. The resulting one-thousand-page report excoriated Adrian. The last I heard about him was that he was living on Salt Spring Island and managing a Nanaimo singer named Allison Crowe shortly after she began performing at age fifteen.

There is even an article excoriating the VSE in the Vancouver Police Museum & Archives. The author concludes: "While no exchange is without examples of fraudulent companies or insider deals, none seemed so plagued as the VSE. With so many recorded instances of fraud and scandal, it's no wonder why an estimated five of every six investors lost money on the Vancouver Stock Exchange. It was a self-regulated system that, whether intentional or not, served the very brokers, promoters, and insiders at the heart of the organization. The VSE perpetuated this ecosystem of fraud and manipulation because of its inability (or lack of desire) to punish the people behind these fraudulent companies."[39]

Reflecting on the never-ending scams on the VSE, I marvel that I kept looking for a positive side of the exchange. It was not inaccurate to call it a sewer. But it is just my nature to look for the best in my fellow man.

---

39   *Vancouver Police Museum & Archives blog:* "The Vancouver Stock Exchange: A Legacy of Fraud and Money Laundering Part I" by Matteo Miceli, January 18, 2020.

Twelve:
S. Hattori's wristwatch

I have many, many memories from the numerous trips abroad that came my way as a writer for the *Financial Post*. Most weekly issues of the newspaper included feature reports on industries and regional economies that could be relied on to buy advertising in the reports. Most of these reports were quite lucrative for the newspaper, but they added a brutal load of work on top of reporters' regular beat responsibilities. For example, before I went to Japan in 1970, I spent about nine months reading about the economy and culture and corresponding with the Canadian embassy and other sources to arrange the itinerary. On the return to Canada, several weeks or a month was required to write supplements that were thousands of words in length. Even so, reporters coveted these assignments because we got to see a foreign country at the employer's expense.

My first travelling assignment was, I believe, to do the report on British Columbia in 1963. I produced a mediocre report because I knew so little about the British Columbia economy. (I might have been better prepared had I taken that tree planting job in the summer of 1957.) I failed to get an appointment with W.A.C. Bennett, the premier, who was not a fan of the eastern media. But his public relations man in Vancouver did arrange a trip for me on the Pacific Great Eastern Railway to Lillooet and back in one day. It is one of the most scenic rail trips in North America, even on the short February day when I did it. Later, I had much better access to Bill Bennett, W.A.C.'s son, when he became premier. That even included having tea with him in his office one slow afternoon in Victoria and talking about the British Columbia wine industry. Unlike his father, Bill was not a teetotaler. After Bill became premier under the Social Credit banner, the party began opening its annual meetings with a tasting of British Columbia wines. I believe Bill's alcohol of choice was whisky.

The first foreign trip was to Mexico in May 1964, just a few weeks after Alison was born. Marlene was left to fend for herself with two small children and, as I learned later, a Volkswagen that would not start because the battery was dead. It was not the last time that my career made considerable demands on her to look after the family at home while I travelled to exotic places. The eight-week trip to Asia in 1972 was long enough to be compared with widowhood.

My report on Mexico was not that insightful either, since I got a sharp critique after it was published from Paul Deacon, the new editor at the *Financial Post*. I don't recall what annoyed him except for one point: he objected to me calling a Mexican businessman a tycoon. It had never occurred to me that it was a pejorative term, but Paul was a member of a Toronto business family that may well have been tycoons. In any event, the Mexican business class of that period, although not that large, was certainly a tycoon class. Even the state-owned companies were little empires whose employees enjoyed remarkable perquisites for a poor nation. The best lunch I had was with the public relations director for Pemex, the state oil company, who took me to an elegant restaurant. Most of my two weeks on this assignment was spent in Mexico City, but I did fly to Acapulco, as a guest of some hotel for a day or so.

To visit a steel mill at Veracruz on the east coast, I took the overnight train, expecting the 250-mile (400-kilometre) trip would take the scheduled eleven hours. But, because of track construction, the train spent most of the day standing idle under the baking sun of the plains, beside a small community. We arrived in Veracruz about 5:00 p.m., after a twenty-one-hour trip. I was famished, having eaten only a ham sandwich before going to sleep and a beer or two while we were idle. There was food available. I bought a chocolate bar, a brand called Wong's after the local Chinese manufacturer of the confection. I would have eaten more if I had had the courage: barefoot women alongside the train were constantly hawking enchiladas, bananas, and various beverages. I went to the steel mill even though I was hours late, knowing there would be someone I could meet because Mexicans kept offices open well into the evening. I finally had dinner at 8:00 p.m. When I found the hotel in Veracruz to be unappealing, I returned to Mexico City on a midnight flight. I never redeemed my return rail fare, the equivalent of $2, because I would have had to go to the ticket office at main station.

One highlight of Mexico was an impromptu forty-cent round trip on an elderly local diesel bus (accompanied by an American student) to the great pyramids of Teotihuacan, about forty miles (sixty-four kilometres) outside the city. The site then had barely been developed for tourism; there was only one rustic tavern. There were few other visitors at the site, and it was possible to sense the spiritual aura that the pyramids must have cast over the Spanish conquistador Hernán Cortés as he led his troops toward the Aztec capital in 1519. I had read a book about him before my Mexican trip; the author vividly described how awe-inspiring the pyramids would have appeared to Cortés. I was also awed by the site.

During a weekend in March 1977, Marlene and I were at the pyramids again when we were part of a group flown there on a Japan Airlines inaugural flight from Vancouver to Mexico City. Teotihuacan had become overrun with tourists and tacky souvenir shops. The spiritual aura was absent. However, the Museum of Anthropology and the Rivera art museum in Mexico City were impressive. (I could not say as much of a Santo Tomas Chenin Blanc we had at dinner one evening.)

The Japan Airlines trip gave me the opportunity to interview Grace McCarthy for a profile in the *Financial Post Magazine*. She had been hard to pin down because she was quite busy in Bill Bennett's cabinet as Minister of Tourism. However, she had also been invited on board the JAL flight. She agreed to give me an interview as we cruised along from Vancouver to Mexico City.[40] She was very effective in her post.

40 *Financial Post Magazine*, May 14, 1977, pp 10–14, "Amazing Grace."

One of her more creative ideas was the installation of lights on the Lions Gate Bridge that links Vancouver and the North Shore, revealing the elegance of the structure every night.

In August 1966, I was in Sweden for three weeks to do a report on that economy. Some of the other reporters at the paper travelled only to a nation's capital when assigned one of these foreign reports. I made an effort always to find interviews in a number of centres so that I could see as much of the country as was reasonable. To do Sweden, I flew to Copenhagen and, after a weekend to get over jet lag, took the ferry to Malmö where I began interviewing businessmen. One hosted me to a dinner at which he drank just half a glass of beer. He explained that the Swedish laws against driving under the influence of alcohol were draconian. I heard later in the trip of an employee of the Canadian embassy who was jailed briefly for driving under the influence. At the time, the penalties in Canada for DUI were modest by any measure.

Next, I went to Göteborg by train to visit the Hasselblad camera factory, a surprisingly humble place for a major brand. Hasselblad was then an international sensation because its cameras were being used in the Apollo space program. Eventually, I worked my way by train across the country to Stockholm, where I enjoyed both the sightseeing and the interviews. I borrowed a folding bicycle for a day and a half and cycled all over the city, once even finding myself on the median of a freeway. The confusion arose because the Swedes at that time drove on the left, like the British. (They changed in September 1967.) I attended my first opera, a performance of *Madame Butterfly* that was marred only by the uncomfortable cheap seat I had. Among my interviews was one with an industrial designer, Count Sigvard Bernadotte. He was the king's younger son but had renounced his title to marry a commoner. He was an excellent designer in the Swedish tradition that function comes first. I came home from that trip with various items, including wine glasses and a languorous salad bowl, that reflected the functional elegance of Swedish design.

The next foreign report, in the spring of 1967, was the British edition. London was not yet prohibitive: my expense account stretched to dinner at Simpson's on the Strand which compensated for the dreary hotel I had just down the road from the BBC. For reasons that now escape me, I arranged an interview with Anthony Wedgwood Benn, a charismatic young Labour politician who later called himself Tony Benn to distance himself from his aristocratic heritage.

I took the train to Manchester to interview astronomer Sir Bernard Lovell at the Jodrell Bank observatory. It was a dubious business story, but I had long been fascinated with space and even considered studying astronomy until deterred by the requirement of mathematics. From there, I carried on to Glasgow to visit a steel mill, a gritty plant whose condition reflected Britain's slow and prolonged recovery from war. I spent the Easter weekend in Edinburgh, where I did an interview on Good Friday because the Scots work that day. I still have the robust Harris tweed jacket I bought at a shop on Princess Street, although it no longer fits. During the course of a three-week trip, I packed in my share of sightseeing, which included Westminster Abbey, accidentally coming across the grave of Handel, and taking in a concert by the Soviet Army Chorus at the Royal Albert Hall. There was much more but, unaccountably, I was not a diligent diarist during that trip.

In June 1968, I was assigned to do the German report and once again arranged interviews all over the country, starting in Cologne because it was near Bonn, the capital of West Germany. I decided to exercise my childhood German, telling the hotel desk clerk that I had a *stube* reserved. He laughed and suggested I mean *zimmer* because the former referred to a drinking room. I had not grown up speaking such elegant German. In my childhood house, a room was always *stube*.

The interviews over the next week likely were with German and Canadian bureaucrats, generating nothing for my diary, probably because I was busy filling notebooks that have since vanished. I did learn of a weekend-long Mozart festival in Augsburg and got a ticket to hear the opera *Ideomeneo*. When I discovered it was a black tie event, I rented a tuxedo (for about $8.50) since I was travelling with brown suits. As I dressed for the concert, I realized that I only had brown shoes. The following evening, I heard the Bavarian Radio Orchestra under Rafael Kubelik do three Mozart symphonies. I assume I wore a brown suit.

In Munich, I met Victor Sabal, a beer salesman for Löwenbrau, who briefed me on his brewery for an article and who became a lifelong friend. He had been born in the Ukraine and made it to West Germany after World War Two. While he earned a living selling beer, he was keenly interested in politics, serving as a broadcaster for Radio Free Europe's Czech service. I learned of that late in our acquaintance when Marlene and I, on one of our German trips, were being hosted by Victor and his wife, Helen. We actually visited them several times in Munich, beginning with a visit in May 1984. He toured us around, including a visit to Oberammergau. That happened to be the three hundredth anniversary of the Passion Play, which was to be staged again that summer. We also welcomed Victor to dinner at our home in Canada on several occasions and had long conversations about European politics. Until he joined a different brewery, he sent us two dozen bottles of Löwenbrau every Christmas. He died in 1990.

I arranged some interviews in Berlin, which was a surreal city because of the Cold War. West Berliners pursued a frantic lifestyle. The city never seemed to sleep and was illuminated with huge neon signs showing off its affluence in stark contrast with the Lutheran and Marxist dreariness of war-damaged East Berlin. The Berlin Wall was then seven years old. It was disturbingly ugly; its dirty concrete slabs were topped with barbed wire or broken glass or lengths of concrete pipe. It was evident that the East Germans had erected it quickly, running it through buildings and even cemeteries. The windows of one building that formed part of the wall had been bricked up so fast that the curtains remained between the bricks and the glass. On Saturday, June 15, I spent a day in East Berlin. At one point that afternoon, I was standing beside a couple with a young child whose relatives were seated on bleachers on the western side of the wall. As the couple prepared to leave, they instructed their boy to wave farewell to his grandparents on the other side. Then they shouted the date for their next rendezvous. For me, this captured the banal evil of that wall. Back in West Berlin that evening, I found solace in the Berlin Philharmonic's superb performance of Beethoven's Pastoral Symphony.

JOHN SCHREINER

There was no foreign trip for me in 1969, unless I count the Newfoundland and Labrador special edition. My travels there began less than two weeks after John was born, but this time, my mother had come to Montreal to help Marlene. We moved back to Toronto that summer.

In 1970, I was assigned to do my first report on Japan. During the following decade, I wrote two more reports on Japan. I also visited Japan in 1975 for a Japan Airlines inaugural flight. The tradition at the paper had been to pass these assignments around because the staff viewed them as plums. I discovered that Japan, while exceptionally interesting, was perhaps the most difficult because one had to understand a culture as well as an economy. H.O. Moran, the Canadian ambassador in Tokyo at the time, told me he thought the *Financial Post* should send the same reporter more than once, perhaps to reduce the demands for service we made on the embassy staff. I passed this on to Neville Nankivell, our editor, and I appreciated the value of that advice when I returned to Japan in 1972. I had to spend three weeks in Japan in 1970 but only two weeks in 1972 because I had learned how to use my time more effectively and how to avoid time-wasting interviews. In 1976, however, I spent three weeks in Japan, doing my third report on the economy. In many instances, I was able to interview much more senior executives when I visited a company a second or third time. Where I got no higher than vice-presidents of Nippon Steel in 1970, I met with the chief executive two years later.

I arrived in Tokyo on Saturday evening, February 21, 1970, and quickly learned that I should have arrived at least a day earlier in order to get over jet lag. I found myself waking at three or four in the morning for several days and collapsing with fatigue in the early evening. However, my room in the Tokyo Hilton (now demolished) stands out in memory as one of the most comfortable hotel rooms I ever stayed in: a large room finished with the clear, knot-free wood so prized by Japanese architects. The windows must have been triple-glazed because the room was very quiet.

The trade officers in the embassy generally organized my schedule of interviews based on requests made by letter well before the trip. In this era before the internet, organizing these foreign trips was challenging and time-consuming, with the program depending so much on help from the embassy. It was obvious from time to time that I was used as an excuse for them to meet some business or political contact more important to them than to me. Often, a Japanese staff member from the embassy came along to translate during interviews. However, I generally found such interviews frustrating and thin of content because the usual give and take of interviewing was absent. During one trip, I had an interview over lunch with a Japanese winemaker from Suntory, accompanied by an English-speaking publicist who doubled as a translator. She knew nothing about winemaking, did not understand my questions, and probably did not understand his replies. We had a pleasant lunch, but I got little of value from it.

Japanese culture intrigued me and sometimes appalled me. There was then an incredible degree of male chauvinism. One Japanese executive who had lived in Canada told me his wife wanted to work in Japan, but he was opposed to that. Another time, I was being led to the elevator in the Mitsui & Co. head office by a senior man. We arrived there at the same time as a group of women. When I stepped aside to let them enter the elevator first, he grabbed my arm and said: "Come on. In this country, we're number one."

During a business lunch in a Tokyo hotel, I noticed that the waiters all wore red arm bands. My companion from the embassy explained that they were on strike and that was how they signalled their grievance. If that was the extent of widespread labour disruption, no wonder the trains always ran on time.

Aside from dull interviews with various economists, I had many interesting meetings. One that stands out to me happened during the 1970 assignment. One of my final interviews at the end of three weeks was with S. Hattori, the president of the Seiko watch company whose products were gaining global market share against traditional watch makers. At the Seiko office, Hattori-san met me alone in a small boardroom. This was unusual because senior Japanese executives were generally flanked by aides, at least one of whom handled the translating. Hattori-san, a tall, elegant man in his seventies, spoke flawless English and answered my questions with easy confidence.

The interview lasted a pleasant hour. When I asked my final question, Hattori-san took off his wristwatch to illustrate his reply. I have forgotten the question, perhaps because what happened after his answer was so unexpected. He slid the watch across the table and suggested I keep it as a memento of the meeting. Accepting such a gift was not strictly ethical but giving back a watch he had taken from his own wrist would have insulted him, given the importance of gifts in Japanese culture. In a feeble attempt at reciprocating, I gave him a photograph of mine, a small Canadian scene in a paperboard frame. I had taken a number of them with me to Japan in order to respond, at least in a small way, when someone gave me a gift. The Japanese have a tradition of generous gifts. On another occasion, I received a small camera in exchange for addressing a business group on the Canadian economy. But I don't recall any gift as valuable as the watch. When I examined it later in my hotel room, I realized that it was a new watch that Hattori-san had put on his wrist before our meeting. The initial impression that it was his personal watch had totally disarmed me. Later, I priced it in a Tokyo store, discovering it had a retail value of about $115. In 1985, when the watch broke down and could not be repaired, I replaced it with a $200 Seiko, keeping alive my memory of Hattori-san. In 2020, when this watch developed a problem, I spent another $200 to have it repaired.

Another interesting connection occurred during a visit to a Nissan car plant outside Tokyo. Here is an example of connections paying off. Nissan's Canadian operations were then run from Vancouver by Hiraki Miki, one of the warmest Japanese executives I have ever encountered. When I first met him back in Vancouver, he had been in Canada for four years and loved it so much that he had rocks from all over the country, including Peggy's Cove, in the rock garden at his Annacis Island office. He paved the way for a good meeting in Tokyo. Several years later, I had also come to know Toyota's senior man in Canada and then had dinner at his Tokyo home. On another occasion, I interviewed a senior Honda executive months before the company diversified from motorcycles to cars.

In my usual fashion, I found opportunities to travel outside of Tokyo, including two days in Hokkaido (to see an agriculture project that was buying Alberta breeding stock) and to the site of the 1972 Winter Olympics. Hokkaido in February was a lot like Canada in February—crisp and snowy. From there, I flew to Kyoto, site of the 1970 Expo, where I was given a cultural tour of temples and shrines by a professor named Makoto Irie, to whom a colleague, John Irwin, had referred me. Irie was a teacher of Russian, having spent the war in Manchuria as a liaison between the Japanese military and the Soviets. He packed a great deal into the nine hours we were together, including a visit to the astonishing gallery of artist Inshō Dōmoto, described by Irie as the Japanese Picasso. Dōmoto died in 1975, but the art is still displayed in a museum dedicated to his career.

Irie was so intent on showing Kyoto's finest temples and attractions that he did not want to stop for lunch in order to "make the most economical use of my time." Our only nourishment had been a glass of warm sake at one of the temples. Starving at 3:30 p.m., I had to insist that we stop for a bowl of curry rice. We parted at 7:00 p.m. after one of the richest Sundays of my life.

The next few days included visits to the Expo site (this was two weeks before the fair opened), a tour of a prefabricated house builder's factory, a Kobe shipyard, and the Yamaha piano plant in Hamamatsu. Then I returned to Tokyo and completed my round of interviews before heading off to exhilarating Hong Kong for another week or so to do a supplement that the *Financial Post* cancelled when I got back. I got back to Canada a month after leaving, and I see from my diary that I stopped off in Vancouver again for a few days as well as in Regina. There was a time when the airlines facilitated stopping off along the route. But while this was a long trip, it was nothing compared to the six weeks I travelled in Asia in 1972.

John at Yamaha piano factory in Japan

My increased familiarity with Japan led to some quite substantial interviews, including the chairmen of several trading companies. The chairman of Sumitomo invited me to interview him on the flight from Osaka to Tokyo. I enjoyed the deference showed to senior business executives: we were allowed to board the aircraft after everyone else was seated, and we were seated side by side in the first-class cabin.

One of my more memorable experiences occurred one Saturday morning, May 20, which seems to be the Japanese memorial day for war dead. I left the Palace Hotel, where I was staying, to wander around Tokyo with, as always, no definite itinerary. I soon stumbled across the Yasukuni Shrine, whose grounds were full of Japanese families, including men in military uniforms. Not realizing that I was intruding on what must be a sacred day for the Japanese, I wandered around the adjoining museum for an hour or two, trying to puzzle the meaning from displays on which there was no English (understandably). It surprises me that I was not asked to leave. Here is what the Japan Guide says about the shrine: "The spirits of about 2.5 million people, who died for Japan in the conflicts accompanying the Meiji Restoration, in the Satsuma Rebellion, the First Sino-Japanese War, the Russo-Japanese War, the First World War, the Manchurian Incident, the Second Sino-Japanese War, and the Pacific War, are enshrined at Yasukuni Shrine in form of written records, which note name, origin, and date and place of death of everyone enshrined."

On another evening in Tokyo, I attended a farewell party for a Canadian hockey player and coach, Terry O'Malley. He had spent seven years in Japan, ending his career there as coach of a team sponsored by owners of the Seibu department store chain. An estimated 1,600 people, mostly Seibu employees, attended a grand and emotional evening. O'Malley had helped the team win a number of trophies, which were on display. Japan's top pop star sang a song called "Love Letter from Canada." (Bruce Rankin, the Canadian ambassador to Japan, took it on himself to jump on stage and coach the singer, who was mispronouncing Canada. I thought the behaviour embarrassing.) O'Malley subsequently spent twenty-three years at Athol Murray College in Wilcox, Saskatchewan, including three years as president.

The 1975 trip was a week-long junket in April, hosted by Japan Airlines, which had just begin to serve Vancouver with Boeing 747s. This junket included an excursion to the Hakone National Park and a shrine of Buddha. Our group also went to Kyoto and Nara for several days touring temples and gardens. The tour began in Tokyo where we were put up in the New Otani Hotel, a multi-storey tower. At 4:00 a.m. one morning, a moderate earthquake shook the tower. The swaying, which the tower was designed to do, woke me. It did not last very long, and I decided not to walk down twenty or so floors. I was even able to get back to sleep. Japan, of course, has a lot of earthquakes. I thought the people had come to take them in stride until one morning during my 1976 trip to Japan. I was in a different hotel, having breakfast in the basement, when my seat began to shake, the lights above the table began to sway, and one of the servers screamed in terror. But the shaking stopped, and I chose to finish my breakfast.

In 1976, I was assigned the Japanese report again. The power interview this time was with Tokoshiro Shiina, the vice-chairman of Sumitomo Shoji, one of the major trading companies. We met in his office in Osaka for a three-hour interview that began at 2:30 p.m. Then he gave me a ride to the airport in his limousine. Sumitomo must have purchased my ticket as well because I was assigned seat 1-B on Japan Airlines, next to Shiina.

One Sunday, I was invited to dinner with Tak Fujita, a senior Toyota executive, and his wife, Eiko. He had spent nine years in Canada. He furnished his custom-built suburban Tokyo home with Canadian appliances (all larger than typical Japanese appliances). The living room was dominated, and I mean *dominated*, by a large stuffed moose head. On the wall, he had a framed letter from Pierre Trudeau, congratulating him on something or other. I was served a substantial meal (appetizers, chicken yakitori, barbecued ribs, potato salad, and apple pie), along with a non-vintage Margaux and a rather good 1971 Sauternes from McWilliams in Australia, of which I had three glasses. The wine had been imported by an Australian affiliate of Toyota in some arrangement to grease the wheels for Toyota car exports.

The rapid economic development and opening up of Japan in the decade was quite evident. A little example: in 1970 it was difficult for a foreigner to use the subway system because the station names were almost exclusively in Japanese script only. By 1976, the much expanded subway system had English and Japanese signs in the stations. Armed with a system map, I travelled to many of my appointments by train. Because of congested streets, the trains usually were faster than taxis. Many of the larger stations had become anchors for underground shopping plazas. In the Shinjuku station one evening, I enjoyed lasagna at a restaurant called Pub Cardinal, where I was served by a waiter who had spent a month in Vancouver during the summer of 1975.

During this trip, I made it a point to drink wine from one or other of the Japanese producers. The wines generally were mediocre, tasting like blends of imported wines. Some perhaps were made with concentrates. Like Canadian wineries at the time, the Japanese branded the wines with European names. The most pretentious one that I noted was Château Lumiére 1967 Premier Cru Grand Classé—a light red "mis en bouteille" in Yamanashi. Many years later, I suggested to Marlene that we should visit Japan, for she had never been there with me. She was not interested and I have never been back there since.

Thirteen:
Becoming an old China hand

I booked a four-day Beijing tour on the spur of the moment while Marlene and I were vacationing in Hong Kong in 1992. I wanted to see again the society that I had visited on my first trip to China in 1972, in the final years of the Cultural Revolution. We had what I called "our own Tiananmen experience" in a column I wrote in June, 1992.[41] Our tour bus disembarked its passengers on a side street near the square, which is immense, and turned us loose to wander for an hour.

It is said to be the largest city square in the world (800 metres by 500 metres). It is an unattractive, flat expanse of pavement with government buildings on several sides and a huge portrait of Mao Zedong on the north side. After a leisurely walk around the square, we had begun to retrace our steps to where the bus was parked when the police and military suddenly began to herd all of the people off the square—in the direction opposite to our bus. The task was carried out with a frightening menace, an echo, perhaps, of how the square had been cleared of protesters five years earlier. This time, they were clearing the square in advance of the arrival of the president of India. We had to walk all the way around the perimeter of the square. We returned to the bus, dripping with sweat and shaken by the experience, only to have the tour guide grumble that we were late. I snarled right back at him. The experience showed me that, while China had changed dramatically

41 *Financial Post,* June 22, 1992: "China has taken two steps forward."

since my first visit, it remained a police state prepared to roll over the individual on the slightest pretext. That had been displayed for all the world to see in 1989 when the military crushed student demonstrators at Tiananmen Square.

My first glimpse of China had been in 1970 when I went to Hong Kong on assignment for the *Financial Post*. Then Hong Kong was a showcase of laissez-faire capitalism. When I checked into the Hong Kong Hilton (now demolished), the book in the table beside the bed was not a Gideon Bible but the Red Book of the colony's manufacturers' and exporters' association. The hotel guidebook included advertisements for escort services and warnings for tourists to negotiate the rate in advance before getting a shoe shine or a rickshaw ride (the escort service rate was stated with the comforting comment that there is "no charge if dissatisfied"). The contrast between the colony's affluence and its poverty startled me. I have a newspaper clipping in my diary in which the letter writer deplores that there are beggars in the street—thirty years before the Vancouver newspapers began publishing similar complaints.

Hong Kong was a complete assault on the senses, from the aroma of night soil when I disembarked at the airport, to the raucous Cantonese spoken loudly in the crowded streets and markets. Hong Kong had been a British colony since 1841 and acquired its substantial population (around four million) when millions of mainland Chinese fled there after the Communists took power in Beijing in 1948. According to the treaty between Britain and China, Hong Kong reverted to Beijing's control in 1997. Under British administration, it had developed into a strong economy with limited democratic government and appalling social services, such as no compulsory elementary schools because there were not enough schools. Primary education was only funded publicly in 1971.

One of the most interesting characters I met there was Derek Davies, the editor of the *Far Eastern Economic Review*, a keen and critical observer of Hong Kong and a figure of some influence. At his recommendation, I went to the Matsuya Jewellery Co. store to buy Marlene a ring. When I mentioned that Derek Davies had referred me, it seemed that the prices quickly became much more favourable. On my last Saturday in Hong Kong, I accepted his invitation to lunch with a group of his drinking buddies, mostly older journalists, who called themselves "Alcoholics Synonymous". That also was the only clear day of the week, and I was determined to see the view from The Peak, the mountaintop overlooking the city. I left lunch about 3:00 p.m. with a skin full of Guinness and Beaujolais, took the tram to the top, and then walked down to work off the alcohol. Dead tired when I returned to the hotel at 6:30 p.m., I lay down for a nap. I woke up a few hours later, thought it was 4:00 a.m., changed into my pyjamas and, when I could not sleep, finally realized it only 9:25 p.m. So I dressed, had some food, and tried to go back to sleep with indifferent results. I was happy to fly home the next day. Ironically, the trip produced only a few articles because the supplement planned by the *Post* was cancelled.

China was in the grips of the Great Proletarian Cultural Revolution from 1966 to 1976. Chairman Mao Zedong, then old and increasingly unwell, set out to nip opposition before it broke out by sending intellectuals to labour on farms and by persecuting, and even executing, the populace indiscriminately. One method was requiring abject public self-criticism, enforced by vigilante committees. "The Communist Party does not fear criticism because we are Marxists, the truth is on our side, and the basic masses, the workers and the peasants, are on our side," Mao said in a 1957 speech. This is a typical gem from my copy of *Quotations from Chairman Mao Tsetung*. Better known as *The Little Red Book,* this was a 312-page book that every literate Chinese carried in his pocket during the Cultural Revolution. I brought an English language copy back from China in 1972 along with a Mao lapel button, mementoes of China when it was in the grips of political lunacy. It was a fascinating time to be there. The stories just wrote themselves.

The 1972 trip came about when the Canadian Importers Association organized its first buying mission to the spring trade fair in Guangzhou (formerly Canton). They invited the *Financial Post* to send a journalist, and I, having spent a month in Asia two years earlier, drew the assignment. It proved a very onerous assignment because after eight or ten days in China, I went to all the rising economies of Southeast Asia and to South Korea and wrote the Pacific Rim report that had been cancelled in 1970. To say the least, it was an exotic adventure.

I started planning this trip on January 30, almost three months prior to departure. It required an enormous amount of reading on China and the other nations, including nine books. Part of the research also involved locating the China experts in Canada and interviewing them. I did a long article for the *Financial Post* on April 1 on some of the academic experts that business people and others were besieging for advice—experts like Paul T.K. Lin at McGill, John Melby at the University of Guelph, and William Saywell at the University of Toronto.[42] These, along with the other academics I interviewed, suddenly had become stars at their universities, leading seminars and sometimes even leading groups to China. There was an enormous curiosity about China as it was emerging from the cultural revolution.

There was a great deal to organize for my trip and some nail-biting until the Chinese granted my visa on March 13. I was the only person in the group of about seventy businessmen and wives officially identified as a journalist. However, a *Globe and Mail* writer named Richard Dolman joined the group as the alleged president of a small importing company interested in Chinese spirits. Even though he roomed with me briefly in Beijing, his cover seems not to have been discovered. The Chinese often rejected applications from journalists. For example, so many journalists had attached themselves to an Ontario trade mission to China in March that none were given visas. Zena Cherry, a social columnist at *The Globe and Mail* married to a genuine importer, was unable to get a visa with our group. The Chinese were so capricious that they even refused the travel agent who organized our tour. I have no idea why my visa was approved.

There was no hotter travel destination in 1972 than China, a few months after Richard Nixon, the American president, made his famous visit there. The country had largely been closed to all but the pluckiest of tourists since 1948. Pierre Trudeau and his friend, Jacques Hébert, a Montreal labour lawyer, managed to get into China in 1960 and wrote

42   *Financial Post*, April 1, 1972: "The questions Canada's own China-watchers get."

a book about it. It may have seemed ground-breaking at the time, but when I read it, after having been there myself, I was bemused to learn they had travelled to the same points of interest as our group. It was an indication that the Chinese were managing their tourists, not giving them free reign.[43]

Ours was an eclectic group. Most of them had recently joined the Canadian Importers Association because it was a ticket into China (as it was for me). One was Harry Barberian, the owner of a well-known Toronto steak house and an irrepressible character. In China, he collected acupuncture dolls, tried to buy a uniform cap from a Chinese soldier, asked a taxi in Beijing to take him to Chairman's Mao's house, and tried to talk politics with our Chinese guides. There were serious businessmen among the group as well, including Fred Eaton of the department store family and Pat Brodeur, who ran Cassidy's, then a major importer of chinaware. All of the serious people had a common problem: China was opening so suddenly to foreign business that the manufacturers could not meet the demand. Time and again, people in our group were told what they wanted was out of stock. The managing director of Boosey & Hawkes in Canada ordered one thousand violins which the Chinese were selling at about $8 each; and he was only allocated 150.

We flew to Hong Kong on April 23 and, after an overnight stay, embarked by a rather decrepit train for the border where the Chinese processed us through a series of waiting rooms, which took several hours. Then we were seated for an enormous Chinese lunch, the first of many good meals, before taking our seats in an air-conditioned train car for a two-hour run to Guangzhou. This was as luxurious as China would get. My large room at the Tung Fang Hotel had dirty walls, a worn carpet, and no hot water between 8:30 a.m. and 6:00 p.m. Richard Dolman was given a different room, so I now roomed with a Montreal textile merchant, Marvin Carsley, who had been coming to the trade fair since 1968. Breakfasts were spartan. The real old China hands travelled with their own jars of instant coffee and strawberry jam. It was

---

43 Trudeau, as Prime Minister, recognized the government of The People's Republic of China in 1970 and went there in 1973.

a huge hotel, about 1,200 rooms, with what passed for a concierge on each floor, keeping an eye on the guests. On checking out, we waited in our two buses for some time while the staff went through our rooms, perhaps to see if we had taken souvenirs or if we had left anything behind. A rather large woman on our bus was mortified when a hotel staff member arrived, holding her capacious pair of used panty hose retrieved from her waste basket.

I was intrigued with the English-language brand names on products at the fair and wrote about them: Double Red Horse shirts, Flying Pigeon bicycles, Seagull cameras, Flying Dove sewing machines, Spring Thunder radios, Happy accordions, Double Sheep water colours, Golden Cock shoe polish, Deer Brand rifles, Double Fish fishing nets, and so on. My favourite was "Double Happiness, the most luxurious toilet paper." (That was better than the rugged quality of toilet paper provided by the Tung Fang.) Of course, these brands might not have been at all funny in the pictorial Chinese language; these were simply translations of those pictographs. During the two days spent at the sprawling trade fair, these provided me with a good deal of amusement. I also found some wine to taste, including a palatable white called Peking Weisswein.[44]

The Chinese kept us immersed in propaganda, including an evening at the opera. The Peking Opera Troop (*Beijing* was just coming into general usage) performed *The Red Lantern*, a so-called "modern revolutionary Peking opera." I believe there were four approved operas at the time, all heavily political. In this opera, the Chinese, despite a traitor in their midst, defeat and execute a Japanese villain named Hatoyama. "New China will shine like the morning sun," the translated libretto reads. "Red flags will fly all over the country." It was two hours long and staged with spectacular gymnastics. Whatever entertainment we attended inevitably revolved around the cult of Mao's personality and the glorification of the Communist party. "There is a golden sun in Peking, and he is Chairman Mao," went the refrain sung by a group of school children performing in a cultural park. We went to the municipal

44   *Financial Post*, May 20, 1972: "Brand names of China—heroic or romantic?"

museum to see a display of antiquities and were told that the beautiful vessels had been available only to the rich in feudal times. We heard the same thing at the Ming Tombs. Even if true (it probably was), it was irrelevant today. The Great Proletarian Revolution was twisting and denigrating China's splendidly rich cultural heritage. There was also a ghastly tableau in the museum depicting peasants rising up against the rich, arrogant landlord.

Of course, we were shown how peasants lived now. We travelled to a communal farm, the Ta Li People's Commune, near the city. It was a commune with a population of 63,000, about 1,100 hectares (2,717 acres) of arable land, a mill, a cement block plant, a slaughterhouse, and five other factories. Mr. Lin, the vice-chairman of the Revolutionary Committee, told us there were six tractors but 9,300 bicycles. That seemed a surprising small number of bikes until one saw how many people rode on the same bike (unless it was transporting night soil or other commodities). We were introduced to a "brigade leader" who lived with a family of five and a pig in a four-room house. He was especially proud of his transistor radio, a rare luxury since most of the commune relied on a public address system with speakers in every village, playing patriotic music and broadcasting announcements.

On another day, our entire group was allowed to watch one stoic Chinese woman have kidney stones removed and another have an ovarian cyst removed, with, apparently, only acupuncture against the pain of surgery. Some in our group turned green and left the observation rooms, which were on the floor above the operating table. I focussed my camera on the action and snapped away. (I had brought nineteen rolls of film and supplemented that later with a few rolls of dreadful Chinese black and white film.) We were told the doctor was actually a brain surgeon. The woman whose kidney stone was removed got off the table after being stitched up, waved to us, and walked out on her own. The peanut-sized stone was sent up for us to see, and the patient also appeared and answered a few questions. It was all rather bizarre.

That evening we flew to Beijing. The Beijing of 1972 was a grey city filled with stolid Marxist architecture and sprawling neighbourhoods of low buildings, quite unlike the modern high-rise city it has become. The fine sand of the Gobi Desert, lifted by persistent spring winds, sifted across the city and onto everything, including camera lenses. There was not yet much pollution from vehicles because private vehicles then were bicycles—throngs and throngs of robust black bicycles locked in vast parking areas when not in use. Our next day was dedicated to seeing the Ming Tombs and the Great Wall, then as now China's best-known tourist attraction. In 1972, there was one restaurant at the Great Wall. There were not many visitors; we strolled the short section open to the public, taking photographs of what seemed the vast and empty expanse of the wall. The wall was an hour or two north of Beijing, snaking over the far horizons. When Marlene and I were there again in 1992 (after our Tiananmen experience), we found the wall completely overwhelmed with camera-toting crowds. There were even Chinese with camels on the wall itself, posing for the tourists for a fee. Meant originally to keep the hordes out, the wall attracted thousands once China tourism opened to the world.

In 1972, I was in Beijing for May 1, a big day for all Marxists. Our group had guided tours of the Summer Palace, a former imperial residence, crowded with Chinese on a rare day off to enjoy folk dancing and other May Day entertainment. During one of these events, Marshall Ye, the vice chair of the government's military committee, arrived and got, as one would expect for a veteran of the Long March, a standing ovation. Authority rested casually on him as he lounged in the front row, watching the folk dancing, while the Chinese government's paparazzi snapped photos of him. A few years later, he was one of the generals that overthrew Mao's widow and the rest of the Gang of Four.

We returned to Hong Kong the next day, all with stories on which we could dine for years. I wrote a number of pieces on China, some of them undoubtedly naïve. I certainly did not appreciate the banal evil of the Mao administration, nor how fast China would modernize after the Gang of Four were gone. In the China of 1972, virtually everyone dressed in denim smocks and pants, with Mao's button on the breast. No one talked politics other than to repeat Mao's thoughts. Twenty years later, the Chinese were wearing the same jeans and sport shirts they exported to the West. The tour buses were modern, and the guides bitched about local (not national) politicians. And Peking Weisswein had been replaced by a rather decent Chardonnay, which may or may not have been grown in China.

The 1992 visit to China was on the back of a visit to Taiwan in May 1992, so that Marlene and I could spend a week with John and Elizabeth, who were studying there. (My luggage included thirty-six hours of recorded hockey games for John.) They had immersed themselves in the local culture, even taking up dragon boat racing. We went to watch an early morning practice. We also took in some of the city's major attractions, including the National Palace Museum. During the revolution, Chiang Kai Shek had moved a large number of treasures from the Palace Museum in Beijing to Nanking and then to Taipei. This is one of the great museums in Asia. Whether on our own or with John's help, we managed to get around by bus and train, including a weekend excursion to Taroko National Park, a very scenic park on the east coast of Taiwan.

My engagement with China resumed in November 1994 when I won a two-week Taiwan work study fellowship from the Asia Pacific Foundation. I was there during one of those politically fevered periods that made it a lively visit. Elections were underway for the governor of Taiwan. That office was separate from the presidency, left over from the time when Taiwan was a province of China, but still with major authority. The governor led the Kuomintang, the party of Chiang Kai Shek when he fled to Taiwan after his defeat by the Communists in 1948. For years, the administration of Taiwan maintained that it was the legitimate government of China. The rival Democratic Progressive Party in Taiwan sustained those who wanted to declare Taiwan an independent country. Meanwhile, the regime in Beijing, which also considered itself the legitimate government of all China, including Taiwan, routinely stated that it would meet an independence declaration with military force (as it does to this day). The relationship between the two regimes was tangled and even absurd. That fall, officials from Beijing were in Taipei to discuss "borrowing" treasures from the National Palace Museum for an exhibit in China. It seem unlikely this would happen since Beijing also insisted that the treasures had been stolen when Chiang brought them to the island in 1949.

I happened to be there when Winston Chang, one of the illegitimate twin sons of Chiang, suffered a stroke in Beijing while he was at an academic conference (he was president of a university in Taiwan). He could not be put on a mercy flight directly from Beijing to Taipei because such direct flights were not allowed at the time. Chang, deep in a coma, was put on a plane that touched down in Hong Kong en route from Beijing. An English language newspaper in Taipei explained it thus: "John Chang, chairman of the cabinet-level Overseas Chinese Affairs Committee, and the twin brother of Chang, said he believes his brother would not want to violate the government's policy of no direct links with Beijing, and would choose to come back via a third area." Chang remained in the coma until he died in February 1996.[45]

The Canadians living and doing business in Taiwan had negotiated the diplomatic absurdity quite creatively. Canada had broken diplomatic ties with Taiwan in 1971 when Prime Minister Pierre Trudeau established ties with the People's Republic of China. At lunch one day in Taipei, I fell into conversation with Pierre Loisel, a Quebecker who had come to Taiwan in 1964 and was now president of the Canadian Society.[46] The lack of an embassy in Taipei had been a huge inconvenience for Canadians doing business there. Clearing routine paperwork typically involved trips to the Canadian consulate in Hong Kong. Taiwan businessmen asked Loisel to go to Ottawa and devise a sensible approach. Loisel hit a brick wall with the Trudeau bureaucrats. However, Governor General Roland Michener, a distant relative of his, suggested that the Chambers of Commerce in each country should reciprocate with offices in the other country. The idea was not only implemented, it worked so well that the Chamber was allowed to open a Canadian Trade Office in Taipei in the early 1990s to operate as an embassy in everything but name.

My program of interviews included numerous bureaucrats but also some notable businessmen. The most prominent was Stan Shih, sometimes referred to as the Bill Gates of Taiwan because, in 1976, he led a

45 *Financial Post*, December 3, 1994: "China closely eyes Taiwan vote."

46 *Financial Post*, December 17, 1994: "Taiwan is the back door to China."

group that founded what became Acer Computers. As I recall, he spoke English well and gave me a good interview.

Typically, when I travelled in Asia, I was blessed with an iron stomach. That was not so on one evening midway through my Taiwan trip. Some bug got to me, manifesting itself while I was at the National Concert Hall to listen to the Sapporo Symphony under Kazuyoshi Akiyama. My stomach began to growl in the second half, and I began to plan a dash to the bathroom as soon as the concert ended. Would you believe that Akiyama did two encores? I fled to the bathroom as soon as he finished the second and was able to evacuate into the toilet. When I stood up, I was light-headed and sweating. I spent ten or fifteen minutes seated in the lobby until the world came back into focus. One of the volunteer ushers drove me back to my hotel. I felt beaten up the next morning, but I was able to carry on with the program, which included tours of a steel mill, an industrial park, and ultimately, some time at Kenting National Park at the very tip of Taiwan.

After two busy weeks in Taiwan, I relaxed several days in Hong Kong with John and Elizabeth before returning to Vancouver. Ironically, in view of the extremely loose bowels in Taipei, I had such a case of constipation at home that I went to the doctor. He prescribed a powerful suppository that put me right with the world again.

Fourteen:
A gun fight in Manila

The ten days in China in 1972 were a prelude to a month of travel in Southeast Asia and South Korea to gather material for another *Financial Post* supplement. One of the first things I did on returning to Hong Kong from China (after ordering a tailored suit for $50) was to apply for a South Korean visa. Approval would have been routine except for the fact I had just been in China. The Korean consular officials quizzed me in detail on my impressions of China, asking, among other things, whether the Chinese people were happy. I replied that they seemed happy to me. In retrospect, my answer was naïve in the extreme. After all, I had just spent time in one of the most oppressive dictatorships, so oppressive that one could not expect candour from the people. The society was still decked out with Mao buttons and copies of *The Little Red Book.* I made a diary note of seeing an elevator operator reading the book. Perhaps what I interpreted as a sign of devotion to Maoism was rather a fear of not seeming ardent enough. There was a guide on our bus in Beijing who spoke excellent English but who was distinctly uncomfortable when one of our group tried to get him to make political comments. He totally sidestepped such questions. How could I have believed these were truly happy people? My diary indicates that I was unduly impressed with China's efficiency and with the apparent honesty of a society surrounded by corrupt governments. How could I have been so wrong?

The Southeast Asian trip started on May 6, 1972, with a visit to the Philippines. My flight from Hong Kong arrived about midday on a Saturday. That evening I went to Mass. I was walking back to my hotel at dusk—which in the tropics is always around 6:00 p.m.—when I heard what sounded like firecrackers and saw several figures scurrying across the sidewalk toward a car. One seemed to be carrying a rifle that was aimed at a nearby restaurant, while another was helping someone into the car. My first thought was teens playing cops and robbers. Then I realized that Filipinos are slight; that was a real rifle and real gunfire. I quickly took cover behind a large tree until the car roared away. The incident left me shaken. When I told an officer at the Canadian embassy about it later, he advised me not to worry. "They only shoot their friends," he laughed. I learned from the *Manila Times* newspaper that I had witnessed a gunfight between three narcotics police seated in the restaurant and five assailants. No one died but one of the policemen and one of the assailants were wounded. On a subsequent evening, I decided to dine at the Taza de Oro restaurant near the American embassy to get over the incident. There were bullet holes in the wall, but the dinner—fillet of fish with cantaloupe for dessert—was excellent.

The Philippines did not impress me. At the time, both the politics and the economy were a mess. The Filipinos explained this away by pointing to the country's colonial history: three hundred years a Spanish Colony, fifty years an American colony, and then independence after World War II. "What can you say for a country that spent three hundred years in a convent, fifty years in Hollywood, and thirty years in hell?" one Filipino asked me. As I write this in 2022, the outgoing president of the Philippines is a thug who has turned police and vigilante squads loose to eliminate drug trade criminals. To mid-2020, about four thousand had been eliminated. That president's successor is the son of Ferdinand Marcos, the autocrat who was in power when I visited the country in the 1970s.

The country was then promoting tourism, and I was invited to an evening dance entertainment in the company with German travel agents. One told me the country had a great tourism future: visitors could do anything they wanted because "they have no Puritanism," unlike Malaysia; and no curfew, unlike Thailand (which had recently had a military coup). He said he would not go to Thailand because the cost was so low that "you might find your housekeeper there."

I spent the following morning in the company of a public relations man from San Miguel Corp., very likely the largest company owned by a Filipino businessman. I don't recall if I got an interview; I did get an aerial tour of Manila by helicopter. Then I moved on to interview the secretary of commerce (who was called away, leaving a hopeless bureaucrat to fill in) and then the president of the University of the Philippines. One kept hearing tales of inefficiency and corruption. Manila's air terminal, I discovered, was a shambles because much of it had been destroyed earlier in the year by an arsonist. The tale told to me was that the fires were organized by a contractor who had installed used telex machines instead of new ones and wanted to obliterate the evidence. The story sounded far-fetched, but one never knew with the Philippines.

From Manila, I flew to Jakarta, the capital of Indonesia, arriving there on a public holiday. The Hong Kong representative of the Toronto Dominion Bank had his Jakarta counterpart send a car to the airport, lest I be held hostage by a local taxi driver. That actually happened to the *Financial Post's* advertising salesman when he came through a few weeks later; the taxi drove him all over the city until he came up with some extra cash. The sum was modest, but the experience was harrowing.

The Indonesians made a better impression on me, starting with an interview with Sumitro Djojohadikusumo, the trade minister, one of the cadre of foreign-educated leaders in the government. He was an impressive man who had a doctorate in economics from Erasmus University in the Netherlands. He had become head of the economics faculty at the University of Indonesia. I did not get much time with him because, like the so-called Berkeley Mafia in government, he was extremely busy.

The government of General Suharto also was dictatorial, having come to power by overthrowing General Sukarno in 1966. The Communists who had supported Sukarno were brutally crushed, with somewhere between five hundred thousand and two million being eliminated in a genocide still not widely discussed in Indonesia. None of the business people I spoke with even mentioned the pogrom. No doubt, the foreign business people closed the door on it because the Suharto government had stabilized the economy and encouraged foreign investment.

Most of the senior Indonesians I met seemed overwhelmed with the demand for their attention because, I concluded, the veneer of educated managers was still rather thin. My appointment with the senior legal official at Pertamina, the state oil company, was delayed by ninety minutes while other officials paraded in and out. Many people I spoke to, including the Canadian ambassador, offered negative accounts of the Sukarno government and the disastrous results of its reliance on Russian aid (fertilizer plants, pulp and paper plants, and a steel mill that did not function). The inflation rate had hit 650% in 1966 but had been contained by the Suharto government.

One of my contacts here was Frank Vymetal, the senior Jakarta officer for the Bata shoe company. Before leaving Canada prior to this trip, I had gone to the Bata headquarters in Toronto for a briefing from one of the senior executives, Dr. C.K. Herz. In his office, I got a taste of Bata corporate culture. When the voice of Thomas Bata boomed over a loudspeaker in the office, Dr. Herz stood while replying to the voice of his boss. The shoe company had factories and representatives throughout Southeast Asia. They were well-connected and well-informed, and I relied on them as much as on the Canadian trade commissioners for briefings. Bata's factory had operated in Indonesia at least since the 1930s. The Japanese occupiers did not take it over but, in 1965, Sukarno did. Bata got it back two years later when Suharto came to power. Vymetal, who had previously run Bata factories in Africa, was nearing retirement. He and his wife were not happy in Indonesia and did not remain there after retiring. Since he was Dutch, it would have been surprising if he had stayed since the Indonesians were not sympathetic to their former colonial masters.

The other major Canadian company in Indonesia at the time was International Nickel, which had just begun building a plant to process nickel. The deposit had been discovered in 1901, but development had been delayed more than half a century until Inco negotiated a contract with the new Suharto government. One of the senior Indonesian executives at Inco was named Hitler Sangawinata. At the end of a good interview, I just had to ask how he got his first name. It seemed that his father was an Indonesian nationalist who detested the Dutch in Indonesia so much that he named his son Hitler when the son was born just after the Nazi armies invaded Holland.

My next stop was Singapore. It was then, and remains so today, the best-organized economy in Asia; a city state that has been governed with very firm but clean hands. I was impressed with its society's sense of purpose. For some reason, I interviewed a leader of the trade union movement who recounted how, after considerable labour turmoil in the 1960s, the unions had fallen into line with the government's development objectives. "We cannot afford to practise the way our counterparts in the West can," he told me. "We just cannot afford to let Singapore down."

Singapore was well into urban redevelopment during which most of the charming British colonial architecture was being replaced with gleaming office and residential towers. My Bata guide, G.C. Thio, lamented the pace of development. "People who were here a year ago say they don't recognize the city," he said to me as he showed me some of the remaining old Singapore. That included the Cold Storage Supermarket parking lot, which was indeed a daytime parking lot. When the cars left about 5:00 p.m., the lot was taken over by the stalls of food vendors. It was a marvellous place to eat; unlike much of Asian street food, this food was safe because Singapore enforced rigorous sanitation. The supermarket subsequently grew to a retail chain and the food carts, to the best of my knowledge, no longer set up in the parking lot. However, Raffles Hotel still maintained the standards of luxury it set in colonial times. I stayed at a much cheaper hotel, but I went to the bar at Raffles for a drink. The matchbooks bore a Somerset Maugham quote that Raffles "stands for all the fables of the exotic East." I was back in Singapore in 2002 when Singapore Airlines flew me there to observe (but not take part in) the selection of wines for the airline. The city gleamed with modern buildings. As Thio predicted, I did not recognize it. It had become a major financial and shipping centre and had managed not to come under the thumb of Beijing.

(In 2002, Singapore Airlines also arranged several days for me in a Bali resort called Begawan Giri. It is one of the most luxurious resorts at which I have ever stayed. The air was redolent with floral aromas and the sound of tropical birds. Aside from spa treatments, there was little to do but relax in tropical luxury. I did walk into the local village and once took a taxi to Ubud, a nearby city, to buy some batik for my daughters. As lovely as the resort is, a longer stay would have bored me with the sheer idleness.)

Kuala Lumpur in Malaysia, my next stop, also no doubt is dramatically different from what I found: "a sleepy little place, very picturesque, with the Moorish railway station (built in 1910)." I spent Sunday afternoon at the Batu Caves, a Hindu shrine in a collection of limestone caves, taking a local bus for the seven-mile (11.2 kilometre) ride from the city. I did not record whether I climbed the 272 steps to the highest cave, but I did note the haunting shrieks of the bats high above, among the stalactites. I found the caves an eerie experience.

My Malaysian guide, a dull fellow named Nathan, took me to sit in on a debate in the Malaysian Parliament where I got to listen to banal speeches about sugar cane production and about the need to modernize the thinking of farmers. We went for dinner at a hotel with a program of Malay dance and shadow plays in the garden. We even had coconut "Champagne" that I found "not very good."

Malaysia then as now was an interesting study in politics. The country had endured serious race riots in 1969 in which the Malay majority asserted its political rights against the ethnic Chinese and ethnic Indians. The latter groups had been settled there when this was a British colony to provide the colonial masters with a cadre of administrators and business people. The Chinese had come to dominate business, while the East Indians dominated retail, services, and the professions. After the race riots, the Malaysian government adopted policies deliberately favouring the Malays, involving that group in the economy beyond agriculture. Some of the Chinese Malaysians I spoke with were bitter but also resigned, knowing that the government would not allow the country's ethnic majority to languish in third place economically. Some potential foreign investors were not impressed: I encountered a German businessman at a dinner party who dismissed Malays as "lazy."

In the aftermath of the race riots, there was a real push by the government to get job-creating development going. The major Canadian project at the time in Malaysia was a lumber and plywood plant designed by Canadian consultants. The drive there, 145 miles (232 kilometres) east of Kuala Lumpur, was terrifyingly memorable. We set out in the dark at six in the morning on a four-hour drive on a twisting jungle highway; there was always a chance of meeting a truck loaded with logs on a blind curve. My guide was Frank Wilfert, a consultant on the project. He drove his Holden sedan[47] with abandon, sometimes lighting a cigar with a cupped match while negotiating a curve. It proved to be a long day in stifling heat.

In Bangkok, the capital of Thailand, I had booked a room at the Oriental Hotel where, famously, Somerset Maugham had lived. My room had a view of the Chao Phrya River. The terrace restaurant overlooking the river was wonderful, both for the food and for the views of busy life on the river. Once again, one of my guides was a Bata manager, Chalerm Chanurai. He took me to a Buddhist temple (it was the holiest day of the year for Buddhists) and then to an excellent dinner and evening of classical Thai dancing. The next day, a Sunday, he drove me to Pattaya, even then a popular beach resort but not as crowded as it became in later years.

Thailand had been through a military coup the previous November (and has had several since). I did not form as positive a view of Thailand as I had of Malaysia and especially Singapore. In fact, my impression was largely negative because the country was struggling with corruption, illiterate farmers, a communist insurgency, and who knows how many other problems. And it did not help that, after a month on the road, I was wearing down in the suffocating heat and unbelievably congested traffic of Bangkok. When I was back there for a few days in 1976, I found the traffic was even worse. I have never wanted to go

47 Holden was a General Motors brand made in Australia. The brand was retired in 2021.

back, even though Thailand has since become a major tourist destination and, individually, Thais are quite charming people.

I interviewed several representatives of Canadian consulting companies based in Bangkok. One was run by a German-Canadian. He was free in expressing his contempt for Thais; his wife had the vocabulary of a truck driver. Another of the Canadians who did not know about the hard-cursing wife was chagrined that he had proposed the individual for membership in "the club."

After Thailand, I had two or three days in Hong Kong for more interviews and then flew to South Korea. This had been a late addition to my trip at, I recall, the suggestion of a South Korean trade representative in Toronto. The Sejong Hotel in Seoul, where I stayed, made it a practice to place flags of the country at the doors of guest rooms. The Canadian flag in front of mine was upside down! But it was obvious that the Koreans had it together when it came to economic development.

Of course, there had also been a military coup there: in 1961, a general named Park Chung-hee had become president and was still running things with a firm hand and with other military people throughout government. (He was assassinated in 1979 by his own security chief.) I had a long interview with a Major-General Park—Park is a common Korean surname, along with Kim and Lee. A former Marine commander, Park was then vice-president of the Korean Trade Promotion Corporation. He told me that the president's strong hand had been necessary to marshal the phenomenal energy of the Korean people and open up the economy, which even then was one of the most dynamic in Asia. "We work up under the direction and control of the leadership of President Park," I was told. We got along well. He invited me to his home for drinks (beer for me, Scotch for him). I was struck by the personal security measures. The house was walled with barbed wire topping the walls and with a pair of menacing watchdogs caged inside the walls. His home also was full of mementoes of his career. The strangest was a collection of about three hundred cigarette lighters, each with the crest of a military unit with which the general had been associated.

My Southeast Asian excursion, which began on Sunday, April 23, ended on Thursday, June 6, with a flight back to Canada through Tokyo. I got to relive it again when I put together the most complex expense account I have ever done. I did each segment separately in the local currency and converted the totals into Canadian dollars. To my surprise, there was no challenge at all from my employer's accounting department.

The 1976 Canadian trade mission led by Trade Minister Don Jamieson covered the same countries in Southeast Asia, but compressed it into about ten days. The minister's presence meant our group had access to both political and business leaders. The most senior leader we met was Ferdinand Marcos, president of the Philippines. It was a bizarre meeting. The Canadian group waited an hour before Marcos popped in, speaking to us for about five minutes and rationalizing why there was martial law in his country. In my diary, I commented that: "Martial law has put an end to the endemic gunfights. All the expatriates enthuse about the new peace and security which exists (along with a 1:00 a.m. curfew)." Our return to Canada included an overnight stop in Hawaii.

In June 1978, on my second trip to South Korea, I visited the demilitarized zone at Panmunjom, the truce village about twenty-five miles (forty kilometres) north of Seoul and a thoroughly menacing place. It flourishes as an attraction for tourists who want to see the room where the truce ending the Korean war was signed. On their side, the North Koreans had erected a two-storey building so that their soldiers could look down on the other side. Not to be outdone, the Americans had deployed the tallest and most menacing black Marines who towered over the North Korean soldiers. In 1976, two American soldiers clearing trees near the truce line were attacked and killed by an axe-wielding North Korean. I expect that Panmunjom today still has a menacing feel, given that the North Korean government, now a nuclear power, remains repressive, and that there still is no peace treaty.

My week or so in Korea on the second trip included comfortable stays at guest houses of both Pohang Iron & Steel Company (spartan) and Hyundai Shipyards (rather grand). I had tours of industrial plants, meals with publicists, and interviews at Samsung and with a cabinet minister. The obvious energy of the country was impressive, but the extensive security everywhere, while understandable, was suffocating. I was happy to leave and, unlike Japan, had no desire to go back.

Fifteen:
No promotions for me

When I negotiated my transfer from Toronto to Vancouver in 1973, Robert Herz, one of our Toronto friends, warned that I was removing myself from opportunities to be promoted at the *Financial Post* head office. What Robert did not know was that I did not want those promotions. I did not expect there was much chance of continuing the climb through the ranks. I had joined the paper in 1961, an inexperienced business reporter paid $500 a month. By June 1970, I was in charge of a pod of about six reporters and was being paid $1,175 a month.

During the two years in the Montreal bureau (1967–1969), I had come to appreciate the more productive work environment of a bureau—at least for someone with my self-starting work habits. While the *Financial Post* newsroom in Toronto was small compared to most big city newsrooms, I always found it difficult to work in an open office. There was no privacy when the desks were right against each other. One overheard neighbouring reporters doing telephone interviews. One or another reporter was always wandering around, casually visiting others. For several years, I was seated beside Terence Robertson, a British-born writer of military books. He was completing a book on the Dieppe military landing in 1941, and we were all knew that he was working on it. In fact, the editor's secretary actually typed the manuscript for him.[48]

---

48 Terence Robertson committed suicide in New York in 1970 while working on a book about the Bronfmans.

The newsroom distractions were so numerous that I often took my work home. In Montreal, there were only three or four of us in the bureau. There were far fewer distractions and more self-directed opportunities to write. I believe my career flourished in this atmosphere.

Back in head office after Montreal, I had to adjust again to working amid distractions, this time while also running a group of other writers. More than ever, I was taking work home to finish because so much office time was spent on shaping the copy of those in my group. There was John Fennell, a 1953 Ryerson journalism graduate, who was a workmanlike writer. Ultimately, the *Post* let him go, and he moved on to edit trade magazines at Maclean-Hunter and then, I believe, work in public relations. There was a bright British reporter, David Bentley, who left to work in Halifax after Neville Nankivell had criticized his work. I thought he was capable. He started a weekly newspaper, converted it to the *Halifax Daily News* in 1981, and sold it later in the decade to a local businessman. Perhaps the most challenging member of the group was Basil Jackson. He was more qualified to write business than I was. He had been an aircraft draftsman in Britain and, after coming to Canada, had done both advertising copywriting and technical writing for an aircraft manufacturer. He may have come to the *Post* through the MH trade magazine division. A quiet man, he churned out many feature reports dependably. (He did the Japan report the year before I did it.)

Basil was also just beginning his career as a novelist. He was fifty when I took over the group. His first novel, *Epicenter*, had been sold and would be published early in 1971. Fifteen years before the Chernobyl nuclear plant disaster, the book posited a major radiation leak at a nuclear power plant near Toronto. Chernobyl breathed a second life into sales of Basil's book.

His second manuscript was with a publisher, and he was working on his third book. (In all, he churned out ten fictional thrillers, mostly about aviation. An eleventh failed to get published.) Basil's well-researched prose was workmanlike and his characters were wooden, but his productivity spurred me on and perhaps, in a small way, pushed me to write books.

Basil became a close friend, but was a complicated man to manage, sometimes blurring the lines between his two writing careers. "To my irritation, he has been working on his book at the office," I complained to my diary. "His preoccupation with it probably accounts for his dismal production of recent months, although he puts it down to problems with the 'desk'." Basil was not on the front page as much as he had been, and some of his copy was being rewritten. Basil once told me that he rose at 5:00 a.m. to write because he wanted to do his best work when he was fresh.

Not long after I transferred to Vancouver, Basil just walked out on his wife, Eileen. After six months back in Britain, he came to Vancouver and worked for many years as a business writer for *The Province* while completing more novels. I think Basil tired of Eileen after his first trip to Japan; he became so infatuated with Japan that he courted several Japanese women and eventually married one named Kyoko, who was thirty years his junior. We were invited to his wedding, a civil ceremony followed by a reception in a Richmond hotel. When I saw that Basil had not remembered to order celebratory sparkling wine, I ordered several bottles of Henkell Trocken and paid for it, so that we could enjoy a toast.

The best member of my pod was Steve Duncan, a talented writer who did not need much direction. To my chagrin, he was transferred to our Ottawa bureau, where he blossomed into a fine political reporter. In early 1971, Philip Mathias, who had also been in the Montreal bureau, joined my group and later became an exceptional investigative reporter with an irritating habit of arguing about everything. He was not happy that he had to report to me. I had to talk long and hard to convince him not to quit. He was happier when he managed to switch his reporting to Neville; I was happier, too. There were others I noted in my diary who were either journeymen or unmotivated writers. I did not enjoy administration and doubted I had much talent for it. "Trying to write and administer is one hell of a chore," I told my diary.

What I really wanted to do was write, not manage, and that became clear when I did a good colour story in early 1971 on a Canadian Pacific Airlines marketing coup. The airline had switched its flight attendants into high-fashion uniforms, including ultrashort-skirts, and that created controversy, to say the least. Jack Gilmer, the airline's president, told me he personally received about 250 letters of protest in the first days after the uniforms were unveiled. Many came from the business travellers CP Air was trying to win. There were plenty of people who also approved of the new uniforms. In my story, I write that one executive typed his own protest letter when his secretary, who favoured the new fashions, refused to do it.[49] The airline extracted itself from the controversy by having a public plebiscite. Of the 35,000 who voted, only 14% liked the so-called midi skirt. The plebiscite was milked for all the publicity it could get, giving the airline valuable profile to counter the impact of Air Canada introducing the Boeing 747. The ultra-short skirts were discontinued. As Gilmer told me: "We made lemonade from what looked like a bunch of lemons."

I don't know whether the airline or our editors initiated the assignment, but I was sent to Vancouver to interview CP Air managers. I continued on to San Francisco to interview the advertising agency involved in the campaign, Hoefer, Dieterich & Brown. In the middle of a Toronto winter, it was an incredible experience to stroll around San Francisco in the balmy mid-February sunshine. This alone whet my appetite to move to Vancouver when the job came along. My story about CP Air drew compliments from Paul Deacon, Neville Nankivell, and Carlyle Dunbar (then the editor on the copy desk). "I've felt my writing ability is improving noticeably, and has for the last three or four years," I confided to my diary. I assigned some of the credit for the habit I had inquired in Montreal of reading *The Wall Street Journal* and copying some of its prose style. (I continued to read that newspaper until I retired in 2001, and I continued to structure my feature stories in much the same way the *Journal* did, always leading off with arresting anecdotes.)

My transfer to Vancouver turned out very well on every level. I had never really put down roots in Toronto, but Vancouver felt like home within months, both for me and for Marlene. We were closer to our

49 *Financial Post*, March 6, 1971: "Veni, vidi, vici (or how midis came, travellers saw, and the public conquered".

families in Saskatchewan and, after joining a so-called Newcomers Club, we quickly had a much larger circle of friends than we ever had in Toronto. And, of course, I discovered the wine industry.

In addition, my reporting repertoire expanded considerably when I went to Vancouver. For example, I wrote a lot of political stories, a topic I almost never covered when I was in the East. Dave Barrett's government had come to power in British Columbia in 1972, soon generating an avalanche of news. In August 1973, I covered the Western Economic Opportunities Conference in Calgary, where Prime Minister Pierre Trudeau hosted the four western premiers. Barrett's behaviour, compared to that of the other premiers, struck me as juvenile—swinging in his chair, sometimes turning his back on the table, making sotto voce remarks, and generally getting under Trudeau's skin. When I read my article today, I doubt much was achieved at the conference.[50]

In that time, we published one feature report after another. My first from the Vancouver bureau was a report on forest industries on September 15, 1973. It was an eight-page national report, and I shared the writing with others on our staff. One of the lead stories dealt with Robert Williams, the very clever man who was minister of Land, Forests, and Water Resources. The forest industry feared him because he could be radical and determined. Ironically, I did some wine consulting for him thirty years later when he had a wine store and pub in Mission. It was a lucrative assignment: in 2005, I was paid $3,300 for my advice.

In October 1973, I went to Mackenzie in Northern British Columbia to do a feature on the town's twenty-nine-year-old doctor, Corey Brown. I do not recall what prompted that piece, but it is one of the better profiles I have written. The doctor was quite candid. He was one of two doctors in Mackenzie, taking the position because he could earn money quickly—money he needed to develop a silver property he controlled in the Yukon.[51]

---

50 *Financial Post*, August 4, 1973: "When the kings have left the West."

51 *Financial Post*, October 27, 1973: "I'm a good doctor, what am I doing in Mackenzie?"

When I transferred myself to Vancouver in 1973, one motive was to get away from administration and focus on reporting. That changed in mid-1978, when the *Financial Post* decided to launch *Western Business*, a supplement to be circulated to our subscribers in the four western provinces. The rationale was that Western Canada was booming; we would cover some of those stories in a regional supplement, and it would be supported by advertising. It was assumed there would be abundant advertising revenue, given the region's economic buoyancy.

Western Business was edited by me from Vancouver. Now I found that I could actually manage. We hired Richard Osler for the new Calgary bureau and Jim Lyon to work with me in Vancouver. A British-born journalist, Jim had started his Canadian journalism career with the *Toronto Telegram*; when it closed, he moved to the *Vancouver Sun*, where he was covering forestry when we hired him. It was fortunate for him because the Vancouver newspapers were closed by an eight-month strike that finally ended in late June, 1979. Years later, Jim told me that his happiest time in journalism was the five years during which he worked with me. I had also come to regard him as my best friend.

Western Business debuted in the first week of January, 1979—and my salary was raised by $300 to $2,505 a month. That was a long way from my starting salary of $500 a month when I joined the *Post* in 1961. The launch, however, was not smooth. My lead story in the first edition suffered at the hands of the editing in Toronto, and Neville killed a column. Then at a reception in Vancouver, Paul Deacon, the editor of the *Financial Post*, did not bother to ask me to speak. By March, the advertising manager in Toronto wanted to cancel one of the weekly editions because there were not enough advertisements. Later, I discovered one of the fundamental errors by the advertising department: they had neglected to include *Western Business* in the free copies of the *Post* sent to advertising agencies in Eastern Canada. Most of the advertising buys were made by those agencies and their clients. Many of those agencies were unaware of the supplement and thus did not steer their clients to it. When an effort was made to rectify this a year or so later, it involved giving a white Stetson to a black salesman in Toronto when he called on the agencies.

Things were better by May. "I no longer have stomach and chest pains—and I know we are doing a decent job," I wrote in my diary. *Western Business* created numerous opportunities for me to travel in Western Canada and California. In May 1979, I was in Los Angeles in the midst of panic over supplies of gasoline. Oil markets had been destabilized by the overthrow of the Shah of Iran and a consequent drop in oil production. The actual shortage of oil was not as great as people believed but, in the United States, there was panic buying. Everyone I met was talking about nothing else. I noted in my diary the experience of the CP Air representative in Los Angeles. He was driving to dinner in his wife's car, which had the even number licence plate permitted to travel that day. But when he spotted a service station that was pumping gas, he returned home, got his own car, and lined up for fuel. He was two cars from the pumps when the station ran out of fuel.

In February 1980, on the first anniversary of *Western Business*, I wrote that "it disappoints me. It remains thin in content, and I am not sure it has much impact." I had begun to think the problem was being an afterthought to a national publication. But when I look at how much I travelled, I also wonder how much editing I could do. For example, I accepted a two-week study tour of New Zealand in March 1980. Marlene came along and I insisted on reimbursing the New Zealand government for her. David Paterson, who had been assigned by the New Zealand Ministry of Foreign Affairs as our minder, estimated her costs and I sent them a cheque for $800.30.

The trip was an exhaustive introduction to the New Zealand economy and generated a good deal of copy on my return. In my diary, I made extensive notes on the wines I managed to taste at lunch and dinner. The New Zealand wine industry was just making its big transition to quality, pulling out hybrid varieties and replacing them with vinifera. One day, I spotted a Montana Chardonnay 1978 in a wine shop and bought it for dinner that evening. I made the mistake of placing it in a small refrigerator in the corridor outside our hotel room in Queenston, confident in the honesty of New Zealanders. The bottle had vanished by dinner time. A few days later, I was lunching with Irene Johnson, the Canadian high commissioner. I spotted that Chardonnay on the restaurant wine list and told her of my experience. Taking the bait, she ordered that wine—and it was very good.

Perhaps the pinnacle of my New Zealand trip was an interview—37.5 minutes—with Prime Minister Robert Muldoon. He had a pudgy, bulldog appearance. I did not know it at the time, but his appearance and his confrontational style had earned him the nickname "Piggy". Equally memorable was a night that Marlene and I spent at the Huka Lodge, a luxury resort then run by two eccentric brothers who took turns at serving dinner and breakfast. The restaurant served game (we had venison), and diners selected their wines from a rack in the kitchen. The brother who hosted dinner at one of the communal tables on the evening we were there was Harland Harland-Baker. He was a flamboyant man, a former advertising copywriter, whose white hair and white beard matched his white garb. His brother, Charles, was equally as thespian. Guests assembled at 7:00 p.m. for drinks. Dinner began an hour later, ending at 11:00 p.m., without a moment's lag in conversation. And it was all paid for by the New Zealand government! The resort, which opened in 1924, is still operating a century later.

In May 1980, I wrote that *Western Business* is "finally perking." The sales department was selling more advertisements. The *Post* hired a bright young writer, Giles Gherson, for a new Edmonton bureau. He was the son of two influential Ottawa bureaucrats and, after he left us, he had careers in both the Ottawa bureaucracy and with a think tank. Later that year, we hired Dunnery Best for the Calgary bureau and, in 1981, Edward Greenspon, our Regina stringer, convinced us to open a bureau there. Both had fine careers: Edward eventually became editor of *The Globe and Mail,* while Dunnery became managing editor at the *Post* before leaving for the investment business.

Western Business was struggling, however. We had a management conference in Vancouver in February 1981, trying to figure out why the advertising revenues were not building. Aside from the shortcomings of the supplement, the Liberal government's National Energy Policy had begun to precipitate a recession in Western Canada. As well, inflation was raging and interest rates were soaring. I renewed a term deposit at 18% a year compounded for the maximum five years, and the bank clerk suggested I not lock it in because the rates could go higher.

I attended a meeting in Toronto that November on *Western Business*. It seems the publication would run a $400,000 deficit in 1981. The proposed action plan included an advertising rate increase and better marketing. But for the first time, I noted in my diary that the section might be folded—although Neville and I wanted to take it out on its own in 1983. In retrospect, that was an impractical idea.

The decision to close *Western Business* was made in June 1982, with the last issue in July. I argued against it, but the supplement was en route to losing $500,000 that year. Jim Warrilow, the publisher—who was not in that post when the publication was launched, did not believe in the concept anyway. He argued that good western topics should be covered nationally, not just in a regional supplement; and that a successful western supplement would hurt the national newspaper. He was also concerned that *The Globe & Mail* would respond with a western edition and the *Post* would be clobbered. Years later, *The Globe & Mail* did add a British Columbia section to the national newspaper, and it seemed to succeed.

Many things about the *Western Business* venture were flawed. There was not much buy-in among my colleagues in Toronto—both advertising and editorial. The supplement would have been stronger if a member of the Ottawa bureau had agreed to write regularly, or even occasionally, for *Western Business*. That rarely happened. The people in our western bureaus had to split their time and loyalty between regional issues and the national newspaper. I found myself recruiting a group of freelancers across the West just to get enough copy. Managing them was an onerous job, usually involving spending every Monday on the telephone, talking myself hoarse, to find out what the writers might propose. Then I often had to rewrite their copy. I kept them happy by ensuring they were paid regularly.

On occasion, I was dragged into difficult management problems. One of my best freelancers in Vancouver was Catherine Gourley, whose previous experience including working for the Dow Jones news service. She had several assignments in progress in 1981, including a profile of a Vancouver junior energy company called Aero Energy Ltd. After she turned in the article, but before it was published, she traded in Aero shares. Diane Francis, who wrote a money column in 1981 for *Quest* magazine, stumbled onto the fact that Catherine had made at least $4,500 on the shares. Neville Nankivell, our editor at the time, was livid. The ethics of Catherine's actions were questionable. "Our reputation suffers from an incident like this, and I can't take it lightly," Neville wrote in a memo to me on October 20, 1981. "I do not want her byline in *Western Business* or in any other part of the *Post* again." I saw that she had quit payments for her unpublished pieces, even though her judgment on the stock trade was clearly poor.

I wrote copy for both *Western Business* and the national paper. It involved an enormous amount of work. When *Western Business* closed, I found I suddenly had time on my hands. I promptly filled that by writing my first wine book, *The World of Canadian Wine*.

Maureen and David

David Romanick in 2018

*Clockwise: Alison in November 2018, Maureen in 2017, John in 2016,
Joe and Oly Gattinger in 2011, Rodney in 2018*

Clockwise: Joe and Sandy Schreiner in 2011, Alison and Maureen with John in 1969,
Ferd and Apollonia Dietrich, Marlene in 2015

Top to bottom: Joe and Oly Gattinger with Marlene, The entire clan in 2015, John and Marlene in April 2021

Sixteen:
A passion for wine

The first bottle of wine with a cork that I bought was a French Sauternes. This was in 1959. I was living in one room in the basement of an apartment block in Regina, next door to Conrad Rodney, a university chum and one of my best friends. We were best man at each other's wedding. We fell out later when he told me he was going to vote Social Credit, and I asked how someone with a degree in commerce would even consider doing that. But we were still close in 1959. One Sunday I invited him to dinner, having bought the wine the day before. My signature dish at the time was spaghetti with meat sauce. It never occurred to me that Sauternes was not the ideal pairing. It was also a great surprise to discover, when the capsule was cut, that the bottle was closed with a cork. Neither of us had a cork screw. I was able to find one in a nearby drugstore. It was so poorly designed, with a thick screw, that I managed to push the cork right into the bottle. Yet we enjoyed the wine and the spaghetti.

It is a mystery to me why I came to find wine so engrossing. My parents consumed little wine, nor much other alcohol, although my father operated a small still for a few years, and my mother once made dandelion wine. When Marlene and I first moved to Toronto in 1961, we lived a couple of blocks from a T.G. Bright & Co. wine store on St. Clair Avenue west of Bathurst. There had been no private wine stores in Saskatchewan at the time, so this spurred my curiosity. From time to time, I dropped in to read the labels, quiz the clerks, and buy the occasional bottle. The wines, made with hybrid and labrusca grapes, were not very appealing but that did not crush my interest.

From the evidence in my clippings, I know that I took an early interest in the Ontario wine industry. In October, 1971, I wrote a long article about the grape surplus that fall in Ontario (which then produced 90% of the grapes in Canada). The crop that fall was a record 70,000 tons. The surplus was aggravated because the United States had imposed a 10% surcharge against Ontario grapes. On the other hand, the industry was experiencing good growth in wine consumption—and expected to be short of grapes within a few years. Canadian wine consumption had been growing at an annual average of 8.1% since 1965, the result of growing affluence, more interest from younger consumers, and the palates of European immigrants. This was when wines like Baby Duck were being introduced. As simple as those wines were, that is what many Canadians were drinking at the time—unless they were buying Portuguese rosés, as we began to do at home.[52]

We eased into wine drinking with the occasional bottle for Sunday dinner. Then the Liquor Control Board of Ontario put product consultants in some of its stores who helped me expand my knowledge of wine. The sturdy and inexpensive French and Algerian wine that we found in Quebec grocery stores accelerated our wine consumption. By 1972, I was hanging around in the Wine-Art[53] store on Avenue Road in Toronto, screwing up my courage to make wine. Marlene bought me a wine kit that Christmas, and I made wine with it in 1974, once we were settled in Vancouver. I started with kits for Pommard, Beaujolais, and Chablis. I also began making wines from salmonberries and blackberries because those berries were abundant in North Vancouver. Recognizing how little I knew of winemaking, I joined the Vintners of North Vancouver winemaking club in 1975.

52 *Financial Post*, October 2, 1971: "Niagara smothers in grapes—and faces shortage soon?"

53 Wine-Art was a chain of stores selling wine-making equipment and kits to home vintners. Stanley Anderson, its founder, also wrote *The Art of Making Wine*, one of the most widely used winemaking texts for amateurs.

That fall, I bought two crates of California Cabernet Sauvignon grapes. I had almost no winemaking equipment, but I managed to crush them, about fifty pounds (22.6 kilograms), in a plastic bucket with a wooden mallet. The yield was about a case and a half of wine. Even though I made a number of other kit wines over the next few years, it was obvious that the quality of wine from fresh fruit was immeasurably better. I was thoroughly hooked, to the point of planting four grape vines in the front yard in 1977. Two were a red French hybrid called Cascade. Those easily managed vines, along with two grown from cuttings, still produce each fall. The other two vines were Müller-Thurgau; I pulled them out because they were too prone to mildew.

I made wine every year until 2007 (sometimes as much as twenty or thirty gallons or 90 to 135 litres a year), when I was too busy tasting commercial samples to drink my own wines. The quality of my wines was distinctly mixed. I did win a number of trophies, but after I stopped making wine, I also dumped a lot of my wines. The real value of the hobby was the wine education it gave me. It equipped me to do more informed interviews with winemakers.

Two early trips to wine regions thoroughly fired my interest. In early May 1973, I was invited, along with a group of journalists and travel writers, on a Qantas inaugural flight from Vancouver to Australia. In Sydney my host asked me what I wanted to do in addition to some business interviews, and I asked if I could go to the Barossa Valley wine region. I spent a day there, visiting three wineries: G. Gramp & Sons (now Jacob's Creek), Kaiser Stuhl winery (where I had a soft, fruity 1969 Shiraz for lunch), and Seppelts (where I tasted the memorable Para Tawny Port). I had some time to walk around Adelaide and was struck by how readily wine was available in private shops. There even was a display of wines behind the pumps at a filling station in the Barossa.

On a family vacation to San Francisco in March 1975, we toured four wineries. Marlene and I arrived at the Robert Mondavi Winery, three children in tow, and were offered a tour before the tasting. Our guide was Zelma Long, then a young winemaker for Mondavi, who later became one of California's leading winemakers.[54] She was infectiously passionate about wine, and it rubbed off on me. We also visited Christian Brothers, Simi Winery, and Trentadue Winery. I was so impressed with Trentadue that I tried to import a case of Zinfandel. The winery's distributor in San Francisco could not be bothered to handle the order. In retrospect, that was a good thing, because a $3 Zinfandel would have become a $10 wine, which, at the time, was real money. In March 1977, we took the children to Disneyland. On our way back home, we stopped at the Firestone Winery, then at Mirassou and, once we reached the Napa Valley, visited Beaulieu, Sterling, and Beringer.

By this time, I had built a set of shelves in the basement on which to store the increasing number of wines I was accumulating. (I did not build a larger and better wine cellar until 1990.) I made regular trips to Alberta on *Financial Post* business and never failed to return without wines from the excellent selection in the government wine stores there, far superior to that in British Columbia liquor stores at the time. My job involved a lot of travel, with plenty of opportunities to sample wine. In May 1975, for the Alberta report that year, I made my one and only visit to Fort McMurray, which was then a dusty townsite under rapid development. I noted in my diary that I was sipping a white Graves. In my hotel in Grand Prairie, I ended the evening with cheese and half a bottle of Blue Nun. It seems I would try anything: once in Calgary in November 1975, I unwound in my hotel with a bottle of Brazilian Merlot, which I found "pleasant ... for the price."

British Columbia restructured its archaic liquor retailing system in 1974, separating retail from the Liquor Control administration, and moving the retail operation to Vancouver. Robert Wallace,[55] an avuncular civil servant from Manitoba with a master's degree in agriculture, had just retired as Assistant Chief Statistician for Census Canada. In 1978, he was recruited to run the Liquor Distribution Branch, and did

---

54 Zelma Long by then had become chief enologist for Mondavi. She left to be vice-president and then president of Simi Winery from 1979 to 1996. She is still a co-owner of Long Vineyards in the Napa Valley and Vilafonte Wine Estate in South Africa.

55 Bob Wallace died in 2011 at the age of eighty-six.

so with great success for ten years. He began hosting occasional tastings of newly listed wines for the media. More significantly, he engaged Peter Adams, a British wine consultant, to advise the Branch on selecting imported wines. The Branch opened its first speciality wine shop on Pender Street in Vancouver about 1976. Adams arranged to have it stocked in part with inventory from a closed New York wine store. He got some amazing bargains: the store was able to sell a 1945 vintage Port for $6.65 and a Château Yquem Sauternes for just over $20. I was in the store one day, reading the storied labels, when I met and traded business cards with a lawyer and enophile named Sid Cross. As a result, I was invited in 1977 to join the Commanderie de Bordeaux chapter just being formed; I remained a member for twenty years.

The Commanderie gave me the opportunity to learn about Bordeaux wines and taste some of the finest. I had already begun to add some good Bordeaux reds to my cellar, bringing a few bottles back from every trip to Alberta. In my diary, I made note of some of these—two bottles of Château Palmer 1974, several bottles of Château Batailley 1970, for example. (By this time in my life, my curiosity about wines was so extensive that I was buying wines from all over the world, including California, Australia, Spain, Hungary, and Germany.) The Commanderie had a membership capped at forty, all males, and most had good cellars. Restaurateur and bon vivant John Levine, one of the leading members of the Commanderie, had an impressive cellar. The Commanderie executive rejected his first wife's application to join in a decision never put to the entire membership. When they divorced and split the cellar, the Commanderie's executive reconsidered and offered her a membership in order to retain access to the older Bordeaux wines that the Levines had been collected. She turned the Commanderie down!

The Commanderie chapter organized six to eight tastings a year, typically over dinners in excellent restaurants (which wives often were allowed to attend). One of the best was a dinner in 1982 at the Four Seasons Hotel with twelve vintages of Château Mouton Rothschild from 1943 through 1970. The 1945 vintage in Bordeaux was one of the best in the twentieth century. The 1945 Mouton is perhaps the greatest wine I have ever tasted. The top growth wines from Bordeaux generally were beyond what I could afford to buy for my cellar, but they were accessible through my membership in the Commanderie. For our functions, we shared the cost of the wines, and the wineries occasionally provided the wines at no cost. The 1945 Mouton, as an example, was contributed by the château from its cellar. Toward the end of my time in the Commanderie, the annual membership dues, which had been modest, began to climb, reflecting the rising cost of Bordeaux wines. That was one reason why I gave up my membership. Secondly, a turnover in members had brought in many social-climbing professionals. It got boring listening to them compare notes on who had had dinner at such and such château (especially when I could not afford to do the same). Thirdly, I had become quite involved with the Australian Wine Appreciation Society, which had been organized in 1983, and with the emerging British Columbia wine industry.

I had joined several wine clubs—Spanish, Italian, and most notably, the Australian Wine Appreciation Society, where I was twice the president. The position did not involve much responsibility the first time because the Australian consul-general and his staff did most of the work. The second time, in 1994, was much more difficult. The consulate no longer supported the society, not even by bringing in wines for our cellar at the consular discount. But that problem was minor. The previous president, after alienating some members with dull programs, had gone to Asia for a year and a half without arranging a transition in the club's executive, and the society was faltering. The Vancouver agent for Penfolds persuaded me to step in. When I agreed, one of the existing executives would not give me the computer file with the membership list. It took me the entire summer, with the help of our treasurer, Fred Hester, to build my own data base and revive the society. For that effort, I was awarded a life membership. I turned the presidency over to Jim Forbes, a retired University of British Columbia commerce professor and a former wine agent, in June 1997.

I also begin visiting what few British Columbia wineries there were, starting with 1974 visits to the Okanagan and to André's Winery in Port Moody. The brief note in my diary suggests I was not impressed with the wines. But the visits gave me profile with the industry. A diary entry for December 15, 1976, reads: "Last night, the Association of BC Wineries had me (plus a horde of others) to a reception for Leon Adams [the author of *The Wines of America*]. I find I have pretty well established my credibility with the industry in BC." Now, I began visiting wineries in the Okanagan. On September 21, 1977, I stopped over in Kelowna (during a trip from Calgary back to Vancouver) to visit Calona Wines and then to have lunch with Tom Simard, an executive with Casabello Wines. Tom apparently told me that Casabello's Gala Keg wines were actually second-run wines, something that scandalized me. That fall, Casabello opened the first winery store in a British Columbia winery. Similar retail outlets opened later that year at Andrés, Calona, and the new Ste-Michelle winery in Surrey, a $6 million winery that replaced the decrepit Growers' Winery facility in Victoria.[56]

In October 1982, I began writing a monthly wine column for *Vancouver Magazine*, along with any other wine articles I could sell. Neville Nankivell asked me in March 1981 to write a wine column for the *Financial Post*. I wrote numerous wine articles for the paper over the next several decades, but they were not run systematically and few readers realized we had a wine column. The March column dealt with a Canadian, Frank Narby, who had just purchased Château Guiraud. That was a hook for a column on Sauternes.[57] The headline showed how clueless our desk was about wines: "Guiraud investment sparkles."

As a self-taught wine writer, I seldom missed the chance to learn from the many who knew more than I did. In July 1980, *Epicure*, a magazine published in Toronto, asked for an article on Port, a wine about which I knew nothing. When I admitted as much to the magazine editor, he challenged me, saying I was a professional reporter and could surely manage it. My strategy was to pick the brains of anyone in my circle who knew Port. That included Graham Page, who ran the Coal Association in Calgary and who had studied at the Port Institute in Porto. He was also a former military officer who once complimented

---

56 *Financial Post*, November 19, 1977: "B.C. wine industry 'turned corner'."

57 *Financial Post*, March 21, 1981: "Guiraud investment sparkles."

my well-polished shoes! The article, which was published in December, turned out very well.[58] I was especially pleased to include a tip I got from Sid Cross on how to keep half a bottle of Port fresh for a week or two after opening it: drop marbles into the wine to displace the air. I also recycled what I had learned for an article in *Skyword* in January 1981.[59]

One individual I consulted was C. Calvert Knudsen, who was then president of McMillan-Bloedel Ltd. as well as a partner in an Oregon winery, Knudsen Erath, that had been founded in 1972. I had interviewed Cal a number of times about the forest industry; the interviews usually digressed because we were both so devoted to wine. I even got him into the Commanderie de Bordeaux. By the time he got back to me on Port, the magazine's deadline had gone. But he insisted because he did not have much opportunity to drink the Ports in his cellar. He arranged lunch at The Vancouver Club, arriving with a bottle of Sandeman's 1945 under his arm. We repaired to a private room for steak, drinking the Port before, during, and after the meal. There still was half a carafe when we left, both of us in quite a jolly mood.

All the columns I did for various publications drew invitations to wine regions. Over the next thirty years, I visited almost all the major wine regions except for South Africa, usually at someone else's expense. Sometimes I even engineered my own invitation, as happened in Japan in 1978. During my previous trips to Japan, I had tasted a modest number of Japanese table wines. Most were made with concentrates or were blends of imported wine. In 1978, I arranged to visit the Suntory winery in Yamanashi Prefecture, an hour or so from Tokyo by train and not far from Mount Fuji. I was told it was the largest winery in Asia. I only saw barrels of whisky in the cellars and never saw any wine processing facility, although vineyards surrounded the winery. The vineyards were unusual: because of the humid climate, the vines were trellised horizontally two to three metres (6.5 to 9.8 feet) above ground, allowing optimal air circulation. I had lunch with the winemaker. The interview was less than satisfactory because the questions

58 *Epicure*, December, 1980: "Glorious Port."
59 *Skyword*, January, 1981: "Port: the gentleman's drink," p. 117.

and answers were relayed through a translator who did not understand wine growing. I was served a Chateau Lion white (said to be a blend of Sémillon and Chardonnay) and a Chateau Lion red (said to be a blend of Cabernet Sauvignon, Cabernet Franc, and Merlot). The wines were poor. I was sent away with samples, which I gave to a New Zealand businessman at my hotel.

One of the first foreign wine tours to which I was invited was a weeklong trip to Italy and the Vinitaly fair in the spring of 1982. I was one of a small group that included both wine writers and Canadian liquor board buyers. We mostly visited producers near Verona. These included the Luxardo distillery where our host was Franco Luxardo, perhaps the fifth generation of the family to run the business. The company had been founded in Dalmatia. In World War Two, when this was in German-controlled territory, the distillery was bombed by the British and, so we were told, the alcohol burned for six days. The family then re-established the business in 1945 near Padua. One thing I learned from the trip is that lunches and dinners with Italian wine-makers can be gargantuan, and the speeches can be long-winded.

In October 1983, I was invited for the first time to judge at the Banco di Assaggio dei Vini d'Italia, a wine competition originated two years earlier by Giorgio Lungarotti, the owner of the winery bearing his name. The winery and the quaint adjoining hotel, Le Tre Vaselle, were in the hilltop village of Torgiano, an attractive locale with breathtaking views in every direction. The town of Assisi was across the valley. The Tre Vaselle hotel was in a building dating from Medieval times. It had been modernized except for the door locks, which were still opened with skeleton keys. One evening, after a bibulous dinner during my 1987 visit, I let myself into what I thought was my room and was relieving myself when I saw another person's shaving brush on the bathroom counter. I was exactly one floor below my room. Fortunately, the occupant was still at dinner.

The Banco was an easy judging experience. We usually judged just in the mornings. One morning, my panel of five judges had just fifteen wines to score. (I have judged as many as ten times that number daily at other, more taxing, competitions.) We were done in two hours. That pace proved to be typical. We would then have a large lunch; foreign judges usually were taken sightseeing after lunch to work up an appetite for dinner. Once, we all went to a truffle farm; another time, we toured Assisi and then the city of Perugia and its Etruscan ruins. Occasionally, the tours were bizarre—such as a visit to a factory that made prefabricated earthquake-proof housing and insisted on demonstrating by giving a house a severe shaking.

I was disappointed when, during a subsequent Banco, one of the Italian judges told me that the wine scores entered by foreign judges were discarded. I still find it hard to believe that. At the end of my first Banco trip, I arranged a stopover in Siena to visit the Cecchi winery. I was enchanted by Siena with its giant clamshell-shaped piazza and its baroque cathedral, surely one of Italy's most beautiful churches. On a subsequent Banco trip in late October 1989, Marlene came along, and we spent time ahead of the competition in Rome, Siena, Florence, and Pisa. Siena still enchanted me. In Rome, we were awed by St. Peter's Basilica and by the Sistine Chapel. We did not much like the Leaning Tower in Pisa, perhaps because we found the surrounding city dull compared with Siena or Florence.

In October 1984, I joined a group to visit wineries in Piemonte in Northern Italy. The sponsor was Superior Wines, a wine agent in Toronto. The agent's purpose was to gain some publicity for the release of the Vino Novella wine from Fiore, a major Piemonte winery. We actually sat through a rather baroque ceremony in a castle where Fiore launched that season's Vino Novello. Wines of that style, along with Beaujolais Nouveau, were then enjoying considerable popularity in the Canadian market. Even Mission Hill and Calona Wines joined the trend, producing nouveau wines with the Maréchal Foch grape. The wine industry overdid it, flooding the market with these simple grapey wines, and the fad evaporated—but not before I did at least one wine column on Vino Novello in the *Financial Post*.

It was a very eclectic tour, including visits to the Cinzano and Martini & Rossi plants; to Gancia, a producer of sparkling wine; and to the Marchesi di Barolo. The only other wine writer in the group was Andrew Sharp, a large and voluble man then at his peak as an Ontario wine writer. Others in the group appeared to be clients of Superior and may even have paid their own way. One of my favourites was Frank Suma, a Toronto insurance agent of Italian heritage with a passion for art and antiques. One day at lunch in Milan, I began enthusing to him about the beauty of the cathedral in Siena. He immediately proposed we take the train to Siena, so he could show me a masterpiece in the cathedral. He said he had been there at least ten times to see it. I regret not taking up his offer.

There was always too much food served at lunch and again at dinner. One day, the lunch at a hilltop village was so large that I left the table after the pasta course and skipped the meat course to take some photographs of the village. I returned an hour later for dessert and coffee. Then the group went on to a winery where, after a tour and tasting, we were hosted to a big dinner in the cellar of the Ascheri Vineyards. After dinner, a guitar was produced for one of our group who had a fine voice, and a party broke out.

The 1984 group spent a weekend in Northern Italy's lake country at a resort on Lake Orta. Exhausted after several long days and late nights, I slept in until 12:30 p.m. on Sunday morning. Having concluded I had missed Mass, I had a good lunch and spent the afternoon walking through the neighbouring forest, where chestnuts were being harvested. The soft autumn weather and the chestnut pickers and the jangling of cowbells among the trees made it an enchanted afternoon. On my way back to the hotel, I even found a church with evening Mass.

I took advantage of my host's plane ticket to do book signings (*The World of Canadian Wine*, my first wine book, had just been published) and to do media interviews in Winnipeg, at several Niagara wineries and, on returning from Milan, in Ottawa and Toronto. I may have done more radio and television interviews for *The World of Canadian Wine* than for any of my other books.

In April 1991, I was invited to Vinitaly again, with visits to other wineries in Northern Italy, including several uninspiring co-operatives. However, we also visited an outstanding producer, Alois Lageder in Alto Adige. The wines were, and still are, among the best wines in Italy. Lageder was then a charismatic forty-year-old vintner who left a deep impression on me. The tour lasted two weeks, most it with a group of twenty that included a number of American writers, including an attractive New Yorker who wrote for *Playboy*. The size of the group inevitably meant we were usually running behind schedule. The days were long, with elaborate luncheons and later dinners. In my diary, I wrote: "Much of the trip could be called ludicrous. Yes, I probably have notes on two hundred wines and yes, I met a very interesting figure in Alois Lageder." I actually had tasting notes on 207 wines.

In May 1984, Marlene and I went to the German Wine Academy. I was there with one of the "scholarships" awarded to wine writers, and I paid for Marlene's tuition, which because the Canadian dollar then was strong, worked out to about $100 a day, including meals and hotels. The accommodation was excellent, starting with the Hotel Schwann in Oestrich-Winkel, a village on the Rhine. The Academy was (and still is) sponsored by the German wine industry to educate consumers from around the world on German wine. Our forty-person group for the week-long class was an eclectic mix. The daughter of California vintner Joseph Phelps and her husband, a vineyard manager, were there. In the final exam at week's end, he took first place, beating me by three points. On the other hand, there were three Irish operators of a London pub, who had won a scholarship for their window display of German wine. They often remained on the bus drinking beer when we were at wineries and wine lectures. The course content was excellent for those of us who applied ourselves. Most of the lectures and visits were along the Rhine and Mosel, with the examination and final dinner in the lovely and historic Kloster Eberbach. That was where I first met Hans Ambrosi, who intersected with my life fifteen years later when I was to write a book on icewine.

Since we were already in Europe, we stayed for another two or three weeks, which included winery visits in Alsace (Hugel, Trimbach, Leon Beyer) and Baden-Baden. The village of Riquewihr (population 1,300) packed thirty-seven wineries within its medieval walls. It is said the village still looks much like it did in the 1600s because the strict construction and decorating regulations preserve the architectural integrity.

The travel floodgates opened in 1986. I was now writing about wine in numerous publications and that triggered invitations for sponsored wine tours. The first came in March from Wines of Spain—ten days in the company of three other wine writers: Michel Phaneuf from Montreal, Michael Roberts from Ottawa, and David Rodger, a fellow Vancouverite. We packed in a lot of producers in that time, including two Cava producers, several Rioja producers, and the Torres winery in Penedes, then still presided over by the imperious Miguel Torres Sr.

I travelled with Michel on several occasions and developed respect for him. He wrote an annual guide to the wines in the Quebec Liquor Commission, and he was knowledgeable and serious. I had judged wines several times with David Rodger, a founder of the Vancouver Planetarium who was a science writer as well as a wine writer. David was a pleasant travelling companion until something upset him. On our first evening in Barcelona, he complained that 8:00 p.m. was too late for dinner. Of course, for the Spanish, that was early. There was another evening when we were still dining around midnight; David, a staunch monarchist, and Michel got into a long, heated argument about whether Canada should keep the monarchy. There was another day when an enology station near Pamplona put on a large tasting, followed by an enormous lunch. David skipped dinner that evening and went to bed. The rest of us tasted outstanding Riojas and did not finish dining until 1:00 a.m. The following day was one to try anyone's patience. After a lecture and a couple of tastings, we arrived (late) at Bodegas Bilbianas where, after a tour, we were ushered into a room where a big spread of tapas awaited. The problem was that we were to have lunch an hour down the road. The winery owner and our wine industry guide had a loud and unpleasant argument before we could move on. The lunch included several Spanish vintners who spent so much time gossiping with each other that no useful interviews were possible. Then it was back on the bus for a tasting at Marquis de Murrieta, a very fine winery. David by this time had had enough. He remained on the bus where he put one of his opera tapes into the bus audio system while we tasted inside. On the return leg of the trip, David and I had to stay overnight at the Airport Hilton in Montreal to connect with our Vancouver flight the next day. A telephone call jerked me from a deep sleep at 1:30 a.m. It was Sharon Proctor, David's wife, concerned that he was not answering his telephone. I went to his room and woke him. The bell on his room phone had been turned off. Of course, David could not get back to sleep. We remained friends and wine touring companions for many years; he even led an evening of wine and opera for the Australian Wine Appreciation Society when I was its president. *Western Living* dropped his wine column in 1990; then David decided to stop drinking, and he just disappeared from my universe.

My second opportunity to tour Spanish wineries came in May 1990. Our group spent too much time on buses and, as usual, had dinners that started at 9:30 p.m. and lasted three hours. I took to grabbing a few hours of sleep in the early evening. The highlights of this tour were visits to sherry houses in Jerez. The vaulted cellars were vast and redolent with the aromas of the wines. The man who handled public relations for the producers recited a local saying: "One fino before eleven or eleven before one." I drank six sherries that day. Sherries are great wines but, alas, the demand in Canada is not strong.

In June 1986, I was invited to join three French Canadian wine writers for a week in the Loire followed by a week in Alsace. My French fluency was mediocre, unfortunately. When I tired of trying to follow the conversation, I wrote detailed notes on our lavish meals, leaving the pages of my notebook stained with butter and spilled wine. At one restaurant, I wrote that the grilled turbot was "swimming in mayonnaise" but the Muscadet we were served offset the richness. The next day, a two-hour lunch started with hard-boiled quail's eggs and went on to crayfish in pastry smothered in sauce and then to a fish course once again swimming in mayonnaise. As if that was not rich enough, warm camembert preceded the dessert, strawberries in a custard sauce. It was difficult to stay awake during an afternoon tasting where the high point was a 1976 Muscadet. While Muscadet wines usually are consumed within three years, this showed how much richness and complexity the wine develops with age. Another producer treated us to a remarkable pair of Muscadets from 1961 and 1953. Dinner that evening was lamb chops grilled over vine cuttings. Seven of us at dinner drank six bottles of wine.

So it went for the week. At a restaurant in Angers, where dinner lasted from 8:30 pm until 1:00 a.m., the menu was two feet long and one foot wide; the wine list was even longer. We ate "turbot swimming in butter sauce, duck swimming in currant sauce" and wild strawberries. Lunch the next day began with cantaloupe with wine sauce, salmon, strawberries, and cheese. Dinner that evening begin with foie gras and duck a l'orange. I avoided the lettuce, deciding to diet!

The most extraordinary tasting of the week was at Moulin Touchais, a distinguished producer of dessert wine from the Chenin Blanc grape. Our party arrived the day after the winery had expected a delegation of Canadian liquor board buyers—which had not arrived. The wines set out for them were then served to us in the winery's underground cellar. The ambiance was as mystical as the wines. These included a Moulin Touchais 1887, one of the greatest wines I have ever tasted. At 99 years, the wine had a dark amber colour, aromas that recalled plum jam, and had concentrated flavours of figs.

A memorable tasting with done with a producer called Jacques Morin, who hosted us to lunch in a cave on his vineyard. He had a Canadian connection. When he was young, his father told him he was no good, and he needed to prove himself elsewhere. So he moved to Quebec and spent six years managing one hundred cattle on an Eastern Township farm. After his father died, he came back to the Loire and took over the winery in 1976. The day of our visit was hot. The cave, however, was cold and damp, warmed by a wood fire over which steaks were grilled. At the end of lunch, the woman from Montreal who was leading our tour suffered a debilitating back spasm due, I believe, to the damp cold of the cellar after the heat outside. She was taken directly to our hotel in Tours to rest and was in discomfort for the rest of the trip.

The other memorable tasting was in the cellar of Clos Baudoin, a Vouvray producer where we tasted several great Chenin Blanc dessert wines, including Clos Baudoin 1945. The property was then managed by the aristocratic Prince Philippe Poniatowski, a tall man fashionably casual in corduroy slacks and a tweed jacket. His ancestors, relatives of the last king of Poland, had come to France during the Napoleonic wars. Prince Philippe, whose grandfather had bought the Loire property, was a paratrooper with the Free French during World War II. While he was away, his staff bricked up part of the cellar so that occupying Germans would not drink all of the old wines. He took over the vineyard when his father died in 1970. He also spent eight years in the 1970s as president of Massey Ferguson in France. After his death, the property left the ownership of his family.

The middle weekend on this trip was spent in Paris. I got away from the rest of the group so that I could explore at my own pace. Rereading my diary notes on Notre Dame Cathedral is poignant, considering the major damage to the cathedral by fire in 2019. "The rose windows in the transept are quite astonishing in their beauty," I wrote of the very windows that were largely destroyed in the fire. I also climbed the towers, a taxing feat on a hot day in June. I needed a large beer to recuperate when I got back to earth. In the evening, I found a restaurant at Les Halles, where I had dinner at an outside table under a moonlight night sky, with a fine bottle of Sancerre. A few years later, when Marlene, Alison, and John were in Paris with me, we returned to that restaurant for another excellent dinner.

Two of our initial group left us at the weekend, replaced by two other French Canadian wine writers. We met them at a Paris railroad station where they were enjoying steak and fries after a trans-Atlantic flight where the airline food had been poor. Then on the four-hour train ride to Strasbourg, they dug into their stash of candy bars. That evening, we dined on eight courses at Michelin-starred Restaurant Le Buerehiesel, beginning with deep-fried foie gras. By the middle of the week, one of the pair was so sated with rich food that he could not go on after lunch. Dinner was cancelled, and we all found our own light meals and got to bed early. The tour, however, involved some of the finest wineries and vintners in Alsace, including Jean Hugel, Hubert Trimbach, and Guy Dopff. We tasted close to 150 wines in Alsace. The quality, even from the cooperatives, was generally impressive. The Alsace enthusiasm for wine was telegraphed at the Laugel winery, where the owner's grandfather had died in 1985 at ninety-six years. With evident pride, his family calculated that his consumption had averaged two litres a day. The last lunch in Alsace was at a Michelin-starred restaurant in

Ammerschwihr called Aux Armes de France: foie gras, broiled sole, and crêpes filled with raspberries and served with ice cream and raspberry sauce. Ironically, several of us had to rush off to catch trains when we would have preferred to linger over a fine meal.

On November 4, 1986, I joined three other wine writers in Australia on a fifteen-day winery tour hosted by the Australian Wine and Brandy Corp. Our flight—more than fifteen hours from Vancouver, not counting stopovers in San Francisco—arrived in Sydney about 8:00 a.m. I had time to get to the hotel, shower and shave, before our group was hustled off to a restaurant run by Len Evans, then at his peak as an Australian wine writer. We were joined by other wine industry personalities for a big and boozy lunch. It led to a sound ten-hour sleep.

We started with three Hunter Valley wineries: Tyrrell's, Tulloch's, and Lindemans. At the latter, winemaker Gerry Sissingh introduced us to one of the pinnacles of Australian wine—aged Hunter Valley Sémillons. On that first day, we tasted fifty-four wines. Alsace began to look like a walk in the park.

The Australians had been growing wine for more than 150 years, producing mostly fortified wines and some big reds. The first Chardonnay vines were planted in the 1960s. The Sultana grape still was ubiquitous in many vineyards. We were told that in the 1980s, seventy per cent of Australian table wine still was being consumed as simple bag-in-the-box wine. The domestic market was not very profitable, forcing the more ambitious producers to look to export sales of their premium wines. That was why wine writers from promising markets were being invited to Australia by the industry.

Tyrrell's was typical of how quality wines were emerging. Murray Tyrrell started buying French Burgundies in the 1960s to acquaint himself with Pinot Noir, a variety he planted late in that decade. The winery's first commercial release was from the 1973 vintage. "It's a bitch of a variety," Bruce Tyrrell, Murray's son, told us. "It's hard to grow and hard to make. It is like a temperamental woman—but when you get a temperamental woman on the right day, you are away. Pinot's the same."

Much of the rest of the tour was in wine regions within driving or flying distance from Adelaide. One of the worst flights of my life was a short flight to Renmark and the Angove's winery. A brisk wind was blowing in that morning from the ocean, adding velocity to the air currents boiling up from a low range of mountains just beyond the airport. The ten-passenger twin-engine Piper Chieftain we were in was pitched about violently. I was seated next to the pilot, and I hit my head on the ceiling of the cabin even though I had my lap belt fastened. Briefcases were airborne in the cabin. The pilot told me it was one of the worst flights he had had "in quite a while." We spent an hour drinking strong black tea at Angove's to settle our stomachs. Joel Butler, an American who was one of our foursome, was so unnerved that he rented a car to drive back to Adelaide at the end of the day.

The visit, of course, included Penfolds. There we tasted several vintages of Grange Hermitage (as it was still called then), drinking some of it with pheasant and kangaroo in a restaurant called The Pheasant Farm. This is Australia's most famous red wine and one of the best. Over the years, I have tasted about twenty-five vintages before the wine became prohibitively expensive. The last bottle in my cellar, which had been given to me by the executive of a mining company, turned out to be corked.[60]

By the end of two weeks, the heat of the Australian summer, the long days, and late evenings had left us all quite exhausted. But we had covered a number of major producers and had our heads turned by the general quality of the 428 wines we tasted. I was impressed with the wines. When the Australian consul in Vancouver sponsored the Australian Wine Appreciation Society in the mid-1980s, I was a charter member and later served two non-consecutive terms as president.

My next visit to French wine regions was in June 1987 and was self-organized. Marlene and I scheduled a trip to France to coincide with Alison completing her studies at Montpellier and John graduating from Vancouver College. Initially, we flew to Frankfurt and joined a small group hosted by the ZBW wine co-operative in Baden. The wines

60 Corked wines are the result of a winery closing bottles inadvertently with flawed corks. The wines develop an unpleasantly musty aroma and flavour. There was so much corked wine in the 1990s that many producers switched to using screw cap closures.

were not memorable (but good value). More memorable was the party of clean-cut university students staying on our hotel. Their picture of robust health was at odds with their jobs: handing out sample packs of Marlboro cigarettes. After three or four days touring and tasting at ZBW wineries, we rented a car and headed out on our own for Dijon and Beaune in Burgundy. I was awed by the famed vineyards we passed. We even toured the old monastery at Clos de Vougeot.

I had arranged a visit to Maison Louis Latour, which owns choice vineyards in the Corton appellation. The following day, June 25, Marlene took the car to meet Alison at a nearby train station, while I had a superbly informed morning on Burgundy at the house of Noemie Vernaux, followed by a self-guided tasting at the Marché Aux Vins in Beaune. There were at least thirty wines available for tasting in the candle-lit cellars. The fee was a refundable ten francs, which covered the loan of a tastevin. I liked it so well that I took Marlene and Alison there later in the afternoon.

After Beaune, we drove to Paris and stayed for several days, which is where John met us. There was nothing much to recommend our hotel except that it was two blocks from the Louvre. (I like the Dutch Masters but was underwhelmed by the Mona Lisa.) We went to Mass at Notre Dame and had dinner at the excellent restaurant near Les Halles that I had discovered the year before.

Then we set out for Reims in Champagne. I spent the better part of a day with Champagne producer Pierre Lanson and most of the second day with Remi Krug. He took me to a Michelin three-star restaurant called Chez Boyer for a three-hour lunch with several outstanding bottles of vintage Krug Champagne. As the lunch went on, several others—including two Canadians from a neighbouring table—were invited to join us. This generated an article in the *Financial Post* in which I named the Canadian, who was a Toronto investment dealer and a Krug collector. I happened to add that he was there with his wife. A few days after the article appeared, he phoned me and said the woman was not his wife. "But you're lucky," he added. "I am not married."

From Reims, we drove to Trier in the Mosel and then, after a few nights in the Mosel, we drove to the Frankfurt airport. We turned over the rental car, a Volkswagen Golf, to Alison and John and boarded a plane for home. We had barely arrived at home in Vancouver when Alison phoned, in tears. She had driven into a narrow street in some German town and, while backing out of a tight spot, managed to smash a tail light. The car was still roadworthy. So I settled her down and advised her to be forthright with Hertz when turning in the car a few weeks later. Hertz shrugged off the damage.

In November 1987, I was invited to Italy, along with Anthony Gismondi and Bernard Hoeter[61], to judge again at the Banco. We arrived in Rome in the morning and a day early, checked into a hotel near the airport, and took the train into the city to see the Colosseum and the neighbouring Roman Forum. Bernard gave us a vivid and well-informed commentary on the great events in the Forum during the Roman Empire. He had lived near the Forum for two weeks as a German student and had been back many times since. He served with Rommel in North Africa, where he was captured by the Americans in 1943 and spent the rest of the war comfortably in the United States. He emigrated from Germany to Canada in the 1950s to work as a notary. He was the *Vancouver Sun's* wine columnist in the late 1980s. Bernard's commentary at the Forum was exceptional; he had a deep knowledge of Roman history.

Bernard, Anthony, and I ended the day at dinner at a restaurant near our hotel where we gave the restaurateur carte blanch to prepare a menu. We also drank four bottles of wine, including a Barolo. The rest of the experience at my third Banco did not rise to the level of Bernard's guided tour. We ended the week with a gala dinner in a very noisy venue. The food was mediocre, the speeches endless—and our bus to the Rome airport left Torgiano about 4:00 a.m. "I have not learned anything about Italian wine this week," I groused to my diary.

In September 2014, Marlene and I went to Italy at our own expense. We booked a tour of Sicily through Road Scholar, an excellent tour

---

61   Anthony Gismondi was just developing his career as a wine writer and consultant in Vancouver. He later succeeded Bernard Hoeter as the *Vancouver Sun's* wine columnist. Bernard was a notary public in Vancouver as well as the consul general for Guatemala. He was a great wine enthusiast and a bon vivant. He died in 2011 at the age of ninety.

company based in Boston that we had used four times before.[62] The Road Scholar programs are almost all organized under university auspices. The content is stimulating, and the tour guides are well informed. The tour of Sicily was focussed not on wine but on history and antiquity. Sicily was the centre of the ancient world due to its location in the Mediterranean Sea, and Syracuse was a major city (Archimedes lived there). Our tour basically circumnavigated Sicily in ten days, ending up in Palermo, the modern capital of the province and a notorious centre for Mafia activity. We had at least one lecture on that criminal organization.

However, one cannot avoid wine in Italy, and why would you? Some Road Scholar tours allow for a glass of wine at dinner. There is nothing stopping one from ordering more—and we usually ordered more. I was quite surprised by the quality of the white wines in Sicily. Given how hot the climate is, I expected cooked wines with low acidity. The whites that we encountered were fresh and crisp. The varietal I liked best was Grillo, apparently Italian for cricket. When the tour ended, Marlene and I went back to Trapani for another four days. This pretty city is the centre of Marsala production. I arranged private visits and tastings with four wineries: De Bartoli, Donnafugata, Pellegrino, and Florio. The latter are the largest producers of Marsala, and Florio is one of the most historic. Founder Vincenzo Florio was a supporter of Giuseppe Garibaldi, said to be the general who unified Italy into a single state in the nineteenth century. Some of the rifles that Florio supplied to Garibaldi still are on display in the cavernous wine cellar. The cellars, in fact, are so large that the Allies mistook them for a military installation. The winery was bombed heavily in 1943. There still were vast casks of aging Marsala when I toured the winery because, sadly, there is not much demand for Marsala. The wines, therefore, are inexpensive and are terrific value.

In September 1991, I was invited to spend a week in Bordeaux. The long history of French wine has generated a good deal of ceremony.

---

62 We also did Road Scholar tours in Germany (opera and concerts in Berlin, Dresden, and Leipzig) in 2006; the Grand Canyon, and associated Arizona canyons in 2009; New Orleans in 2010; the Bach Festival in Eugene, Oregon, in 2012; and Spain in 2017.

We were plunged into ceremony on our first Sunday there, for it was the Ban des Vendanges in Saint-Émilion, the day when harvest began. The day began with Latin Mass, followed by the induction of members into the Jurade (a local organization dedicated to promoting the wines). That was followed by a massive four-hour wine-soaked luncheon. The Jurats, as they are called, resplendent in fur-trimmed red velvet robes, paraded through the town's cobblestone streets to a tower overlooking the vineyards. Several officers of the Jurade climbed the tower and declared the vintage could begin. The celebration apparently dates from 1611. It was a grand start to our Bordeaux tour.

For several days, our base was Château Magnol, a winery that had been renovated in the 1980s to offer accommodation. To this day, it has twelve rooms and facilities for conventions. It also offers packages that include extensive courses in wine history and tasting. We certainly tasted a lot of wines: one day, we had about seventy young Bordeaux reds. That was an assault on the palate.

We visited some storied wineries, including Château Mouton Rothschild. The barrel cellar there—at least the one open for tours—has an almost spiritual feeling. Flickering candles illuminate the rows of barrels, just one high. Everything in the cellar is surgically clean. No expense has been spared to impress visitors that this is one of the greatest wineries in the world.

On this day in Bordeaux, our group had dinner at Château Cos D'Estournel with Bruno Pratts, then the owner. We had spent a long day in hot vineyards. By dinner, I was sticky with sweat and in need of a shower, except we did not have the opportunity. I was quite uncomfortable sharing a table with the elegant vintner in his rambling, elegant estate.

On the way to France, I had stopped in Toronto to interview the owners of the Marynissen Winery, which had just opened. They have me a bottle of their Merlot. Thus, during one of the tastings in Bordeaux, I decided to share the wine with our hosts. The wine was embarrassingly mediocre. But to give credit to the French, no one said anything negative. Perhaps they realized that Canada was just finding its feet in wine growing.

My next trip to an overseas wine region occurred in the fall of 1996 when I was among a group invited to New Zealand. The travelling companions were three German wine writers and David Lawrason, a freelancer then writing for *The Globe and Mail*. The industry organized a good tour, starting with wineries in Auckland and then continuing to the Marlborough wine region. "This is wine touring country with the clock turned back," I noted in my diary. We stayed at a bed and breakfast owned by John Joslin, a one-time British farmer who, after selling his assets in Britain, spent six years sailing around the world before planting vines and building a spectacular open beam home near Blenheim. I asked if an architect had designed it. "No," he said. "When you hire an architect, you end up living in his dream, not yours." Tastings at the wineries here showed the impressive vivacity and quality of New Zealand's Sauvignon Blanc. It also showed the acidity of the wines. My teeth developed a painful ache after three days. One of the German writers needed emergency dental work to repair a cracked filling that had been exposed by the acidity of the wines.

We concluded the trip with visits to wineries at Hawkes Bay on the east coast of the north island and a final tasting at Villa Maria winery, not far from the Auckland airport. I was impressed at the vast improvement in New Zealand wines since my first visit there in 1987, when there still were many hybrid varieties in the vineyards. The best-selling wine then was Brother Dominic. It was based, apparently, on pineapple juice and came in a box. By the 1990s, New Zealand had world-class wines. I was struck by the number of female winemakers, especially when I was told that, in the 1960s, women were never even admitted to the winemaking school at Roseworthy in Australia.

My final hosted wine tour to Germany was in April, 2000. I took advantage of it to add to my comprehensive research on icewine, along with noting colourful details about the producers. At the P.J. Valckenberg winery in Westhofen, the seventy-eight-year-old chairman was a charming gentleman, Hans-Joachim Steifensand. He had been a submarine officer in World War II, became a prisoner of war, and was incarcerated in Canada. He still remembered how well the Canadians treated him and, thus, he was a very friendly guide around the winery.

Heinrich Vollmer, the proprietor at Weingut Heinrich Vollmer, said he had developed a large wine property in Argentina's Uco Valley to provide jobs for Peruvian labourers who had nursed him back to health after he had a serious mountaineering accident in Peru in 1983. It took him six weeks to recover. When he returned to Germany, he discovered that his French-born wife had declared him dead and had taken up with another man. There was a further ironic twist in the story. When Vollmer originally married the French woman, his father kicked him off the family's wine estate in Baden. That forced Vollmer to start his own winery in the Pfalz.

The week-long tour included several days in the Mosel wine region, a favourite of mine since taking the German Wine Academy course. The many vivid characters included Ernst Loosen, a rising star in German wine production since taking over the family business in 1983, and Johannes Selbach, a Mosel producer who then came regularly to Vancouver to promote his wines.

In April 2002, Singapore Airlines invited several wine writers, including me, to observe how the airline's wine consultants selected the in-flight wines. The three-day affair enabled me to write a few pieces on how airlines chose wines. There was nothing surprising in the experience, although I did enjoy the food and wines on the flights to and from Singapore. The disappointment was that none of the invited writers were given anything meaningful to do to help the consultants. We did get a tour of the airline's flight kitchen, which was rather boring.

In September 2003, I joined a small group invited for a four-day tour of wineries near Lodi, California. This previously had been a region for producing bulk wines and grapes for sale to other wine regions, but a number of producers had decided to go up market. The wines we tasted were delicious, for the most part. I was particularly impressed with a family-owned winery called Michael-David Vineyards, and I wrote about them subsequently when they came to the Vancouver International Wine Festival. The flagship wine at the time included a powerhouse Zinfandel called Seven Deadly Zins.

In October 2003, the Washington Wine Commission hosted a group of wine writers for a week tour of Washington wineries. The wines were impressive but, after the British Columbia wine industry had begun to consume my interest, I wrote very little about Washington.

Seventeen:
Wine touring in South America

In the 1980s, Charles Williams, an Edmonton wine writer and a lovely man long since gone, was invited to taste wines in Chile. The handful of wineries then operating were so delighted to host a North American wine writer that they actually delivered cases of wines to his hotel. He told me that the wines were acceptable, but hardly great. The few Chilean wineries at the time were producing primarily for a local market where the preferred beverage was beer. Sales of Chilean wines to Canada in 1982 totalled a mere 30,500 cases.[63]

Exports to Canada had grown to 260,900 cases in 1990. By the time I joined a small group of wine writers to visit Chile in November 1991, the wineries had begun to export wines crafted for international palates, even while still making traditional wines for the home market. The domestic consumers in Chile had become accustomed to wines that were somewhat oxidized. Almost none of the wineries we visited, with rare exceptions, offered us wines more than two or three years old. We found some on our own in a restaurant one evening. We tried a 1983 Tarapaca Sauvignon Blanc ("reminiscent of a drinkable Retsina"), a Tarapaca 1982 Cabernet Sauvignon ("oxidized"), and a 1988 red from Errazuriz, a pleasant wine pretentiously labelled Corton. The styles did not appeal to us. Obviously, the wineries hosting us had anticipated

----

63   The figures were provided by United Distillers Canada, which organized the 1991 trip.

that. The only producer that offered us older wines was Cousiño Macul, a venerable winery in Santiago renowned for its Cabernet Sauvignon wines.

Getting to Santiago from Vancouver and via Toronto was twenty-three hours of travel. I went to bed as soon as I was settled in a hotel. I was in a deep sleep forty-five minutes later when someone from the Santa Rita winery telephoned to welcome me to Chile. Our first winery visit the next day was to Santa Rita, a winery founded in 1880, with attractive gardens and cellars that had been designated a national treasure. Here we heard, not for the last time, how the three-year socialist regime of Salvador Allende had impacted Chilean winery owners. Shortly after he became president in 1970, he began national-izing industry in Chile. The wine industry was severely impacted by the economic turmoil. One major wine family, the Mitjans, had 90% of their vineyards expropriated and turned over to peasants who pulled out the vines and planted corn.

Santa Rita's owners lost the business, which was taken over in 1980 by an industrialist backed by the largest glass manufacturer. Much was invested in new technology and, with much improved wines, Santa Rita began exporting. At lunch there, we were served a very fine premium 1987 Cabernet Sauvignon. Santa Rita debated releasing it at $25, an unheard-of price for a Chilean wine at the time. Today, such pricing is routine because no one doubts the quality of the wines.

At this time, there were about a dozen wineries in Chile. I believe we visited all of them, including Errazuriz, which is located in the spec-tacularly beautiful Aconcagua Valley two hours north of Santiago (and a winery I visited again on my second trip to Chile). The list of wineries included Viña San Pedro, where we toured the vineyards on horseback, and Viña Los Vascos, in which Château Lafite Rothschild had just invested. There was an Allende story here, as well. In 1975, the Allende government expropriated its vineyards. After Allende's overthrow, the owner, Jorge Eyzaquirre, set out to repurchase the property with revenues from selling bulk wines. The bulk wine market collapsed in 1982. When Eyzaquirre and his wife began peddling it as bottled wine, he discovered the quality was poor. So he hired a French winemaker to turn around the quality. Within two years, the Las Vascos wines attracted acclaim at VinExpo in Bordeaux. That gave Eyzaquirre the courage to approach several Bordeaux producers and to strike a joint venture in 1988 with Lafite, which ultimately took over the winery.

We also visited Miguel Torres Chile, founded in 1979. Torres was the first European winery to invest in Chile and may have been the first winery in the country to store wines in stainless steel tanks, not old wood vats. Later, we met a charismatic, young, independent winemaker, Aurelio Montes, who struck me immediately as a future superstar of Chilean wines, even if I almost fell into an irrigation ditch while we toured his vineyard. One evening in Santiago, we had dinner at the Santa Carolina winery whose cellars were designated a national heritage even if the sanitation was deficient. We spent a morning and had lunch at Concha Y Toro, which, even then, was the largest winery in Chile. Folkloric dancers entertained us, and I was asked to dance by the prettiest young woman at the winery, which flattered my ego. In the afternoon, we went to Cousiño Macul, an historic winery set in a park-like garden in Santiago where the first vines were planted in 1856. Here, at last, we had really mature wines—1970 and 1978 vintages of the winery's iconic Antiguas Reservas Cabernet Sauvignon.

My second hosted wine tour to Chile was ten days in January 2003 and involved about twenty-five wineries. I was one of six wine writers, including Memory Walsh, one of the more vexing writers I travelled with. She had a notorious habit of butting into explanations by our Chilean hosts in mid-sentence to ask unrelated questions.

The trip—twelve and a half hours from Vancouver through Dallas—did not start well. We had arrived in the middle of a hot day. Our hosts in Chile loaded us into an elderly van with no air conditioning for a two-and-a-half-hour drive from Santiago south to Curicó. About 2:00 p.m., we checked into a noisy hotel beside the highway. Winery visits started the next day, Sunday, January 12, with a visit to Aresti for a picnic lunch. (I still wear the Aresti baseball cap, one of numerous souvenirs.) After that, we went to San Pedro, which I also visited in 1991, touring the vineyards on horseback then. Now, it gleamed with new stainless steel. We took wines left over from our tasting back to the hotel and ordered pizza for dinner. The next day, three wineries were on the itinerary: Valdivieso, Torres, and Cono Sur. The latter had excellent wines and also served us dinner before we left for Santa Cruz for the night. A very long Tuesday started with a drive back to Santiago and visits to three wineries and vineyards in thirty-degree heat. We did not get to our hotel until 10:30 p.m. The wineries, however, were among the best: Casa Lapostelle, Caliterra, and Montes.

On Wednesday, we started with Cousiño Macul, at its new winery outside Santiago. Lunch was at a winery called Haras de Pirque, owned at the time by Chile's leading horse breeder. The winery, built in the shape of a horseshoe on a hillside overlooking vineyards, was an architectural spectacle. However, the winemaker told me that the shape made it inefficient for wine production. We ended the day at Portal Del Alto, a winery owned by a professor of enology.

On Thursday, we started at Tarapaca winery, whose vineyards occupied an entire valley. We moved to Undurraga for lunch, a tour, and a tasting. We finished with a tasting at Terra Mater, arriving back in the hotel at 9:00 p.m. I had a sandwich and a beer before collapsing into bed. Friday was another thirteen-hour day, this time in the Casablanca Valley, then an emerging wine region between Santiago and the Pacific Coast. We visited four wineries: Casa Rivas, Veramonte, Casa del Bosque, and Viña Casablanca. Casa del Bosque was the winery that helped sponsor the research to identify Carménère as a varietal distinct from Merlot. The varietal had once flourished in Bordeaux until it was virtually wiped out in the 1870s by phylloxera. (This was a destructive ailment caused when native American vines were planted in Europe, bringing with them root lice against which the European vines had no resistance.) Carménère had been transplanted to Chile prior to the phylloxera introduction to France and thrived because the Chilean vineyards remained untouched by the root louse. Growers identified it as Merlot Chileño until ampelographers concluded it was a distinct varietal, not a subspecies of Merlot. Some producers then begun to promote the richly flavoured Carménère as Chile's flagship red wine.

On Saturday, we visited the Errazuriz winery, beautifully sited amid vineyards in the Aconcagua Valley. It had impressed me in 1991.

The winery had been renovated and updated since then; the wines were among the best in Chile, notably a Bordeaux blend called Don Maximiano. Only one winery visit on Sunday—Santa Carolina—but four on Monday—Concha Y Toro, Santa Rita, Viña Carmen, and Sur Andina. It was a very long day, ending at the airport at 10:00 p.m. for the midnight flight to Dallas and on to Vancouver. Overall, the tour was quite typical of most wine tours, with the host wineries working the wine writers hard.

In October 2002, Marlene and I went to Mexico. I was invited by the Mexican Wine Academy and its director, Luis Fernandez Otera, to lead a presentation and tasting of icewine. I rather doubt the audience shared my host's interest in icewine. We used that trip to do some tourism, including nearly a week in Guadalajara. There, we did a tequila tasting, for want of something to do.

In March 2009, when my manuscript for the third edition of *The Wineries of British Columbia* was nearly complete, I managed to carve out the time to travel to Argentina with Marlene. The wine industry there, whose profile was rising rapidly, had never invited me on a sponsored trip. But we could afford to pay for our own trip. I also realized that if I controlled the agenda, the pace of the winery visits would be more leisurely, and I would absorb more information. When I started planning this, Marlene said that she would stay at home if I intended to spend all three weeks visiting wineries. So winery visits were limited to the third week of the vacation. I discovered this was just right: I got a good taste of the Argentine wine industry without tiring of the experience.

Somehow, we had been put in touch with a travel agent from Fernie by the name of Corinne Thomson. She connected us with a travel agent in Buenos Aires and, with the help of the internet, we made most of our travel arrangements in Argentina, except for winery visits. Those I arranged directly through Wines of Argentina. It was all fairly painless.

Except for the flight. We were booked on Air Canada from Vancouver to Toronto, connecting there to Santiago and on to Buenos Aires. The flight from Vancouver, leaving on March 13, was forty-five minutes late in departing, demolishing the time to connect to the next flight in Toronto. We made it, barely, but our luggage did not follow us until the next day. In fact, it was two days before we got our bags because a huge evangelical rally that congested downtown Buenos Aires prevented the airline from delivering them promptly.

After four days in Buenos Aires, we flew to Iguazu Falls, a spectacular group of waterfalls on the border of Argentine and Brazil. Set in a national park, it is the South American equivalent of Niagara Falls with fewer tacky tourist attractions. For most visitors, the highlight is riding under the falls in a zodiac and getting soaked with water that, fortunately, is comfortably warm.

After two days in Iguazu Falls, we flew back to Buenos Aires and then flew to Salta, a quaint city in northwestern Argentina that has retained its Spanish character. It had not occurred to me to set up winery visits in what was then an emerging wine region. But we had hired a guide and car, and he took us on an day-long round trip north of Salta where the scenery is quite dramatic. The guide, called Adolfo, was a well-informed man in his sixties, quite knowledgeable about the villages we stopped in during the day. He also took us to an excellent restaurant for lunch. On the return journey, he and Marlene had a long conversation about the young women of Argentina who had taken to requesting breast enhancements as a gift for graduating from high school. Adolfo disapproved, quite firmly.

Our next stop was Mendoza. Because Buenos Aires was (and probably still is) the hub for most flights in Argentina, we had to fly from Salta one thousand kilometres (621 miles) to Buenos Aires and change planes for another one thousand kilometres to Mendoza, when a direct flight between Salta and Mendoza would have been less than one thousand kilometres. Mendoza is a large city on the plain that stretches to the Andes in the west. It is the major wine city. Wines of Argentina had arranged my program, so that I visited three wineries a day. The first winery picked me up at the hotel and delivered me to the second winery for lunch. The third winery took me back to the hotel. We did spend one night at the guesthouse of the O. Fournier Winery in the Uco Valley. It is a very modern winery that looks like a spaceship rising amid the vineyards. The wines were excellent; dinner at the winery was very good. But the guesthouse was a rustic farmhouse with dodgy wiring and wind-blown sand on the floors.

The wines I got to taste in Argentine ranged in quality from good value to outstanding. The wine industry there is perhaps two hundred years old and was developed mainly by Spanish and Basque settlers. During much of the twentieth century and into this century, the Argentine economy has lurched from crisis to crisis, the result of unstable military and civilian governments. The local wine market was satisfied with inexpensive wines for the most part. It was only when Argentine wineries began developing export markets early this century that wine quality improved dramatically and investment flooded into Argentina's wine industry. The good value wines are much better than they once were; the premium wines are world class.

After our week in Mendoza, Marlene and I took a bus through the Andes to Santiago in Chile. It is an exceptional eight-hour scenic ride as the road drops down the other side of the Andes. At one point, I counted ten switchbacks from the window of our bus. The founder of the Norton Winery, an Englishman named Norton, was involved with building a railroad through this same pass. Remnants of the rail bed and of the tunnels are still visible. The railroad did not operate very long because the line was damaged by rock slides in summer and choked with snow in winter, when the highway is also impassable. We spent three pleasant days in Santiago before flying home on April 3.

Eighteen:
How I got to spend our
twenty-fifth anniversary in Prague

During Expo 67 in Montreal, the *Financial Post* had published several profitable supplements on countries, including several from the Eastern Bloc, which had pavilions at the fair. I remembered that fact as Expo 86 was being organized in Vancouver, and I helped get similar projects started. One of the countries we were negotiating with was Czechoslovakia which, perhaps coincidentally, invited me to join a group of journalists at a trade fair in Brno in September 1985. The travel overlapped our twenty-fifth wedding anniversary, but I thought I would risk killing the *Post*'s supplement if I turned the trip down. (I can't recall if we ever did run a sponsored supplement.) I tried to take Marlene along at my expense. My hosts said there would be no seats available on the Czech Airlines Ilyushin Il62. [64] So I agreed to go alone. I also asked the Czech government to put together a business tour after the trade fair, which would include visits to the Škoda car plant, the Budweiser brewery, and perhaps a crystal factory, subjects I could write about.

Marlene would have been appalled, had she been with me in Brno. The journalists were accommodated in a tired university dormitory with communal showers. The room I shared with a journalist from Winnipeg

---

64 The Il62 was a two-hundred-seat Russian-made jet launched in 1963..

had one clean hand towel and two dirty hand towels. I managed to get another clean one but no bath towels. It had not occurred to us to travel with our own towels. Even in China in 1972, amidst the Cultural Revolution, hotels provided foreigners with towels. After several days in this dormitory, we were moved to a better residence with single rooms and adequate housekeeping—but always with communal showers and toilets. While the Czechs lived in reasonable comfort, it was a society that had learned to make do without, especially if the amenity had to be imported with hard currency. I did not see an orange for two weeks.

The trade fair and our visits to factories and farms near Brno revealed a lack of industrial development in many areas except light aviation. Czechoslovakia had had a Communist government for about forty years. It had been one of Europe's most industrialized countries before World War II but had been left behind since. It did have a reputation for its light aircraft. While I was at that manufacturer's booth at the trade fair, I found an English-speaking salesperson who took me into a back room for a longer conversation. He poured me the best Sauvignon Blanc I had had in a while. The country, I learned, had a wine industry and the aircraft company had access to the best wines.

The trade fair was excruciating dull. One afternoon, the journalists were all invited to a press conference announcing a big sale of trucks to Russia. One of the other reporters, a journalist from Belgrade, took a photograph of me fast asleep in my chair and sent it to me. On the last Friday in Brno, we were taken on a tour of a farm machinery factory that was hand-assembling and hand-painting ten-horsepower tractors. We then got to spend the weekend in Brno, a drab city that recalled the joke about first prize being a week in Hamilton, second prize being two. I learned to take the trams, and I even found a church for Mass on Sunday evening.

On Monday a group of journalists went on another country tour. One journalist was an Egyptian who wanted to see a collective farm. We were taken to a three-thousand-hectare (7,400-acre) farm. In the three-storey administration building, we were met in a boardroom by managers, all in white smocks. A photo of Gustav Husak, president of

Czechoslovakia, hung one wall. On another, there were wall hangings of Lenin and of Klement Gottwald, the country's first Socialist president.

I had asked to visit a winery. We went to what our guide called a "wine factory" called Moravské vinařské závody. It was a sprawling place with primarily fibreglass tanks and the capacity to produce thirty million litres (seven million gallons) a year. The managing director, the winemaker, and several others—again all garbed in white smocks—led an unenthusiastic tour of the place. The tour ended at an upturned barrel with four glasses of white wine. My hosts watched while I tasted the wines (which were sound but hardly exciting). In my fifty years of wine touring, this was one of the very few times in my experience that the producer did not taste the wines with the guests.

We flew back to Prague on Wednesday, September 17. I telephoned Marlene from the hotel—the Intercontinental—to wish her a happy anniversary. The brief call cost $40. Because the Czech airline then had only weekly flights from Prague to Montreal, my requests to do other visits and interviews meant I stayed an extra week. As it happened, none of the places I wanted to visit were available. Typical of the excuses: the Škoda factory was not running because it was in the middle of a model change (highly unlikely since the design was static for some years). The car driven by officials was the Tatra, a large rear-engine sedan with a V8 engine. Plenty of these cars, invariably black, were on the streets of Prague.

In lieu of my requests, my hosts set up a very easy program of interviews and sightseeing. Prague is a beautiful city, unsullied in 1985 by fast food franchises, billboards, and neon signage. The movie about Mozart, *Amadeus*, had been filmed largely in Prague because the city still had the charm of the Mozart era. "Have you seen Salzburg?" one Czech asked me. When I did get to Salzburg some years later, I could see that the commercial clutter would have made it next to impossible to recreate Mozart's era in Salzburg.

The Czechs had given me a guide, a woman in her fifties called Ludmilla Firtova. Her husband was a surgeon who, a year earlier, had done the first heart transplant in the Soviet bloc.[65] She accompanied me to one concert and, I believe, to a tour of several castles outside the city. I also attended a first-rate concert with the Czech Philharmonic, where Josef Suk played the Bartok violin concerto and the orchestra played Tchaikovsky's Fifth Symphony. Because my few interviews were in the mornings, I had plenty of time for sightseeing. During a long walk one day, I came across the ancient fortress of Vyšehrad on the banks of the Moldau. I was taking photographs of head stones in a cemetery and was surprised to find composer Bedřich Smetena's tombstone in my view finder.

I also enjoyed the many beer halls and the invariably excellent beer. Of particular note was U Fleků, the oldest brewery in Prague (1499). Of course, it was nationalized when the Communists took power. It is now back in private hands. It is an enormous place, with capacity for 1,200 in eight halls and a large outdoor garden. The place was jammed with tourists and local citizens. I had a half litre of a delicious dark beer in the garden.

My last day in Prague was spent with an urbane man who later was a manager of the Czech pavilion at Expo 86. He invited me to his flat for coffee and cake and then took me on a tour of more castles in the country. Our conversation ranged widely. At one point, he complained how the Russians in Czechoslovakia were only interested in the Soviet Union. I laughed and told him he sounded like a Canadian talking about Americans. He was also interested in wine and told me that vines were imported to Czech vineyards from Burgundy in 1348 by Charles IV, later the Holy Roman Emperor as well as the King of Burgundy.

I had not seen an English newspaper for two weeks. On the flight back from Prague to Montreal, only the newspaper of the British Communist party was available on the flight. The aircraft was another tired Ilyushin Il62. The overhead luggage racks were open, and the non-smoking section of the plane was the opposite side of the cabin.

---

65 An internet search suggests that the first heart transplant in Czechoslovakia was done in 1984 by a surgeon named Vladimír Kočandrle. It is likely that Ms. Firtova was using her maiden name.

There was no wine, just spirits, on the bar trolley but, thankfully, there was good Czech beer with lunch.

On returning home, I was determined to make it up to Marlene for missing that trip. Fortunately, I came across a ten-day excursion to Portugal at the start of 1986. John and Alison also came along. Maureen was very disappointed not to come, but she was working. I always regretted not trying to arrange for her to come along as well.

When we departed from Vancouver, Marlene and I were both recovering from heavy colds, quite possibly influenza. My stuffed sinus passages caused considerable pain as our British Airways flight descended into Heathrow. Our excursion included a three-day stopover in London at the start. That gave us time for a morning at the British Museum, seeing among other attractions a display on Halley's Comet which, on each pass-by, was once interpreted as an ill omen. The comet was visible in 1066, linking it to Harold's defeat at Hastings. We also went into Westminster Abbey where I was moved profoundly by discovering Handel's grave in Poet's Corner.[66] Originally, we planned to go to the theatre but instead went to bed early to hasten our recoveries from the flu.

We flew from London to Lisbon, arrived mid-day on December 31, and checked into a hotel near the airport. I immediately made a dinner booking, believing it would be as busy on New Year's Eve in Lisbon as at home. That was not so. The dining room was almost deserted, the food was ordinary, and the service, therefore, was so fast that we were done in an hour. I was asleep by 10:00 p.m. The rest of the family were up at midnight to hear the Portuguese banging pots and pans. On New Year's Day, we spent several hours exploring the city and did not start driving to the Algarve until mid-afternoon. That meant a four and a half hour drive mostly in the dark and in the rain, on a narrow, twisting highway. We enjoyed a good dinner when we reached our hotel, with Alison—always adventurous with food—suffering through an order of salt cod.

---

66 I admire Handel's music—and *The Messiah* in particular. Over the years, I collected a dozen recordings. My favourite is the recording by Sir Georg Solti with the Chicago Symphony. The soprano is Dame Kiri Te Kanawa. Her interpretation of the aria, "I Know My Redeemer Liveth", is what I would program for my funeral.

The Algarve in the first week of January was not overrun by tourists, which suited us just fine. We spent time exploring the towns along the coast, the highlight being Cape Sagres where Prince Henry the Navigator's school of navigation launched Portugal's exploration of the world. When we had exhausted the attractions of the Algarve, we made a nine-hour drive to Porto. While we found a better highway than the coastal road, there were still many two-lane stretches, often behind trucks belching diesel smoke. I was happy to have Alison along to share the driving. Of course, I arranged visits to Quinta do Noval and also to one of the Port houses owned by the Symington family. We returned to Lisbon the night before the flight home. The last dinner was at an East Indian restaurant where I discovered that vinho verde pairs well with curry. As with all the restaurant meals we had, the cost was amazingly low. It is hard to imagine we never returned there for another vacation.

Expo 86 itself generated many stories. I wrote several articles for a *Financial Post* section in May 1985, when a preview centre for the fair opened. The following spring, we got family passes for Marlene and our children. (I had a press pass.) We enjoyed many evenings and weekends at the fair. Predictably, the Saskatchewan Pavilion, with a restaurant serving perogies and Saskatoon berry pie, was one of our favourites. It was a magical summer in Vancouver. As well, the fair changed Vancouver profoundly, transforming it from minor coastal city to a major international city.

Nineteen:
I begin championing wineries

When I started working on my first wine book, *The World of Canadian Wine*, I was familiar with all of the British Columbia wineries then in operation. I had a significant profile with the wine industry after judging several times at the Okanagan Wine Festival (beginning in 1983) and at several competitions sponsored by the Pacific National Exhibition (PNE). The Okanagan competition started in 1980 as "Septober" (which it was called for the first two years as it began in September and continued through the first week or two of October), while the PNE competition was launched in 1983. The wine competition was added to the PNE on the pretext that, even with its location in Vancouver, it was still an agricultural fair. The objective of both competitions was to lift the profile of British Columbia wines. For several years, the PNE imported tuxedo-clad Nathan Chroman, a wine writer and a lawyer from Los Angeles, to add a veneer of sophistication to the chairman's role. When he stepped down, the successor in 1990 was Paul Warwick, one of Vancouver's earliest wine educators. Born in Winnipeg in 1941, he had a long career managing parts departments for automobile dealers before a membership in the Opimian Society fired what became a consuming passion for wine and food. He was teaching twenty-nine wine courses when I profiled him in the June/

July edition of the *BCL Guide*.[67] "He may well be the only person in Greater Vancouver making his living primarily as a wine educator," I wrote. His personalized licence plate was GEWURZ. Paul became a friend and we moved in similar wine circles until his death in 2002.

In the 1980s, acceptable wines were being made in British Columbia by Gray Monk, Sumac Ridge, Gehringer Brothers, and Mission Hill, all frequent award winners at the competitions. In Ontario, Inniskillin's quality was being matched by Chateau des Charmes and Vineland Estates Winery, while T.G. Bright & Co. had perhaps the most aggressive research program of any large Canadian winery. On several occasions, I got absolutely hammered drinking Baco Noir with George Hostetter, the winery's research director. Brights was instrumental in importing and propagating the hybrid varieties such as Baco Noir from France in 1947.

There were still appalling wines being made in the 1980s, notably in Quebec where regional development grants from Ottawa helped finance several wineries. The most disappointing was a winery in the Montreal suburb of Dorval called Secrestat. It was built in 1972 by The Seagram Company, the big distiller that also owned Paul Masson in California, Barton & Guestier in Bordeaux, and G.H. Mumm & Co. in Champagne. Seagram's also owned, or had owned, wineries in Tuscany, New Zealand, and Ontario. I arrived at Secrestat's offices for a pleasant morning of interviews with its executives. There was no wine tasting; they arranged to ship a case of wines to me in Vancouver. Then I was taken to lunch where, to my surprise, my hosts all drank whisky. I discovered why when I tasted the wine they sent. All had been made with concentrates and none was palatable, at least in my estimation.

The World of Canadian Wine manuscript was done on a typewriter, although some may have been finished on a computer. The *Financial Post* office was equipped in July 1983 with Kaypro 11 computers, forty-pound "portables" with 64 K memories. I was so impressed with the

---

67 The *BCL Guide* was published by the Liquor Distribution Branch, with some editorial content wrapped around a listing of all LDB products. The magazine, in a format similar to the *Reader's Digest*, was available without charge in all government liquor stores.

productivity of a computer that I bought my own machine for home later that same year. It was a waste of $2,100. The limited memory slowed the writing process when the document was longer than one thousand words. I replaced it in 1987 with an Olivetti computer that had a 640 K memory, more than enough for a book-length manuscript. I purchased it for $1,901.64 from a shop called Friendly Technology Corp, located further along on Melville Street from my office downtown. Two years earlier, I spent $700 there for a printer. Over subsequent years, I bought a number of computers: a Tandy laptop in 1990 for $1,059; an IPC 486 desktop computer in 1993 for $2,935; a Texas Instruments laptop computer in 1995 for $3,149; a Toshiba laptop; another Toshiba laptop; and finally, an HP laptop.

The World of Canadian Wine was released in October 1984, and the *Financial Post* published an excerpt and an opportunity to purchase the book.[68] Release of the book coincided with an invitation to judge in the Okanagan. The press run for the hard cover was three thousand copies. In the initial three months, it sold very well. I personally sold $600 worth of books (at $19.95 each) at the public tasting during the Okanagan wine festival. The three thousand were sold out by mid-December and the publisher, Douglas & McIntyre, then issued a much larger run in paperback in February. Scott McIntyre, the president of the publishing company, led me to think a second edition might be needed. I invested time and money in the summer of 1985 to visit wineries in Ontario and Quebec, updating some information. Alison was then finishing a French course at McGill; we met in Montreal, went to see an Expos baseball game, and spent several days visiting wineries in the Eastern Townships before coming home.

In the end, there was no second edition because the book did not sell after the burst of sales in the initial three months. To begin with, Douglas & McIntyre released at the same time a memoir by Tiger Williams, a colourful Vancouver Canucks hockey player. His book got most of the promotional budget even though it pretty well sold itself. I usually ended up making my own signing arrangements, especially

---

68 *The Financial Post*, October 13, 1984, p. 17.

in Ontario, building them around *Financial Post* business trips to minimize my personal expenses. Secondly, Canadian wines were not good enough yet to excite much attention.[69]Thirdly, the wines did not sell across the country. Consumers in British Columbia did not care about Nova Scotia or Ontario wines, and vice versa. Finally, wine writer Tony Aspler in Toronto also released a book about the wines of Canada (with a better promotion budget). The royalty income from *The World of Canadian Wine* totalled $4,455.29. The book went out of print in 1990, a year in which one copy was sold. At the time, I did not imagine I would eventually write twenty wine books.

When I began writing about wine, it was because I liked the wine industry and the creative characters running it. It was a surprise to me when I realized I had become the champion of the British Columbia wine industry because of my writing. I was, after all, far more prolific than most of my wine writing colleagues.

There was not much to champion when I started visiting Okanagan wineries in the mid-1970s. The reviews of Canadian wines in *The Wine Consumer*, a newsletter published in Vancouver by Albert Givton from 1985 to 1990, ranged from unflattering to devastating. The most savage critique of a Canadian wine in his publication was of a red wine called Bacaro from Divino Estate Winery in Oliver. "This is the worst I have ever tasted and having tasted more than 7,000 wines over the past fifteen years, this wine will always be remembered," Albert wrote in the spring of 1986. "This product must be removed from our liquor board shelves immediately ...."[70] He knew what he was talking about. Born in Cairo and raised in Israel, he had come to Vancouver in 1973 and eventually founded the three best wine clubs in the city. He had a sophisticated palate, especially for Bordeaux wines, and visited the top châteaux annually. British Columbia wineries at the time were not nearly as accomplished as Bordeaux, to say the least.

I could not disagree with Albert's criticism of Bacaro. It was also one of the worst wines I had ever tasted. It likely was even carcinogenic.

---

69 Hugh Johnson, the renowned British wine writer, refused to even read my manuscript.

70 *The Wine Consumer, Volume II, No. 1*, Spring, 1986: Canadian Speciality Red Wines.

Joe Busnardo, the Italian immigrant who founded Divino in 1983, had made fibreglass tanks in which to age Bacaro, a red blend. The tanks were not properly cured, and the wine smelled and tasted of ethyl acetate. Fortunately for Joe's sales, many British Columbia consumers at the time had uneducated palates. Once, I was signing books at a function in Victoria at which four wineries, including Divino, were pouring samples. I was astounded at how many consumers bought Bacaro after tasting it. One individual even bought a whole case! Joe had good intentions with the wine. On the label, he explained, somewhat cryptically: "The name, 'Bacaro' was given in homage to the God, Bacchus. Just north of Venice, Italy, in the Piave region, the Raboso grapes plus other varieties make up this red wine. The Divino 'Bacaro' is made in a similar manner entirely from BC grapes."

Unlike Albert Givton, I never wrote savage reviews of British Columbia wines. My columns and my books were generally supportive of the wine industry. As I said more than once: "I was a friend of British Columbia wines before they had friends." Winery owners have told me that my support contributed to the industry's credibility and growth. The industry backed that up by giving me a number of major awards. In 2002, the Okanagan Wine Festivals Society gave me its Founders Award to recognize contributions to the British Columbia wine industry. The award was established in 1985, with the first one given to Lyall Denby, the scientist at the Summerland Research Station who created the Sovereign Opal and Sovereign Coronation grapes. The award was Harry McWatters' idea. After his death in 2019, the award was renamed the Harry McWatters Award. The honorees usually were people who had been active in the wine industry directly. I was the first wine writer to get the recognition.

Other awards also came my way. In 2009, the Vancouver International Wine Festival gave me its Spirited Industry Professional Award. In 2014, I was inducted into the BC Restaurant Association Hall of Fame as a "friend of the industry". In 2015, the Canadian Vintners Association gave me its Canadian Wine Industry Champion award. In 2016, the British Columbia Wine Institute gave me its Industry Recognition Award.

My championing of wineries went beyond just reviewing the wines or writing articles and books on the wineries. On several occasions, I even helped wineries find winemakers. In July 2004, I was at the Summerland Research Station to judge wines in the Lieutenant Governor's competition when my cell phone rang. It was Evelyn Campbell, then one of the owners of Blasted Church Vineyards. She was quite upset because their winemaker at the time, Marcus Ansems, had resigned abruptly in the middle of his contract. I do not know why Marcus walked out. He is an accomplished Australian with an impressive winemaking pedigree and a healthy ego. Evelyn and Chris Campbell, her husband at the time, were not easy to work with. I also do not know why Evelyn called me. As it happened, I had a solution to her problem. A few days before, I have been speaking with a sweet-mannered winemaker, Kelly Moss, at Calona Vineyards and had learned she was looking to move to a different winery. At my suggestion, Evelyn offered the job to Kelly. She was the winemaker at Blasted Church until 2007 when she moved to Ontario for family reasons.

In 2010, I helped Saturna Island Vineyards find a winemaker. The winery, now closed, was then owned by Larry Page, a Vancouver securities lawyer, who often struggled to keep a winemaker because Saturna Island is so far off the beaten path. In 2008, he was able to hire a capable young South African couple, Megan DeVillieres and Danny Hattingh, as they were just getting established in the British Columbia wine scene. Her viticultural skills resuscitated a rundown vineyard while Danny made some of the first commercially acceptable wines ever released by Saturna Island. Unfortunately for Larry, they left in 2011 to travel in South America. I heard that Larry was recruiting again just as I was trying to connect a winemaker named Homan Haftbaradaran with a job.

Born in Germany (of Iranian heritage) and trained in Britain, Homan had arrived in the Okanagan in 2008 to take the winemaking job at St. Hubertus Estate Winery near Kelowna. His personality did not mesh with the Swiss brothers who own St. Hubertus. He was fired in the spring of 2010, sued successfully for wrongful dismissal but, as a consequence, found himself blackballed among Okanagan wineries. He related his plight to me. When I saw the Saturna Island job posting, I recognized that Larry and Homan both were in desperate situations. So I referred them to each other. Homan became Saturna Island's winemaker in 2011 and only left a few years later after injuring himself during harvest. The final vintage bottled from Saturna Island was 2012, and the property was sold in 2017 in a court-ordered bankruptcy sale. When he recovered from his injuries, Homan opened City Side Winery in Vancouver in 2015.

The Saturna Island vineyard was purchased by Sea Star Estate Farm & Vineyard on Pender Island—another winery for which I helped find a winemaker. Sea Star formerly was Morning Bay Vineyard, which struggled for several years until it was taken over in 2013 by David Goudge and renamed. I interviewed David shortly after and discovered that he was looking for a winemaker. By coincidence, I knew of Ian Baker, formerly the winemaker and partner at Mistaken Identity Winery on Salt Spring Island. I had visited Ian at Mistaken Identity, which had opened in 2009, and thought he was making sound wines from a dubiously-sited vineyard. In December 2012, he included me in an email announcing that his partners (one of whom was his brother) had just fired him and were evicting him from the property. I recommended Ian to David, who hired him in 2013. Ian made seven exceptional vintages for Sea Star until the winery was sold to new owners in 2020. They found their own winemaker.

On two occasions, I was involved, or was asked to be involved, in naming a winery. I first interviewed Peter Slamka before he opened his winery in 1996. He was debating whether to call it Pine Ridge, after the trees above the winery, or Slamka Cellars, after his family. "What do you think, John?" he asked me. I evaded the question. How could I say that Pine Ridge was far more elegant than his surname? He figured it out eventually, renaming the winery in 2004 as Little Straw Vineyards. In Slovakia, where the family came from, *slamka* means little straw.[71]

The memory of that evasion haunted me when I was interviewing Susan Dulik before she opened a winery in 1997 on the historic East

---

71 In 2021, Little Straw was acquired by Kalala Organic Estate Winery.

Kelowna vineyard operated by her father, Den, and previously by her grandfather, Martin. She told me that the winery would called Pinot Reach because she intended to focus on Pinot varieties and reach for quality—and she asked what I thought of the name. I mumbled a non-answer. That night in my Kelowna motel, I decided I needed to dissuade her from what I considered a silly name. On returning to Vancouver, I wrote that she should name the winery in honour of Martin Dulik. I suggested Martin's View because there is an astonishing view over the city from the vineyard. I added two other suggestions including St. Martin's. That was a big mistake. The Duliks dismissed my idea because Martin, whom I had never met, was anything but a saint. Then Susan made her name not with Pinot but with Old Vines Riesling, the first Okanagan wine to win praise from the renowned British wine writer Jancis Robinson MW. Susan told me she should have taken my advice on the winery name. It was academic: in 2003, the Duliks sold the vineyard and the winery to investment dealer Eric Savics. He renamed the winery Tantalus Vineyards. The Old Vines Riesling is still its best-known wine.

On two occasions, I was flattered when future superstar winemakers sought my advice before committing to making wine in British Columbia. The first was a very long conversation I had with Pénélope and Dylan Roche, who met me at Delaney's Coffee House in North Vancouver, near my home. Dylan was born in Vancouver in 1976, the son of a lawyer and a nurse. After getting a University of British Columbia degree in urban geography, he went to Burgundy in 2000 as a bike mechanic and cycling guide, and developed his interest in wine there. By 2003, he was enrolled in enology studies in Beaune. Pénélope, whom he met in France, had five generations of winemaking and viticulture behind her at the family estate, Château Les Carmes in Haut-Brion. It was sold just before the couple came to Okanagan in 2010. They released wine under their own label a few years later and then, in 2014, bought a vineyard on the east side of Penticton to establish Roche Wines. Their wines are always outstanding.

About the same time that I met the Roches, I had another long conversation by telephone from France with Michael Clark, another

Canadian who wanted to take up winemaking in Canada. Michael, who was born in Ontario in 1972, had been working as an investment banker in Switzerland when he gave in to a lifelong interest in wine. "I read *Champagne Is for Breakfast* when I was probably ten years old," he told me, referring to George Bain's classic Canadian wine book published in 1972. "I don't know other children who loved to read wine books." He began formal winemaking studies in Europe in 2010. Shortly thereafter, he tracked me down as one of British Columbia's most prolific wine writers. He asked me a great many questions about the industry here before choosing a winery in which to invest. In 2012, he joined the partnership at Clos du Soleil Winery in the Similkameen Valley, a producer of some of the most sophisticated wines in British Columbia. Michael soon became the general manager as well as the winemaker.

Given how capable both Michael and the Roches already were, they would have succeeded without my advice. But I like to think I speeded them on their way. I may have played a role in advancing the careers of a few other winemakers, if only by giving positive reviews of their early vintages. I also once gave unsolicited advice to Chris Jentsch, the owner of C.C. Jentsch Cellars near Oliver. "Why are you helping me, John?" he asked. I told him it was just what I did, when I could. I wanted them all to succeed. (Sadly, Chris died of a heart attack in April 2021 and Betty Jentsch, his widow, sold the winery.)

I was a judge for sixteen years on the panel for the Lieutenant Governor's Awards for Excellence in BC Wine. When the competition was established in 2003, the wines were judged in the Okanagan in the summer, but the awards ceremony was scheduled for Government House in Victoria on a Friday afternoon in late November. After the first judging, I was interviewing wineries in the Okanagan for one of my books. The names of winning wineries were not to be disclosed before the awards ceremony—but all the competing wineries had been invited to attend in Victoria. It became obvious to me as I did my interviews that none of the winning winemakers intended to travel to Victoria just as they were putting the vintage to bed. At best, wineries would be represented by local agents. If that happened, it seemed to me that the awards would have little impact. So, I telephoned each winning winemaker (there were ten or twelve) and told each, in confidence, why they needed to be at the reception in Victoria that afternoon. The irrepressible Prudence Mahrer, co-owner of Red Rooster Winery with a winning Gewürztraminer, told me: "Good ... now I can buy a new dress!" I believe I saved that initial awards ceremony from failing to achieve its purpose. Subsequently, the Lieutenant Governor travelled to wine country each summer, presenting the awards at receptions hosted by the winning wineries. That ensured that these awards acquired the intended prestige.

John Schreiner judging wine in 2015

I championed the wineries because I liked the people and I liked their aspirations, even when they did not come off. Joe Busnardo had a good heart but an irascible personality. Harry McWatters, who partnered with Joe to open several private wine stores, once said: "If you were swimming down the river, you know Joe would be swimming up. And if the river changed directions, so would Joe." Born in Treviso in 1934, Joe immigrated to the Okanagan and, while earning a living as a heavy equipment operator, he bought a sixty-eight-acre (twenty-seven and a half hectare) orchard property south of Oliver in 1967. There, he planted only vinifera grapes despite being warned that vinifera would not survive Okanagan winters. When the vines did produce, the existing wineries would not pay a premium for his grapes. Stubborn and determined, he opened his own winery. Tasting with him was always an ordeal, in part because the wines were rustic, and in part because Joe did not believe in spitting. One always left his tasting room inebriated but fired up by his enthusiasm.

Joe had planted a huge number of varietals in an effort to identify the ones that would succeed. Naturally, there were a number of Italian varietals including Garganega and Malvasia. The only one to succeed was Trebbiano. After Joe sold the vineyard in 1996 (the new owners renamed it as Hester Creek), he moved Divino to a thirty-acre (twelve-hectare) property at Cobble Hill in the Cowichan Valley. Joe, after an epic battle with the regulators, was able to bring his Okanagan wine inventory to the island and to sell those wines long after his new vineyard was in production.

Marion Jonn, who opened the Okanagan's first estate winery, was another vintner who did not believe in spitting. Once, I spent a summer evening in 1978 drinking his wine with him on the veranda of his house at Chateau Jonn de Trepanier near Peachland. I doubt if I was fit to drive back to my hotel in Penticton that evening—but I did. Marion was born in Bulgaria and claimed a lineage going back to the Roman Legionnaires. His grandfather had owned a vineyard and made wine for local restaurants. Marion, who had immigrated to Canada in 1954, was working in data processing in Edmonton when he drove through the Okanagan on the way to the Seattle World's Fair in 1962. Smitten by the beauty of the Okanagan, he bought raw land in 1965 and began developing a vineyard. When the province brought in cottage winery licensing in 1977, he was ready. His wines were not quite as rustic as Joe Busnardo's. A year after opening, he sold the winery to Bob Claremont, the former winemaker at Calona Vineyards. I was never quite sure why

Marion cashed out so quickly, but it likely had to do with a divorce settlement. I was in touch with Marion several times over the subsequent decades. He had moved to Toronto where he consulted for a client who wanted to develop a vineyard in Venezuela. When I last heard from him in 1996, he was involved with a winery project in China.

Bob Claremont, with silent backers, paid $1 million for Chateau Jonn. Considering the state of the winery and of the vineyard—located in a notorious frost pocket—he paid far too much. A few years later, the winery (which had been renamed Claremont) failed. His marriage also broke up. Bob went to Ontario and was working in the wine industry there until he died of a heart attack.[72]

Evans Lougheed, who had founded Casabello Wines in 1966 in Penticton, was one of the most influential individuals in my life in wine when I was learning about Okanagan wines. With a commerce degree from the University of British Columbia, he had previously developed a small chain of department stores that he sold to F.W. Woolworth & Co. in 1951. Next, he built a hotel in Penticton and ran a junior hockey team until he had a heart attack in 1961. An Okanagan Valley grape grower named Tony Biollo got him interested in opening a winery, and Casabello was born in 1966. With a production facility including large stainless steel wine tanks, a wine shop, and a show vineyard, Casabello was a landmark on Penticton's Main Street until it closed after merging with Vincor in the mid-1990s.

When I began visiting Okanagan wineries in the 1970s, I always made an appointment to taste with Evans (who had his second heart attack in 1977). My first visit with him, as well as with Bob Claremont, then general manager of Calona Wines, was in the fall of 1974. The Casabello winery had a well-appointed tasting room, but there was regulatory ambiguity about whether tastings or direct sales to consumers were permitted. When visitors to the winery wanted to buy Casabello wines, Evans initially gave them a street map showing where the province's liquor stores were in Penticton. The Calona winery, on the other hand, had begun to do tastings.

---

72 *Financial Post*, December 1, 1979: "Mini-wineries make debut."

Evans employed good people, notably Tom Hoenisch, a talented, if abrasive, winemaker with an affinity for Pinot Noir. Tom influenced Casabello's decision to purchase vinifera grapes from Washington State and to plant some of these varieties in the Okanagan. When I interviewed Evans in 1974, he told me that Casabello had begun planting vinifera vineyards in the Okanagan, with the first significant harvest expected in 1975. "Hybrids are fine to a point," Evans told me, "but you don't get character in wine from hybrids. How do you produce quality wine without quality grapes?"[73] Consequently, the wines at Casabello were among the best in the valley at the time. When the first edition of my book *The Wineries of British Columbia* was published in 1994, I dedicated it to Evans and gave it to him over lunch in Vancouver.

Evans gave Harry McWatters his first job in the wine industry, selling Casabello wines. Harry became a mentor to me and then, as one of the leading figures in the British Columbia wine industry in the 1980s and 1990s, the grist for many articles and books. (We once talked about doing a cookbook together.) Harry took the lead in organizing Septober. I was first asked to be a wine judge for Septober in 1983. And I became a regular visitor and taster at Harry's Sumac Ridge winery in Summerland, either with Harry or with his winemakers.

While generally gregarious, Harry had a volatile side. I discovered this when I was working on *The British Columbia Wine Companion* in 1995. Harry had taken over the LeComte winery near Okanagan Falls, renamed it Hawthorne Mountain Vineyards, and installed Vernon-born Eric von Krosigk as the winemaker. Eric, who had spent six years at the Geisenheim Research Institute in Germany, had been the first winemaker at Summerhill winery before moving to Harry's team. I had made an appointment to interview Eric, but he was not at Hawthorne Mountain when I arrived, and the staff, while clearly embarrassed, offered no explanation. (In his place, I interviewed Michael Bartier, the assistant winemaker.) I heard later that Eric had made an error of some kind, and Harry fired him on the spot. For the rest of Harry's life, he seldom would speak of, or to, Eric.

73 *Financial Post*, September 21, 1974: "It's all a matter of taste (and money and markets and local jobs)."

Harry had a habit of running out of money. Donald Triggs bailed him out in 2000 by buying Sumac Ridge and Hawthorne Mountain and adding them to the stable of wineries in Vincor International. Harry remained involved with Vincor and its successor until he "retired" in 2008. He promptly started a new winery, initially on his vineyard on Black Sage Road. A large cellar had been dug before Harry once more ran out of money. Richter Bai's Phantom Creek Winery bought Harry's unfinished winery and completed it even more grandly than Harry had conceived.

Harry was not done. He decided to re-establish his winery, now called Time, in a closed four-screen movie theatre in downtown Penticton. The winery, which was built with the capacity to make twenty-five thousand cases a year, opened in 2018. Sadly, Harry died in his sleep in July 2019. Christa-Lee, one of his daughters and the new president of Harry's wine company, asked me to be one of the eulogists at his celebration of life. I also dedicated *The Okanagan Wine Tour Guide* to Harry in 2020. I had not dedicated any of my other books to Harry because he was a polarizing figure in the British Columbia wine industry. I could not be seen to be taking sides. Harry was such an influential figure that he locked horns with many of his colleagues, especially over his insistence, ultimately successful, that wineries be subject to the rules of the Vintners Quality Alliance. (Harry refused to drink British Columbia wines that were not VQA.) Harry believed that VQA was critical to assuring consumers that the industry had come a long way from the days when a producer could actually sell a wine that may have been carcinogenic.

Unfortunately, Harry's reputation suffered after his death. In May 2020, Encore Vineyards Ltd., the holding company for Time, slipped into receivership. Harry's daughter, Christa-Lee, outlined the situation in an email to Encore's shareholders. "In late July of 2019, I inherited the operation of the Encore Vineyards business after the death of my father," she wrote. "…It was confirmed that the Company had sustained continued losses since inception." The liabilities were $17.9 million against assets of $3.3 million. "I have worked very hard to make the best of this situation," Christa-Lee wrote, "and I am so very sorry that our investments have not turned out as my father had hoped and planned." A new owner took over Encore with an offer of $5.8 million.[74] Subsequently, the winery was rebranded as Chronos Winery.

Harry's closest allies in the industry included George and Trudy Heiss. Former hair dressers, they had moved to the north Okanagan from Edmonton to plant a vineyard in 1972. That led them to send one of their sons, George Jr., to a German wine school and to open Gray Monk Estate Winery in 1982. Throughout the 1980s, Gray Monk wines—along with those from Gehringer Brothers and Sumac Ridge—won an overwhelming number of medals at regional wine competitions. Gray Monk's advantage came from the grapes in its vineyards. Initially, George Heiss planted Maréchal Foch grapes as his red variety before deciding that it was a mediocre wine grape. For years thereafter, George was fond of declaring that Foch was not exported from France—"it was deported." George did import three white vinifera varieties from Alsace: Gewürztraminer, Pinot Gris, and Auxerrois. These made wines that were vastly superior to those made with Okanagan Riesling, Verdelet, Seyval Blanc, and other white hybrids common in the vineyards at the time.

George and Trudy were an exuberant couple who were very active in advancing the wine industry and, like Harry, unwilling to take "no" for an answer. Trudy once was part of an industry delegation sent to Victoria to meet with politicians. The venue was the Union Club, then a men's club that admitted no women. Trudy was the only woman in the delegation. The taller males clustered around her, hiding her from the eyes of the club steward as they shuffled up the stairs to the meeting room. Trudy repeated that story, with gusto, many times. She and George were very entertaining to be around, and very funny. A regulator once told George that he was not allowed to have seating in the tasting room. "What do I do if a guy in a wheelchair comes in?" George asked. "Make him stand up?" They worked so hard in their vineyards that it took a toll on their bodies. By the time they sold Gray Monk to Andrew Peller Ltd. in 2017, both had had hip and knee replacements. George died in 2021.

74 Documents in author's files.

Steven Cipes was another vivid and eccentric personality. He came to the Okanagan in 1986 from New York in search of a better environment for himself and his family. He bought a thirty-eight-acre (15.3-hectare) vineyard southeast of Kelowna and pioneered organic viticulture in the Okanagan. Since then, many Okanagan and Similkameen vineyards have converted to organic practices.

In 1992, he also established what is now called Summerhill Pyramid Winery, primarily to make sparkling wines. He invited many of his peers—along with a chartered Boeing 737 full of Vancouver wine writers, wine merchants, and restaurateurs—to the grand opening two or three years later. I was among the guests on the charter. There were so many people at the buffet that afternoon that there was no more potato salad left when I lined up for food. That proved to be a good thing. There were several cases of food poisoning from that afternoon, but Summerhill managed to keep the embarrassment quiet.

The winery gets its name from the scale model of the Great Pyramid that Steve erected next to the production facility. He was a true believer in the power that lies in the geometry of pyramids. He insisted that his wines were improved by aging in the pyramid. He and his staff conducted regular tours inside the pyramid, with the guests assembled in a circle and asked to experience the power. I was in the circle one day when my cell phone rang, disrupting the spiritual atmosphere. Steve was not pleased.

Sandra Oldfield, the long-time wine maker at Tinhorn Creek Vineyards, and Jim Wyse, the founder of Burrowing Owl Vineyards, were other driving forces in the Okanagan that inspired so many of my columns and books. Both wineries developed neighbouring vineyards on Black Sage Bench in the early 1990s when it still seemed a gamble to invest in British Columbia wine production.

Tinhorn Creek was launched in 1992 by two Albertans, oil industry executive Robert Shaunessy and his friend, engineer Kenn Oldfield. To prepare himself for the wine business, Kenn went to the University of California at Davis to study viticulture. There, he met Sandra, a winemaker then at the Rodney Strong Winery in California, who was working on a master's degree at the university and was not aware there was wine being made in British Columbia. Kenn persuaded her to join Tinhorn Creek (and to marry him). Tinhorn Creek opened in 1995 with wines measuring up to the standards of California. Ultimately, she also became president of Tinhorn Creek and then, after the winery was acquired in 2017 by Andrew Peller Ltd., she and Kenn became independent wine industry consultants.

Jim Wyse was a Vancouver-based real estate developer working on a project in Vernon in 1991 when he began to look for Okanagan winery opportunities. In 1993, he put together a syndicate of investors to buy vineyard property on Black Sage Road. The property, like the adjoining Tinhorn Creek property, had been fallow since the 1988 pullout of hybrid grapes. Jim planted vinifera and, to make the first seven vintages, engaged another respected California winemaker named Bill Dyer, who had been at Sterling Vineyards. Jim believed the Burrowing Owl vineyard was one of the best sites in Canada for growing big red wines. The style that Dyer stamped on Burrowing Owl's wines—big, ripe, and full of flavour—was widely emulated in the Okanagan.

Jim's environmental leadership has been exemplary. The winery was named for a ground-dwelling owl that had become extinct in southern British Columbia. Tasting room fees at Burrowing Owl were used to fund a breeding program to re-establish burrowing owl colonies. The winery also has protected the habitat for the rattlesnakes native to the Okanagan. In the 1980s, snakes found in the vineyards were usually killed in an exaggerated fear of reptiles which, while venomous, rarely are deadly. A previous owner of one of the vineyards acquired by Burrowing Owl once told me how his vineyard workers had nailed dead rattlers onto sheets of plywood. At Burrowing Owl, vineyard workers relocated any snakes they found—and were rewarded with a few bottles of wine for doing so. Burrowing Owl also was one of the earliest wineries to install solar panels, ultimately powering most of the energy needs of the winery buildings.

I enjoyed championing Richard Stewart and his sons, Ben and Tony, the founders of Quails' Gate Estate Winery in West Kelowna. I first interviewed Richard to profile him in my 1996 book, *The British Columbia Wine Companion.* He was a founding member in 1961 of the

Association of British Columbia Grape Growers; in 1963, he began developing a vineyard in West Kelowna. He is credited with planting the first commercially successful Pinot Noir in the Okanagan in 1975. He enlisted his sons to open Quails' Gate in 1989, and the winery eventually emerged as one of the Okanagan's premier Pinot Noir producers.

However, the first Quails' Gate wine that turned my head was the Old Vines Foch, which salvaged the reputation of Maréchal Foch grapes, hitherto known for producing dark but thin red wines from overcropped vines. In the early 1960s, Richard Stewart partnered with the Capozzi brothers of Calona Wines to develop Pacific Vineyards on Black Sage Road, planting winter-hardy hybrid varieties including Foch. Richard initially planted these varieties in the West Kelowna vineyard. He decided not to pull out the Foch in 1988 when most of the hybrids were pulled out in the Okanagan. In 1994, Quails' Gate winery recruited an Australian winemaker named Jeff Martin, who was dismayed to find most of the vines in the vineyard were young. The exception was Maréchal Foch. These plants were about twenty-five years old. At Jeff's suggestion, the yield was dropped to concentrate the flavour and body of the wine. At the time, I was running the Australian Wine Appreciation Society in Vancouver, and we invited Jeff, as the Okanagan's first Australian winemaker, to show his first Quails' Gate vintage at a Society tasting. He ended the evening with a bold red absolutely jammed with flavour. "This is how we do Shiraz in the Okanagan," he told us. We believed him until he told us it was Maréchal Foch. The Old Vines Foch remains a cult wine to this day, even if Pinot Noir has become the flagship wine at Quails' Gate.

Of the three Capozzi brothers, Tom was the one I interviewed on several occasions. To this day, the boisterous Capozzi family remain identified with Calona Wines, even though they sold the company in 1971 to Standard Brands/Nabisco. The winery was started in 1931 by a debonair Italian named Guiseppe Ghezzi. When his syndicate needed more investors, he enlisted Kelowna grocer Pasquale (Cap) Capozzi and his friends for additional funds. Cap did not play a major role in running the winery, likely because Ghezzi's son, Carlo, was the general manager. But when Carlo retired in 1966, Cap's three sons took over the winery. Their strategy for success, as Tom told me several times, was to appropriate ideas from the Gallo brothers in California, right down to copying products and packaging. Eventually, Tom went to the Gallo headquarters in Modesto and proposed that Gallo take a minority interest in Calona wines. When one of the Gallo brothers asked for majority interest, Tom snapped that he would have filled out an application if he wanted to work for Gallo. Tom told me this anecdote at least twice. He also admitted that Calona might have become an even bigger success in Canada if he had accepted the Gallo offer.

I began visiting the Calona winery in the early 1970s after Montreal-headquartered Standard Brands, who bought it from the Capozzi family, had installed several professional managers and a trained winemaker. However, the back end of this sprawling winery remained a step or two back in time. The cellar hands, who became unionized, consisted largely of men of Italian origin hired by Carlo Ghezzi. The cellar, redolent with aromas of wine and wood, was dominated by vast redwood storage tanks aging fortified wines, red table wines, and fruit wines. To a novice wine writer, the Calona winery seemed romantic. What brought me back to the winery were the efforts of the Standard Brands team to add European-styled table wines with faux European labels to the portfolio. The biggest success was Schloss Laderheim Riesling, which briefly was the largest selling white wine in Canada. Schloss is German for castle. There were no castles in the Okanagan at the time (although a castle-like bed and breakfast was erected a few years later). Calona had come up with a label replete with German typography that enabled the wine to masquerade as a German wine, but at $1 a bottle less. It almost fooled me once. I was halfway to the liquor store checkout counter with a bottle of Schloss Laderheim before I realized it was not the Mosel wine I intended to buy. The wine was drinkable, however, as were Sommet Rouge and Sommet Blanc, two of Calona's other faux European wines. Such marketing gimmicks kept Calona, and other Canadian wineries, in business in the 1980s against a rising tide of imported wines.

It also enabled Calona to foster the development of Howard Soon, one of the most capable of Canadian-born winemakers working in the Okanagan. Toward the end of his long career at Calona, Harry McWatters and I teamed up to nominate him for the Order of British Columbia because we believed his winemaking—especially in what was the Okanagan's most rustic large winery—deserved recognition. We were not successful (one never knows why these nominations fail!), but we were delighted a few years later when Howard was awarded the Order of Canada.

The grandson of Chinese immigrants, Howard was born in Vancouver in 1952 and earned a biochemistry degree from the University of British Columbia. After five years working for a brewery, he joined Calona in 1980 as a quality control supervisor. His big career break came when Calona launched Sandhill Wines in 1997, and he was put in charge of making premium single vineyard wines. The wines under the Calona label were not perceived as premium, and the winery could not shake the Italian peasant image persisting from the Capozzi days. Sandhill, on the other hand, had no such baggage. Indeed, many consumers regarded Sandhill as a sister to the prestigious Burrowing Owl winery because the two wineries had developed Black Sage Bench vineyards together. The early Sandhill labels even included the image of an owl until Burrowing Owl threatened litigation to have the owl removed. Howard had nothing to do with those corporate shenanigans. He just made incredible wines once the Black Sage Bench vineyards were providing better grapes than Calona had ever received in earlier decades.

Another excellent winemaker nurtured in British Columbia is Ann Sperling. Her Okanagan roots go back to Giovanni Casorso, an immigrant from Italy who came to the valley in the 1880s to work for missionaries. His sons planted some of the first commercial vineyards near Kelowna in 1925. Ann's mother is a Casorso, and Ann's late father, Bert, operated the vineyard called Pioneer Ranch that supplies grapes for Sperling Vineyards, the winery that Ann and her siblings launched in 2008.

Ann began making wine in 1984 at Andrés Winery in Port Moody. At the time, the only other female professional winemaker in British Columbia was Lynn Bremmer at Brights. She was then known as Lynn

Stark, having kept her maiden name to avoid confusion when both she and husband John Bremmer worked in the same winery. She was born in Kinnaird, BC (a community since absorbed by Castlegar), the daughter of a Cominco smelter worker. After completing a two-year food processing program at the British Columbia Institute of Technology, Lynn joined Andrés in 1973 as a laboratory technician. Ron Taylor, then the head winemaker, named her assistant winemaker over the objection of John Bremmer, the general manager. "John decided that winemakers were traditionally male and probably should continue to be male," Lynn recalled in 2021. "He told Ron perhaps I was not suited to become a winemaker, and he should look for a replacement. Ron stood by me, and we continue as good friends to this day." John recalled the incident differently. He told me he was not objecting, just asking whether the candidate could handle a particular job responsibility. "I did not care of which gender and that was never an issue," John told me. "I was raised with two older sisters that totally dominated me, so I thought that it was normal that the female was in charge. I had no problem in the work place." Nor was this a problem with their relationship because John and Lynn subsequently married.

Lynn left Andrés in 1980 to join John on the Similkameen vineyard that he and Robert Holt had purchased in 1978 as the basis for an estate winery. After the vineyard had been almost wiped out during the hard winter of 1978–79, the Bremmers accepted employment at the new Brights winery in Oliver, selling their interest in the vineyard to Holt. Starting with the 1981 vintage, Lynn was the senior winemaker at the Oliver winery—the first female winemaker in British Columbia and just the second in Canada at the time. She remained at Brights through to the end of the 1992 harvest. She also made the initial vintages for Gray Monk Estate Winery. Subsequently, she and John set their own consultancy and also planted a vineyard south of Oliver. One of her many services to the industry was compiling an occasional census of varietal acreage in British Columbia vineyards. I published her data in several editions of my *Tour Guide*. As well, I would report new plantings to her as I learned about them while interviewing emerging wineries.

Ron Taylor also hired Ann Sperling for Andrés in 1984 in spite of stiff opposition from the winery's vice-president of production in Ontario. "I remember the phone call very well," Ron told me. "'What have you *bleep, bleep* done'?" [the vice-president snapped.] "'You know that's not our policy!'"[75]

I first met Ann and tasted her wines at CedarCreek Estate Winery. Senator Ross Fitzpatrick had recruited her in 1991 not long after he acquired a struggling winery called Uniacke in 1986 and renamed it CedarCreek. In the 1992 vintage, Ann made a Merlot so good that the judges at the 1993 Okanagan Wine Festival competition (I was one of the panelists) insisted it be given a platinum award rather than merely a gold medal. To this day, CedarCreek's top reserve wines are released as platinum wines.

For obscure reasons, the senator and Ann had a falling out after the 1995 vintage, and she moved to Ontario, carving out a distinguished career in the Niagara wine region. "It was always in the back of my mind that I wanted to make wine here [Pioneer Ranch], because I am so familiar with every foot and every slope and every grape on the property," she told me when she returned to Okanagan winemaking in 2008.[76] Sperling Vineyards became a producer of outstanding sparkling wines, Rieslings, and natural wines.

Vintners who did not see eye to eye with Harry McWatters included Ian Mavety. He and his wife, Jane, established Blue Mountain Vineyard & Cellars in 1992 on a beautiful Okanagan Falls property they had already farmed for twenty years. They had made a good living with hybrid grapes. Ian also was president of the Grape Marketing Board, an effective advocate for growers until the 1988 grape pull-out. By then, Ian had realized the future was with vinifera grapes. He converted his vineyard to Pinot Noir and other Burgundian varieties and launched Blue Mountain with the help of a French-trained consulting winemaker. After getting VQA for Blue Mountain's initial wines, he dropped out of the program because, as he told me, the standards were

75 Exchange of emails between Ron Taylor and the author in 2021.

76 *Icon: Flagship Wines from British Columbia's Best Wineries* by John Schreiner; page 256.

not high enough. That was not empty arrogance: Blue Mountain was perhaps the best Okanagan winery at the time. I wrote a wine column early in 1998 after a Blue Mountain tasting—a fundraiser for the BC Children's Hospital—in which I commented on the winery's cult following. "The wines are as hard to get as the truth from Bill Clinton," I wrote.[77] They were not that hard to get if one ordered wines within days of their release. This was called "getting on Jane's list"—a reference to the customer list that Jane Mavety policed.

For many years, Blue Mountain's wine shop was strictly by appointment only. The winery became notorious for turning away people who had made no prior arrangements. In 2003, a forest fire burned to the edge of their vineyard before it was stopped. Within a few weeks, the joke being repeated around the Okanagan was that the fire had not been allowed into the vineyard because it did not have an appointment. The winery opened a no-appointments tasting room only after the Mavety children, Christie and Matt, joined the business. My own relations with the Mavety family have always been good, to the degree that I was able to secure hard-to-get Blue Mountain wines for two family weddings (John and Elizabeth, and Alison and Rodney). Ironically, many wineries adopted a policy of tasting by appointment in 2020 to control tasting room crowds safely during the COVID-19 pandemic. For employee safety, Blue Mountain kept its tasting room closed in both the 2020 and 2021 wine touring season. It was closed again in 2022 after the winery decided not to bottle any of the 2021 vintage. Forest fires nearby had left a residue of smoke taint in the wines and the Mavety family, which has never relaxed its high standards, decided not to release those wines.

Viticulturist Ted Brouwer taught me a lot about grapes. When I met him in the early 1980s, he was managing the Inkameep Vineyard north of Oliver. Ted was a Dutch agriculturist who had come to Canada in 1955. When the Osoyoos Indian Band got federal funding to develop a vineyard in 1968, Ted was hired to manage it even though his previous experience had been with poultry. Ted embraced viticulture with

77 *Vancouver Echo*, February 4, 1998, p. 20: "Blue Mountain wines hard to find but worth effort."

singular enthusiasm, overcoming the vineyard's chaotic start until it became of the Okanagan's premier vineyards. Ted was fired in 1986 when he fell afoul of band politics. (He was actually evicted at gunpoint but later got a cash settlement for wrongful dismissal). Subsequently, he planted his own vineyard on what is now the Golden Mile Slopes, and he advocated, without success, for a vineyard project in the Similkameen Valley. Ted and I kept in touch over the years. One night about a week before he died in 2014, he telephoned me to say goodbye. I delivered a short eulogy at his funeral.

Vera Klokocka intersected several times during my life in wine. In 1989, she and her late husband, Bohumir, emigres from what was then Czechoslovakia, established Hillside Estate Winery, one of the first of the farmgate wineries.[78] When I first visited Hillside shortly after it opened, Vera and Bohumir were operating from a clapboard farmhouse with a wine shop so small that my tasting was done outside. The tasting was accompanied by Vera's legendary freshly baked bread. The story is told that when the presumptive farmgate producers went to Victoria to lobby politicians, Vera took along several loaves of her delicious bread to help persuade them.

Bohumir's terminal cancer led to the sale of Hillside in 1996 to a partnership that included John Fletcher. The partners expanded the winery massively, ran out of money, and lost Hillside to a group of investors. The next time I encountered Vera, she was John Fletcher's partner, and they were running the new Therapy Vineyards winery near Naramata. Subsequently, they were consulting winemakers in Eastern Canada and in Florida. Vera helped me when I was writing *Icewine: The Complete Story*. I needed information on two Czech wineries that were making icewine. She translated letters with my queries to both of them and then translated their replies.

Donald Triggs, who I interviewed often for articles and books, was one of the most important figures in the Canadian wine industry. Born

---

78 Farmgate wineries were licensed by the Vander Zalm government to accommodate small vineyards which refused to pull out vines in the 1988 grape pull but were not big enough for the twenty-acre (eight-hectare) minimum required for estate wineries. Farmgate wineries typically had five to ten-acre vineyards.

in Manitoba in 1944, he started in wine in 1972 as marketing director for Parkdale, an Ontario winery. When the Labatt brewing company put together a group of wineries (five in Canada, one in California), Don became president of the group and then went to California to turn that winery around. He left the wine business to work for a British fertilizer company. When Labatts decided to sell the wineries in 1989 to their managers, Don, who had just been transferred to Britain, returned as chief executive of the wine group. Getting into the Canadian wine business then was a leap of faith. "We had no money, let's be clear about that," Don told me. "I sold my chalet at Whistler, and we all borrowed the maximum on our homes." By 1992, the group was able to buy Inniskillin and then, in 1993, T.G. Bright & Co., Canada's oldest winery at the time. This became Vincor International Ltd., which I profiled for the *Financial Post* when it went public. Later, I also bought two hundred shares and enjoyed a modest gain when Vincor, which had become one of the world's largest wine companies, was taken over in 2006 by the largest, Constellation Brands of New York.

Don and his wife, Elaine, a chartered accountant, then moved from Ontario to the Okanagan to start over by developing a winery called Culmina—as in culmination. "Retirement to me is a nasty word because it implies stopping," Don told me. "I don't think life is about stopping. It is about continuing and doing what you love." For health reasons, however, Don and Elaine in 2019 sold Culmina to Arterra Wines Canada and moved back to Ontario. As it happens, Arterra is a wine group formed when Constellation sold its Canadian wineries to the managers, one of whom—Jay Wright—had been Don's right-hand man at Vincor.

Don made a number of decisions profoundly important to the development of a flourishing Okanagan wine industry. In the late 1980s, he leased close to one thousand acres (405 hectares) in the South Okanagan from the Osoyoos Indian Band to plant the vineyards supporting Vincor. In the early 1990s, he recruited an Australian viticulturist, Mark Sheridan, to manage the vineyards. At the time, there were almost no professionally trained viticulturists in the valley, a critical deficiency. The evident improvement in the quality of Vincor's wines led others to recruit trained viticulturists. British Columbian wines showed dramatic improvement once the winemakers had well-farmed grapes with which to work.

In 1988, Don also attracted Groupe Taillan, a major Bordeaux wine company, to develop a joint venture winery called Osoyoos Larose. The objective was to bring Bordeaux expertise to the Okanagan. (He made a similar joint venture in Ontario with a Burgundian wine producer.) When Constellation took over Vincor, it showed little interest in advancing Canadian wines. The Burgundy joint venture closed, and Osoyoos Larose drifted until Group Taillan bought total control.

A major driving force in British Columbia wine has been Anthony von Mandl, the owner of a stable of premium wineries led by Mission Hill Family Estate. Born in Vancouver in 1950, he started his career as a wine merchant in 1972 when he was barely old enough to drink and looked even younger. Josef Milz, a Mosel winery owner wanting to sell wines in North America, backed Anthony in forming Josef Milz International Ltd. Anthony's initial applications to list imported German wines in British Columbia were rejected four times. Anthony went public with his frustrations, criticizing the Liquor Control Board to Vancouver Sun columnist Jack Wasserman. "That was the beginning of my reputation as an *enfant terrible*," Anthony told me in 1981.[79] He persisted and, six years later, had Milz wines listed in key Canadian markets and had begun to import wines from other European producers. Anthony then took full control of the agency and renamed it Mark Anthony Wine Merchants.

In the early 1970s, Anthony and the Milz family discussed a joint venture winery in the Okanagan. That venture never advanced, but Anthony, his interest aroused, partnered in 1981 with Nick Clark, a former Liquor Distribution Branch executive, to acquire the Mission Hill winery. Mission Hill had opened in 1966, struggled through several receiverships, and was then being run as Golden Valley Winery, owned by brewer Ben Ginter. "I really believed that someone was going

---

79 *Vancouver Magazine,* September, 1981, pp 40–44: "From Wine Merchant to Maker."

to, and would, make world-calibre wines in the Okanagan," Anthony said later.

Ben Ginter, whose primary business was roadbuilding and operating heavy equipment, was one of the most irascible people in the wine industry. I did a profile of him in December 1973,[80] when he was trying to do an underwriting for his proposed Richmond brewery. That seemed like a new definition of chutzpah: he had failed three times with brewery projects elsewhere in the country. He did have a brewery in Prince George only because he had bought it with the intention of converting it into storage for heavy equipment. The employees talked him into continuing to brew beer. He believed the big national brewers were behind many of his problems with regulators and in the market. He also sparred with unions and politicians.

"The whole strategy behind negotiating with Ben was that Ben was clearly a rogue, and his behaviour could never be accounted for," Anthony told me. "To keep him happy and at the table, you needed a bottle of Glenlivet because he wouldn't drink anything else." In the final purchase negotiations, which lasted late into the night in a Vancouver law office, the two found themselves $200,000 apart. Anthony suggested they flip a coin, each flip being worth $25,000 to the winner. Anthony won the majority of the eight tosses. The final price of the winery was $2.9 million. At the closing of the deal, Ginter was dissuaded from backing out only by a confrontation with von Mandl's lawyer so ugly that Clark and von Mandl lost all desire to open the celebratory bottle of Champagne they had put on ice. "That's the last time I ever saw Ben Ginter."[81]

"The place was absolutely disgusting," Anthony discovered when he took over the winery on June 1, 1981. There were dirt floors and burnt-out light bulbs, along with portraits of Ginter on the walls. And the wine inventory was "a catastrophe." Subsequently, he credited his father, Martin, who died in 1994, as "the driving force through all those desperate years, starting out in 1981. By 1982, interest rates hit 25%,

---

80 *Financial Post*, December 15, 1973: "An unconventional underwriting for Ben Ginter."

81 *The British Columbia Wine Companion*, p. 239.

and I had no idea of how this dream of producing world-calibre wines in the Okanagan could ever be realized."

Publicly, he maintained a brave face. "When I look out over this valley," he said in a speech to the Kelowna Chamber of Commerce in October 1981, "I see world class vinifera vineyards winding their way down the valley, numerous estate wineries each distinctively different, and charming inns and bed and breakfast cottages seducing tourists from around the world, while intimate cafes and restaurants captivate the visitor in a magical setting. In short, the dream is the Napa Valley of Canada, but much more!"[82] About twenty years later, when I was interviewing Anthony on his spectacular renovation of the winery, I suggested this had been his "I had a dream" speech. I was stunned to learn he did not have a copy, so I sent him copies of the one I had on file.

Mission Hill's best wines in the 1980s were made with grapes purchased in Washington State. The winery succeeded initially by producing apple cider and wines with faux labels (like Schloss Weinberg) meant to suggest the wines resembled European wines. Mission Hill turned the corner in 1992 when Anthony recruited winemaker John Simes from New Zealand's largest winery. John was the first winemaker from the Southern Hemisphere to work in the Okanagan. He paved the way for other winemakers to come from New Zealand and Australia, and for Canadians to study the profession there.

In his first Okanagan vintage in 1992, John made Grand Reserve Chardonnay which, in 1994, won the Avery's Trophy as the best chardonnay that year in the International Wine and Spirits Competition in London. "I can't describe how significant an event that was for Mission Hill and, in my mind, for the entire Okanagan Valley," Anthony told me later. "It was the watershed in consumer confidence here in British Columbia and in other parts of Canada that wines that we were now producing at Mission Hill were truly of top international character. It gave me personally, and all of us, a huge inspiration. It took twelve years to get there. This was really the key that we'd been searching for to open

---

82   Address by Anthony von Mandl, October 2, 1981; in author's files.

the door to what I believe, going back to my talk in 1981, is the real future for the Okanagan valley."

Mission Hill bought its first vineyard in the mid-1990s on the Black Sage Bench. As the business prospered, Anthony has acquired about one thousand acres (404.6 hectares) of premium sites in the Okanagan and Similkameen valleys. He also acquired or developed six other wineries. Key to his ability to invest has been cash generated by the alcoholic refreshment beverages developed by Mark Anthony. The best known was Mike's Hard Lemonade, which was introduced in 1996. Inspired by a comparable Australian beverage, it generated the millions Anthony spent on turning Mission Hill into what resembles an elegant hilltop palace in Tuscany. Mission Hill's international appeal to wine tourists is due as much to the magnificent architecture as it is to the wines. Once in 1999, when I was interviewing Anthony for an article on the winery rebuild, I started by asking whether Mike's was financing the project.[83] He fixed his bright blue eyes on me and said, "John, we never speak of Mike's Hard Lemonade and Mission Hill at the same time." Mike's seldom came up again over the next ninety minutes once Anthony acknowledged the role that such products played in developing Mission Hill. "You either need to be fabulously wealthy or you find another source of income," he told me. "I am staking my personal fortune on this project and on my belief and my vision that this will be my legacy."

The Mike's brand eventually was sold. But in 2019, Mark Anthony Brands launched a vodka-based seltzer called White Claw that has been even a bigger success with Canadian and American consumers. No doubt, Anthony would not discuss White Claw in any conversation involving the portfolio of wines from Mission Hill and the other wineries that Anthony owns. The wines, some selling for more than $100 a bottle, have more than realized his 1981 vision. CheckMate Artisanal Winery, for example, was launched in 2013 to make just Chardonnay and Merlot. I have awarded one hundred points three times to CheckMate Chardonnays.

83   *Financial Post*, August 28, 1999: "Winery's success spiked by Hard Lemonade cash."

Almost every winery owner or winemaker that I interviewed answered my questions freely. If I had not met the individual, I usually started by asking where and when he or she was born. I was genuinely interested in who these people where. As well, I believed it important to get personal information into my books and articles, anchoring the wineries with human details. And I was digging for colorful anecdotes. There was one occasion when a winery's owner's candor left me almost speechless. I just had time to open my notebook and turn on the tape recorder for an interview with Vasilica Nemtanu, who, with her husband, operated Constantin & Vasilica Winery, a fruit winery near Cultus Lake in the Fraser Valley. She related how the couple had smuggled themselves into Canada in 1992. I recounted the story in the third edition of *The Wineries of British Columbia*.

"Both are from Romania. Vasilica was born in 1968 into a family of sixteen. She combined work and schooling to earn a university degree in agronomy before marrying Constantin. He had been working in Holland, returned to Romania for a wife, and found Vasilica," I wrote. "In the turmoil surrounding the collapse of Romania's Communist government, they made their way to Belgium. There they arranged to stow away on a container before it was loaded onto a ship bound for Canada. They had one child and Vasilica was six months pregnant. They barely survived the thirteen-day voyage. She remembers that they ran out of water five days before the ship arrived in Montreal. They were rescued after she banged on the wall of the container. 'August 8, 1992,' she says, 'I will never forget. The police opened the container and gave us water and food. They got a translator because I did not speak French; I only spoke Romanian.' Within months, however, they had been cleared to remain in Canada." That was far and away the most vivid origin story I ever unearthed during all my years of researching wineries.

Clockwise: Ted Brouwer, Harry McWatters, Anthony von Mandl, Evans Lougheed

Joe Busnardo

Don Triggs September 2017

Twenty:
How sweet it was

The World of Canadian Wine led to a $75,000 commission (plus expenses) from BC Sugar to write the company's one hundredth anniversary history. _The Refiners: A Century of BC Sugar_ was the most lucrative book I ever wrote. It came about because I covered an annual meeting of BC Sugar in 1986 for the _Financial Post_. Noticing that the company was approaching its centennial, I wrote a note to Peter Cherniavsky, the chairman, encouraging the company to do its history. Unknown to me, he was already discussing a sponsored book with Scott McIntyre of Douglas & McIntyre. When Scott asked him who should write the book, Peter produced my letter. I signed the contract late in 1986.

I had two and a half years to complete the book, more than adequate considering the languorous rhythm of the weekly _Financial Post_. After all, in 1986, I had found time to go on three international wine tours. I was accustomed to working evenings and weekends, and I had five weeks of vacation. BC Sugar had an extensive and professionally organized archive, which made it much easier to research the project than I had anticipated. I jumped into the BC Sugar book quickly, drafting 1,900 words of the first chapter before the Christmas holiday was over. The book began with an anecdote about company founder B.T. Rogers speeding in his Pierce Arrow in downtown Vancouver on a Saturday evening in June 1906. That was intended to set the tone: he was a hard charger. The policeman who observed him did not ticket him, evidence that Rogers was also a prominent citizen. His hard-driving personality, along with the personalities of his four sons, animated much of the book, making it so readable that *The Refiners* was the runner-up (among forty books) in the national business books competition in 1989. That earned me another $5,000.

This was one of my best books and that is remarkable, since it was a sponsored book. The sponsor, by definition, makes the final decisions on the contents of the book he or she is paying for. Sponsors can emasculate and even kill books. My former colleague, Jim Lyon, once was contracted to write the history of the BC Gas Company. He was the second author hired for the job after the directors would not approve the manuscript done by the first writer. They also killed Jim's manuscript, and a book was never done, although both authors were paid. The book was stillborn because too many of the company's people had their fingers in the pie, from the public relations staff to the chairman, leaving the authors guessing just what the sponsors wanted and thus not satisfying the ultimate decision makers. Just as I had begun writing the BC Sugar book, the Archbishop of Vancouver approached me about writing the history of the archdiocese. I turned him down. Even if I had had the time, it surely would have involved many constraints about content.

At BC Sugar, I was dealing just with Peter Cherniavsky, and there was no ambiguity. At one of our first meetings, he gave me copies of histories of other sugar companies. He thought the books were dull (I never read them) and said that he did not want the BC Sugar book to be dull. There was just one occasion when he asked that some text be removed. I had included a lot of stultifying detail on the suppliers of equipment for a major refinery renovation. "Nobody wants to read that," he told me. He was right. He did not remove any detail about controversial events in the company's history, even allowing a chapter about a failed diversification during his time as president that had cost the company $1 million.

Peter was the grandson of B.T. Rogers. His Ukrainian surname came from his father, classical pianist Jan Cherniavsky. The pianist was a member of a musical trio who had once played for the Russian Czar and had performed widely around the world.[84] They were on their way to perform in San Francisco in 1915. Felix Cherniavsky, a descendant, picks up the story in his book, *The Cherniavsky Trio*. "As was their custom, they planned a series of concerts en route to San Francisco ... In Suva, the sleepy capital of Fiji, they stayed at the Grand Pacific Hotel, where they gave at least two concerts while awaiting the ship to Honolulu." Also at the hotel was J.W. Fordham Johnson, a BC sugar vice-president, inspecting the BC Sugar plantation in Fiji. His party included Mary Rogers, the eldest daughter of B.T. Rogers. In short order, a romance blossomed between Mary and Mischel Cherniavsky (Jan Cherniavsky's brother). B.T. disapproved, forbidding his daughters to marry these "fiddlers." After B.T.'s sudden death in 1918, his wife relented. Mary wed her fiddler, and Elspeth, her younger sister, wed Jan. Peter was born in 1926. He began working in BC Sugar in 1942, just before enrolling in mechanical engineering at the University of British Columbia. By 1954, he was general superintendent of the refinery. He was a decisive executive with a sharp tongue that had earned him a reputation for gruffness. We already knew each other because I had covered the company for the *Financial Post*. By the end of the book project, we had profound respect for each other.

His attitude toward the book was one reason why it succeeded. The other reason was the company's superb archive, which was in the museum beside the refinery on the Vancouver waterfront. It was open to the public for many years until the Port of Vancouver's security fence enclosed the refinery property. Sometime before the book was commissioned, BC Sugar had retained a professional archivist, Nicholas Dykes, to file and catalogue most of the significant documents from the company history (along with such personal artefacts as the lock of an ancestor's hair). It was an excellent resource, and I had full access to it.

Benjamin Tingley (B.T.) Rogers had been born in Philadelphia in 1865. His father had run several sugar refineries in the United States and, after a technical course in sugar chemistry, B.T. also went into this business; first for his father and then for a refinery in Brooklyn. He

---

84 The history of the trio is recounted in a book, *The Cherniavsky Trio* by Felix Cherniavsky, published privately in Vancouver in 2001.

spotted the opportunity in Vancouver while installing equipment at a refinery in Toronto. He was building his own refinery in Vancouver by 1890, with a $30,000 grant from the city and backing from investors including directors of Canadian Pacific. BC Sugar quickly dominated the sugar business in Western Canada, with freight costs keeping out the Eastern Canadian sugar producers while tariffs gave protection against American competitors.

I was a few months into my research when I discovered the first significant skeleton. After B.T.'s death in 1918 from a cerebral haemorrhage, the company was run sequentially by his four sons and by one non-family executive. Blythe, the oldest son, and the first to succeed his father, died within a few years from a wartime injury. The reins were handed to J.W. Fordham Johnson until Ernest Rogers, the second son, came of age. Ernest drowned in 1938 and was succeeded by the third son, Philip. His alcoholism became such a problem that the family forced him to resign. I was told of this while interviewing—and drinking Dewar's Scotch—with the fourth son, Forrest Rogers, who took over from Philip. Forrest said he had to tell me the truth, but he did not know how it could be printed. It was printed, an example of juicy details that Peter did not censor. I did not have a second interview with Forrest because he died from cancer.

Typically, I worked fast. By June—even after spending a week on a California wine tour—I had written thirty-five thousand words, and Marlene and I decided to go to France to meet Alison at the end of her course. John, who graduated from Vancouver College that month, joined us in Paris; he and Alison spent another few weeks in Europe after we came home.

It was good I had worked quickly. In October, the *Financial Post's* managers decided that the newspaper would become a daily, beginning in February 1988. The formerly languid pace was to become frantic. I did not make it any easier on myself by accepting a ten-day trip to Italy in early November to participate in judging wines at Torgiano. On the way back, I stopped several days in Ottawa to do research relative to BC Sugar in the National Archives. I had returned from Italy with a heavy head cold. Fortunately, the archive was then open twenty-four hours. Being jet-lagged and unwell, I did most of my research at night when I could not sleep anyway.

John Schreiner on the grounds of Shannon, the Rogers mansion in Shaughnessy, while he was researching the book on BC Sugar.

By the end of 1987, the manuscript was seventy thousand words long. "The last six weeks have been hell," I wrote in my diary on Sunday, March 13, 1988. "The daily has added a huge amount of extra work. It is almost as if I were working for two newspapers. In effect, I really am. On several Fridays I have come home from work (once at noon) so exhausted that it was unreal." I pressed on; by May, the manuscript was at one hundred thousand words. In July, I was able to get a two-month leave of absence to concentrate on the book. The first draft of the manuscript was finished by the end of August and was with the book editor. I was revising one chapter at the end of the year, but the book was basically complete. I finished reading the final proofs at the beginning of September 1989. BC Sugar paid me the final $15,000 owing—and then asked me to write a brochure that could be given to their shareholders. I was paid extra for that.

The book was released on November 30. Peter Cherniavsky called to tell me he was getting a lot of "good reactions" to it. Douglas & McIntyre released a modest number to bookstores, and it was available for the next few months. Most of the print run was delivered to the refinery; there may still be copies there.

And I was already itching for another project. Monsignor Greg Smith called with the news that the archdiocese was still planning to have a history written. Nothing developed from that conversation, and the contract eventually went to someone else. In retrospect, that was fortunate. I doubt I would have written as spritely a book as *The Refiners* under the controlling hand of an archbishop.

Late in 1984, I also proposed writing a one-hundredth anniversary history of Pemberton Securities Ltd., then the largest brokerage house in Western Canada. I developed an outline and wrote a sample chapter about Joseph Pemberton, who arrived in Victoria in 1851 as a Hudson's Bay Company engineer and surveyor. My outline hints about at least one dramatic event that I intended to develop into a chapter called "Major League". "In 1969, shortly after Pemberton Securities first acquired a seat on the Toronto Stock Exchange, the company was asked to execute major floor trades for client Jim Pattison, then quietly trying to take over Maple Leaf Mills Ltd.," I wrote. "Robert Wyman [the chief executive of Pemberton] quietly leaves a Christmas party at the Capilano Golf and Country Club and, still wearing his tuxedo, catches the midnight flight to Toronto to take command of the next day's floor campaign. He succeeds in buying the shares. Flushed with success and more than one celebratory drink, he takes the evening plane back to Vancouver. But there's a panic the next day, initiated by one eastern bank: does Pattison have the cash to pay for the shares? If not, Pemberton's faces financial collapse. However, Wyman is not a man to violate the most basic of all rules in the brokerage business: he knows his client. Pattison indeed has the money. [And] Pemberton Securities has earned respect among the eastern establishment." It would have been an interesting book, but a market downturn ended my discussion with Wyman, who decided the company would not underwrite the history. Subsequently, Pemberton was taken over by RBC Dominion Securities Ltd.

I stopped looking for commissioned projects. However, in 2014, a public relations agency familiar with the BC Sugar book, offered me a $90,000 commission to write the history of Pan American Silver Co. on the eve of its twenty-fifth anniversary. I was tempted because I had written about the company and its chief executive when I was at the *Financial Post*. But I turned it down when I realized I would have no time at all for what had become my major preoccupation, writing about British Columbia wineries.

Twenty-one:
Writing books on Wine

For a writer, at least in my opinion, the pinnacle of achievement always is to produce books. I had discovered early that I had little aptitude for either fiction or poetry. But I was capable of writing non-fiction, which, after all, is a matter of organizing facts coherently and with as much literary grace as I could manage. I am proud of my bibliography, if a bit surprised at how many books I have written.

Bibliography

Transportation: The Evolution of Canada's Networks: McGraw-Hill Ryerson, 1972.

The World of Canadian Wine: Douglas & McIntyre, 1984.

The Refiners: A Century of BC Sugar: Douglas & McIntyre, 1989.

The Wineries of British Columbia: Orca Book Publishers, 1994.

British Columbia Wine Companion: Orca, 1996.

Chardonnay and Friends: Orca, 1998.

Icewine: The Complete Story: Warwick Publishing, 2001.

A Wine Journal—CedarCreek Estate Winery, 2003.

British Columbia Wine Country: Whitecap Books, 2003.

The Wineries of British Columbia (Second Edition): Whitecap, 2004

The Wines of Canada: Mitchell Beazley, 2005.

The Wines of Canada (Paperback edition): Whitecap, 2006.

John Schreiner's Okanagan Wine Tour Guide, Whitecap, 2006.

John Schreiner's Okanagan Wine Tour Guide (Second edition), Whitecap, 2007.

British Columbia Wine Country (Second Edition): Whitecap, 2007.

The Wineries of British Columbia (Third Edition): Whitecap, 2009.

John Schreiner's Okanagan Wine Tour Guide (Third edition): Whitecap, 2010.

John Schreiner's BC Coastal Wine Tour Guide: Whitecap, 2011.

John Schreiner's Okanagan Wine Tour Guide (Fourth edition): Whitecap, 2012.

John Schreiner's Okanagan Wine Tour Guide (Fifth edition): Whitecap, 2014.

Icon—Flagship Wines from British Columbia's Best Wineries: Touchwood, 2017.

Okanagan Wine Tour Guide (with Luke Whittall): Touchwood, 2020.

My respect for people who wrote books is shown in a charming piece I wrote for the *Financial Post* in August 1993 about an author named Geoffrey Taylor who had recently died at age 92.[85] He was a soft-spoken, well-dressed man who arrived in my office unannounced in 1982 to sell me a self-published book—*Builders of British Columbia: An Industrial History.* Because I bought it, he showed up every

---

85 *Financial Post,* August 31, 1993: "Bequest will help preserve the history of business."

two years with another volume on one or another aspect of British Columbia's commercial history. Those titles also included *Shipyards of British Columbia; Timber: History of the Forest Industry in B.C.; Mining; The Automobile Saga of British Columbia 1864–1914;* and *The Railway Contractors.* When he died in 1993, he left $540,000 to the provincial archives to support the purchase of business archives. It was a remarkable gift at the time—the first time anyone had left a bequest of that sort to the archives. I thought it a splendid thing for him to have done.

My first book, *Transportation: The Evolution of Canada's Networks,* was published in 1972 by McGraw-Hill Ryerson and Maclean Hunter Ltd. A paperback only 136 pages long, it was my training wheels book. I was writing about transportation for the *Financial Post* when I was asked by Robert Perry, one of the *Post's* editors, to take on the book. Ryerson Publishing Co. had initiated a project to do five high-school resource books, with James Forrester, the superintendent of geography for the Hamilton Board of Education. I don't recall ever meeting him, but then the whole project was strange. *Transportation* was the fifth and last in the series. Shortly after I submitted the manuscript, Ryerson went into receivership and the manuscripts were returned. I got a poetry manuscript back (!), which shows how disorganized Ryerson was. I am not sure how that was resolved; I assume I sent the poetry back, and I still had a copy of my manuscript. McGraw-Hill took over the Ryerson assets and my book was published. About six thousand copies were sold, and my total royalty income was about $2,000. I was no longer daunted by the challenge of writing a book.

Just as the *Western Business* section of the *Financial Post* closed, Douglas & McIntyre approached me to write my first wine book, *The World of Canadian Wine,* which was published in 1984 in hardcover and in 1985 in paperback. The book was dedicated to my wife: "To Marlene, who denies she had to drive me home." Both the publisher and I believed that the Canadian wine industry had "come of age," as the cliché had it. "The year 1979 was a benchmark in the acceptance of Canadian wines," I wrote. "For it was in this year, for the first time, that the influential Opimian Society, a national body based in Montreal and dedicated to the importing and tasting of wines, included Canadian vintages in offerings to its twelve thousand members."

At the time, the Canadian wine industry still offered a mixed bag of wines to largely unsophisticated consumers. The turning point was not recognition from the Opimians. It was in 1974, when Major-General George Kitching, the general manager of the Liquor Control Board of Ontario, awarded Inniskillin Wines the first winery licence issued in Ontario since 1929. The partners at Inniskillin were Donald Ziraldo, the dashing son of Italian immigrants, and Karl Kaiser, an Austrian-born science teacher turned winemaker. Kitching paved the way for their wines to get on liquor store shelves. "I liked the look of Don," Kitching told me later. "We wanted to make damn sure, if he was going to be the first, that he wouldn't fall down."[86] When I was researching the book and stretching my dollars, Donald let me stay for a week at his house beside the winery near Niagara-on-the-Lake.

I travelled across the country to interview winemakers and winery owners. There were about forty wineries throughout the country, not counting multiple branches established in several provinces by the national producers. I even got to Nova Scotia, staying overnight with Roger Dial at Grand Pré Winery in the Annapolis Valley. A political scientist at Dalhousie University, he had once sold wines for a California winery and brought his wine passion with him to Nova Scotia. His personality was infectious and his wines, including a rustic red from Michurnitz, a Russian grape variety, were interesting. The Nova Scotia government then was not particularly supportive. Roger, who was not well financed, lost control of the winery. Some years later—around the turn of the century—our paths crossed again when Roger and his son started a website called Appellation America. I wrote for it for several years, reviewing British Columbia wines at the astonishing fee of $25 a wine, until this venture also failed.

In the spring of 1993, I began working of the first edition of *The Wineries of British Columbia*. My previous book on the wineries of Canada had not done that well, but the environment for Canadian

---

86 He had retired to Victoria, where he died in 1999, and I interviewed him at his home.

wine had changed dramatically since 1984. The free trade agreement with the United States in 1988 required Canada to remove the domestic preferences that formerly protected sales of Canadian wine. The attitude of the trade negotiators was that the Canadian wine industry was not worth saving. Grape growers in British Columbia were paid to pull out mediocre grape varieties; two-thirds of the vineyards were pulled out after the 1988 harvest, leaving only 1,100 acres (445 hectares) under vine.

Those who continued to produce wine refused to give up. In 1991, the newly formed British Columbia Wine Institute copied the Vintners Quality Alliance program from Ontario. When the VQA seal began appearing on wines made just with vinifera grapes (hybrid varieties were not eligible for VQA at the time), consumers interpreted it to be a seal of quality. Sales of VQA wines began growing. Then Harry McWatters, the founder of Sumac Ridge Estate Winery, took a huge leap of faith by planting one hundred acres (40.5 hectares) of Bordeaux varieties in 1993 on a Black Sage Road vineyard property that had been fallow for four years. Several others, including Burrowing Owl founder Jim Wyse, soon replanted vineyards that had formerly grown hybrids. At the same time, half a dozen smaller vineyard owners who had refused to pull out vines opened what were called "farmgate" wineries. By the time I started researching the book, dynamism was returning to the industry.

I needed a publisher. I may have approached Douglas & McIntyre; if so, Scott McIntyre was not interested since *The World of Canadian Wine* had been just a modest success. One morning I heard a CBC radio interview with Bob Tyrrell, the owner of a small Victoria company called Orca Book Publishers. He mentioned on air that he had written a guide to pubs in British Columbia. I concluded he might be a kindred soul when it came to alcoholic beverages, and I sent him a book proposal, which he accepted. Published in 1994, *The Wineries of British Columbia* was 220-pages long with seventy-eight thousand words and profiled forty wineries (two of which never opened). Ten years earlier, I had profiled or referenced just fifteen British Columbia producers in *The World of Canadian Wine*.

One unexpected reader of *The Wineries of British Columbia* was the Rev. Edwin Searcy, a United Church minister in Surrey. Early in 1995, he wrote to Orca for permission to copy excerpts from the book in a course called "To Gladden the Human Heart—The Theology & Art of Wine." He taught it that summer at the Naramata Centre, which was then operated by his church. "As a United Church minister I have a high interest in recovering a positive interest to wine in circles that still feel the lingering effects of prohibition," he explained. "The course at Naramata this summer is intended to encourage such a shift in thinking within the church." I was happy to help, especially since he planned to have the book stocked in the local bookstore.

The Okanagan Valley in the early 1990s was not as upscale as it would become when, with the proliferation of wineries making good wine, it would attract thousands of wine tourists. During my initial research trip, I spent several days in a cheap lakefront motel in Okanagan Falls, which lacked a telephone but did have a gas stove that leaked. I spent three days at the CedarCreek Estate Winery's guesthouse—a three-bedroom house with a resident mouse, which later became the winery's office. On Vancouver Island, Marlene and I stayed at a bed and breakfast that the founders of Cherry Point Vineyards ran for a year. The stay is fixed in my mind because their dog, Pinot Noir, chewed up one of my toe rubbers.

In October 1993, I noted in my diary that a University of British Columbia geneticist, Michael Smith, had been awarded the Nobel Prize. A year later, the Hainle Winery staged an event in Kelowna during the wine festival and invited me to sign copies of my new book. I was thunderstruck when one of the consumers who approached me for a signature was the Nobel laureate. Perhaps it was a sign that British Columbia wines were really being taken seriously. The book was launched formally in September 1994 at a wine festival in Whistler. I did a number of signings and media interviews over the next month, and the book was well received. By the end of October, 1,800 copies had been sold, almost half of the print run. In March, Orca, which had already given me an advance of $1,000, issued a $4,600 royalty cheque.

One of the wineries most appreciative of the book was Bella Vista in Vernon, which had been built by a group headed by Larry Passmore, the former operator of a home winemaking store. Its official opening coincided with the release of the book. As was my practice, I included wineries under development in the book as well as operating wineries. When people started arriving at Bella Vista a few days after it opened in the fall of 1994, with my new book in hand, Larry was ecstatic. In November, when I was in Taipei, he arranged to have a Vernon radio station interview me by telephone—at three in the morning Taiwan time! Unfortunately, Larry's world then fell apart after his wife left him. He comforted himself with drink; his partners abandoned him; the winery became a shambles and ultimately went bankrupt.

Another winery that opened after the book came out was Scherzinger Vineyards at Summerland. I was just finishing the manuscript when I learned of Edgar Scherzinger's plans from a winery in Keremeos. When I arrived for an interview, Edgar and his wife Elisabeth laid out their plans over lunch in their charming cuckoo-clock house. He was a one-time wood carver from the Black Forest and the style of their furniture reflected that. He had been growing Gewürztraminer since 1978. A few days later, during an interview at Sumac Ridge, then the only Summerland winery, I told founder Harry McWatters about Edgar's plans. To my surprise, Harry was enraged because he did not know. He had been buying Edgar's Gewürztraminer for one of Sumac Ridge's most successful wines. Harry came very near to suing for breach of contract. I was told later that the staff at Sumac Ridge were forbidden to provide directions to Scherzinger Vineyards, on pain of being fired. Harry subsequently denied that, but I am inclined to believe the story.

The Wineries of British Columbia was dedicated to Evans Lougheed, the founder in 1966 of Casabello Winery in Penticton. When I started visiting Okanagan wineries, no one was more generous with his time and his wines than Evans. He was in Vancouver in late September, shortly after the book came out, and I took him to lunch to present a copy. The restaurant I had chosen involved climbing a set of stairs which left him breathless because he had a bad heart. I was mortified at my thoughtlessness. He died in his sleep on December 17, 1994. I could not get to the funeral, but I decided to mark the occasion by opening my last bottle of Casabello Pinot Noir 1972, one of many wines we had had together. I found that the wine, like Evans, had also expired.

By March 1995, I was researching and writing my second wine book with Orca: *British Columbia Wine Companion*. The concept was a collection of historical vignettes and biographies of individuals, past and current, in the British Columbia wine industry. I wanted to dig out and preserve historical details, largely from private files, that might eventually be lost. When I was writing *The World of Canadian Wine*, I was surprised at the paucity of records on the Ontario wine industry. Very few winery documents had been given to the Ontario Archives, although I did stumble on considerable published material there about temperance movements and prohibition in Canada. Only the Chateau-Gai winery had a room full of records and clippings, apparently because one of the senior executives made a point of saving such things. I hope those files went to the archives when he retired, but that would also have surprised me. That experience was what led me to prompt BC Sugar to commission its history, and to write *Wine Companion*.

A trip to Toronto for the *Financial Post* editorial day gave me the opportunity to dive into the files of Lloyd Schmidt, a founder of Sumac Ridge, who by then had moved to St. Catharines and was selling vine stock to vineyards across Canada. His father, Frank, had been a long-time grower for Growers' Wines in Victoria; there was invaluable correspondence about Growers' in Lloyd's files. Lloyd also had been a wine salesman for Casabello Wines. He related a touching story about Evans Lougheed. Just before Christmas Eve in 1974, Lloyd was returning to Penticton after a successful sales trip when he encountered a blizzard in the south Okanagan. He stopped at a pay telephone to report that he was running late. Having no coins, he tried to reverse the charges— only to be refused because Casabello strictly forbad accepting reversed charges. He was livid when he finally arrived at the winery that evening, but was totally disarmed when Evans Lougheed, after reminding him of that policy, presented him with a $1,000 Christmas bonus.

The format of *Wine Companion* gave me many opportunities to interview fascinating individuals. One of the toughest subjects was Sam Baptiste, the former chief of the Osoyoos Indian Band before taking over management of Inkameep Vineyards. Clearly, Sam had never been interviewed before by a writer. I interpreted his attitude as a chip on his shoulder when, on reflection, he was just nervous. He spent much of the hour of the interview riffling the pages of a thick magazine. On the recorded tape, it sounded like a waterfall. All subsequent contacts with Sam, who became a very good grape grower, were friendly and relaxed.

The book was published in the fall of 1996, with a print run of 5,900 copies. I promptly proposed a third book to Orca, *Chardonnay and Friends*. I began working on it the following February and did much of the research that summer when I was on sabbatical from the newspaper. My motive was to occupy the British Columbia wine book real estate so thoroughly that I would own it. My strategy worked, even if *Chardonnay and Friends* was significantly less successful than the other two. The book profiled forty of the varietals used by British Columbia wineries. I provided some viticultural history, information on the producers, and on how the wines of each varietal tasted. I assumed that the burgeoning number of British Columbia wine consumers would snap up the book. Perhaps one of the book's problems was the title. The book was released in 1998 just as Chardonnay was falling out of fashion. This was my final wine book for Orca, which had decided to focus on publishing books for children.

Twenty-two:
Icewine: The Complete Story

In 2001, the Gourmand World Cookbook Awards lauded my book, *Icewine: The Complete Story*, as that year's winner in the category of Best Book on History of Wine in English. In fact, it was the first history of icewine and, to the best of my knowledge, remains so. I regard the book as a great personal achievement. Unhappily, the publisher was ineffective and the book was a commercial failure.

The book emerged from a suggestion made to me by Eric von Krosigk, an Okanagan winemaker who had studied and worked six years in Germany. In 1998, I had just released *Chardonnay and Friends*, my third wine book with Orca Publishers of Victoria. It profiled forty wine grapes used in British Columbia. Eric was one of the winemakers quoted in the book. "You should write a book on icewine," he said to me when we met at a wine event.

I plunged right in because I thought it such an excellent idea that finding a publisher would be the least of my challenges. In fact, the Toronto publisher Anna Porter kept me dangling for the better part of the year before proposing an unacceptable format. By that time, I was too far into research and writing to turn back. So I retained a Vancouver book agent, and he sold the book to Warwick Publishers in Toronto. It was not a major house, but it published *Wine Access*, a national wine magazine. The agent said that the synergy between the magazine and the book would lift its sales. That is not the way it worked out. The magazine never even ran a house advertisement for my book.

My research began by observing an icewine harvest in the Okanagan in December 1998. Sandra Oldfield, the winemaker at Tinhorn Creek Vineyards, knew I wanted to do this and called me as a cold front was advancing on the Okanagan. I was offered accommodation in the winery's guest cottage. I flew down on a Friday afternoon and was up by 7:00 a.m. the next morning to join Sandra and the picking crew in the vineyard. But the temperature stabilized just above the legal minimum, which is -8°C. Sandra called off the pick at 9:00 a.m. and did not reschedule for Sunday morning because the winery staff had a social function. Fortunately, the nearby Gehringer Brothers Winery, which had begun making icewine in 1991, did schedule a harvest. They had two tractors with light bars with which to illuminate the vineyard at night so that the pickers could remove the grapes. I spent several hours talking to the brothers about the process. Then I went there around midnight and watched the pickers for an hour or so until the freezing cold got to me. Then I spent another hour on the crush pad, observing the painfully slow process of extracting juice from grapes that are nearly as hard as marbles when frozen. Without doubt, I cannot think of a wine that is more unpleasant to make. On that occasion, Walter and Gordon Gehringer had arisen about 3:00 a.m. Saturday morning, waited around all day for the temperature to drop, and then worked through the night, managing a crew of about fifty pickers. Some twenty-five tons of grapes were picked and pressed during at least a thirty-six-hour period. "The real world and the romance [of icewine] are two separate things," Walter observed wearily.

In 1999, the Okanagan Wine Festivals Society began hosting a January wine festival at the Sunpeaks ski resort north of Kamloops. For at least the next ten years, this was called the Icewine Festival. My education began here since, in that inaugural year, there were several extensive icewine panels and tastings, a recognition by the wineries of icewine's rising stature. The Canadian wine industry was emerging as the world's largest producer of icewine. It was logical that a Canadian write the first thorough book on the wine. When I began my research,

I expected to find that a German wine writer, or even a British writer, was already ahead of me. Gradually, I understood why that was not the case: icewine was simply a niche product in Germany and Austria. In Canada, it had become our signature wine.

The first icewine was made in Canada by Walter Hainle, a German immigrant who was an enthusiastic home winemaker. The Okanagan Riesling grapes he ordered in 1973 arrived frozen, so he made thirty or forty litres (between six and nine gallons) of icewine. I met Walter in 1983 when I was doing interviews for *The World of Canadian Wine*. Hainle Vineyards did not open until 1988, but his son Tilman was already working with several cottage wineries and was planning the family winery. At his suggestion, I met with Walter on a warm June morning to talk about plans for the winery. We sat in the sunshine in front of his Peachland home for the interview and wine tasting. At the end, he sent his wife to fetch a small sample of icewine from the cellar. It was the first time I tasted icewine, and I was swept away by the experience.

Several wineries in Ontario had also begun icewine production trials in the late 1970s. Three of the four who sought to make commercial volumes in 1983 failed when birds devoured the unnetted grapes. Pelee Island Winery did net its vines because the vineyards are on a major flyway. So many birds became tangled in the netting that a conservation officer began destroying the nets. The winery saved enough grapes for a small volume of icewine (which proved difficult to sell because of its novelty) and, in 1984, deployed nets with a tighter weave. Inniskillin, where the winemaker was Austrian-born Karl Kaiser, emerged as a leading icewine producer, winning a Grand Prix medal with its Vidal 1989 Icewine at a 1991 wine competition in Bordeaux. That was one of the first major international awards for a Canadian wine. By the time I began researching my book early in 1999, Canadian icewine had an international reputation, especially in Asian markets.

After the Icewine Festival, I quickly expanded my research. Even though the *National Post* had been launched, I had time on my hands along with six weeks of annual vacation. Getting to work on the icewine book was the perfect cure for the boredom that had set in for me at the newspaper.

I began in late February, 1999, with a week of interviews with the leading icewine producers in Ontario. In May, I flew to Germany for two weeks. I began my research by interviewing Dr. Hans Ambrosi, considered to be the father of icewine. He had earned a doctorate at Geisenheim in 1953 and, after working in South Africa, returned to Germany to manage the Hessische Staatsweingüter at Eltville from 1966 until he retired in 1990. Eiswein had been made only on those rare occasions when vineyards experienced hard freezes in early autumn. In 1966, Ambrosi covered some vines with plastic skirts, protecting the grapes from rain and birds until a freeze occurred. In almost every year thereafter, the wine estate made eiswein regularly, basking in the prestige and high prices the wines earned. Ambrosi recounted this in a long and amiable interview in his sun-bathed garden, not far from Kloster Eberbach. At the end of our interview, we had lunch at the monastery restaurant, where I took a photograph of him. The intent was to use it in the book. However, the publisher used no photographs whatsoever. When the book was published, I sent Ambrosi a copy but, to my surprise, got no acknowledgement or comment from him. (He died in 2012, aged eighty-seven.)

I relied on contacts in the wine industry as well as wine literature to develop a roster of German producers to interview. For example, Brian and Alan Schmidt at Vineland Estates put me in touch with Nik Weis at the St. Urbans-Hof winery in the Mosel. His father, who owned a major vine nursery, had been an initial investor in Vineland, using that vineyard to market Clone 21-B Riesling vines in Canada.[87] Nik arranged several days of interviews with Mosel wineries and recommended the hotel in Leiwen where I based myself for several days. I relied on letters and faxes to get information on wineries that I could not visit in person in Germany.

When I had time during the trip, I began writing segments of the book on my laptop. The first draft of the segment on Ambrosi

---

87 Clone 21-B had emerged from the nursery at the Weis winery. It is now one of the best and most widely planted clones of Riesling in Canada.

was written a few days after the interview. By October 1999, I had written forty-eight thousand words and was in talks with Keyporter Books about publishing it. In fact, I had been in talks most of the year with Anna Porter, a rather imperious woman who clearly did not have much faith in me or in the project. She actually proposed that I engage Karl Kaiser as a co-author. That would have made sense from the point of view of marketing the book, but the book then would have become an authorized Inniskillin book. Some years later, Kaiser and his partner, Donald Ziraldo, did release their own icewine book. It says something about their writing ability that they lifted (with permission) the Inniskillin profile from my book for theirs. Ultimately, Anna Porter backed out early in 2000, leaving me looking for a publisher.[88]

Marlene and I set off in early September for two weeks of interviews in American wine regions south of the Great Lakes. The quality of the icewines seldom measured up to those of Germany, largely reflecting the grape varieties. Some of the wineries made wines with artificially frozen grapes, a technique that is illegal in the major icewine producing countries. Since then, the labelling regulations have been clarified by American authorities. Freezer icewine must have a proprietary name. Only wine made from naturally frozen grapes can be called icewine. I was surprised by the number of icewine producers I found; the best were Konstantin Frank in New York and Chateau Grand Traverse in Northern Michigan.

In Austria, I had fewer contacts and I asked the Austrian Wine Marketing Board for help. This was not my first trip to Austria. In late May and early June of 1998, Marlene and I were there for three weeks, anchored on the Vie Vinum wine fair in Vienna, to which the Austrians had invited me. On that trip, we also visited Salzburg and a number of other small communities. I had interviews with Maximillian Riedl, the wine-glass maker, and with Frank Stronach, the auto parts magnate, who was then at a magnificent estate south of Vienna. That interview gave me material for a major magazine article on him. I also visited a number of wine producers prior to Via Vinum, among them the

---

88 The Ziraldo-Kaiser book, *Icewine: Extreme Winemaking*, was published in 2007 by, of all publishers, Keyporter Books.

colourful Willi Opitz, a dessert wine specialist. He gave me a compact disc of the sounds of fermenting wines by varietal, telling me he had sold enough to pay for a new tractor. The Vie Vinum tasting gave me the opportunity to taste 158 Austrian wines during two days, including the first Zweigelt I had encountered. At the time, no Okanagan winery had yet begun to produce that varietal. I spent an entire morning tasting just Zweigelt wines, to become familiar with the grape and the full-flavoured red wines. By comparison, the Okanagan Zweigelts have seldom measured up to those I tasted in Austria.

The Austrian Wine Marketing Board agreed to help me in 2000, organizing two weeks of interviews with about thirty-five eiswein producers, with the itinerary so well structured that I was late for just one appointment. The Austrians even paid my hotels and loaned me a car for the two weeks, even though I had not asked for this.

I arrived in Vienna on the evening of January 29, 2000. The itinerary set out for me started with picking up my car the next day on Sunday morning, a diesel-powered Nissan station wagon. I asked for, and got, a bundle of road maps. I had two interviews that Sunday: one in the suburb of Grinzing and a second over dinner at a winery with a guest house. It was nearly midnight when I got to bed. I spent the next several days at Rust, a charming little city. The young winemaker at Weingut Peter Standl recounted a story I was to hear again and again about the vulnerability of icewine grapes to birds. The winemaker had left grapes on the vine until January 1, 2000, planning to make an eiswein of the new millennium. Snow on December 28 covered the usual food sources for the birds except the grapes, which the birds then devoured.

En route to Illmitz, a small city across the lake from Rust, my diesel car needed refueling. I pulled into a service station at dusk and, because I needed to get to the bathroom, refueled in a hurry. In error, I put gasoline in the tank. Ten kilometres (six miles) down the road, the Nissan died. I just managed to get it to the guest house at the Willi Opitz Winery. The next day, at some expense, I had the fuel tank pumped out and refilled with diesel. Fortunately, all my interviews that day were in walking distance in Illmitz.

The next day, I spent at least half a day with Julius Hafner, whose father had made perhaps the earliest Austrian eiswein in 1971. We tasted a big vertical of Hafner wines going back to 1971, with the conspicuous absence of vintages from 1985 to 1989. The elder Hafner had been involved in the scandal of adulterating sweet wines, which broke in 1985 and devastated Austrian wine sales. The elder Hafner spent time in jail for this. I ferreted out the story and put it in the book, to the displeasure of Julius.

By the end of two weeks, I had notes on 146 eisweine and probably as many, if not more, other wines. It was one of the best winery tours I ever experienced, even with occasional language issues. By the end, I had recalled enough of my childhood German to do basic interviews, if need be. After the Austrian trip, I stopped over for a week in London, meeting up with Marlene and relaxing as a tourist.

A subsequent invitation to a wine festival in Vienna gave me the opportunity to go to Slovenia after I learned that icewine also was produced by wineries there. By this time, it had become an obsession to write as thorough a book as possible on icewine. After that, I found an opportunity to visit some wineries in Switzerland as well. I had seen a photograph of a Swiss eiswein harvest in an old book. The Swiss Embassy in Ottawa told me there was no such wine being produced there. I was about to give up when Walter Gehringer at the Gehringer Brothers Winery in the Okanagan referred me to his German cork supplier who put me in touch with a winery producing eiswein in Switzerland. Through that contact, I found five or six producers. Marlene and I enjoyed a delightful week in Switzerland. I also found icewine producers in New Zealand, Australia, and the Czech Republic. The final book was ninety-one thousand words long.

Unfortunately, Warwick Publishing was difficult to deal with. Nick Pitt, the man who ran it, was a very poor communicator. He seldom returned telephone calls or emails. He had almost no budget for promoting the book. I actually paid $478 to a publicist in the Okanagan to organize some launch events there for me. I piggybacked on a *Financial Post* event to fly to Toronto where Warwick actually had a reception for me at The Royal York. But I set up my own signing at the

Jackson-Triggs winery in the Niagara Peninsula. A few years after the publication of the book, which had had a press run of 4,500, Warwick decided there must be a demand in the United States and shipped the remaining inventory to its American distributor. When that distributor failed, I no longer had a source from which I could order books. Ultimately, Warwick itself closed.

My next wine book, *British Columbia Wine Country*, fell into my lap. The project had been initiated by Kevin Miller, a Canadian photographer who had proposed it to Whitecap Books. It was to be a small coffee table book with his wine country images and with text by Tim Pawsey, another Vancouver wine writer and a fellow wine judge. Kevin used his advance to finance two years of taking pictures in wine country. Tim, who always had a lot on his plate, never delivered any text. When Whitecap challenged him to produce, he suggested they ask me to take over the project in 2002. I was not working on anything substantial at the time. I had done some business-related freelance writing, and I dabbled unenthusiastically in public relations. I was only too happy to get my teeth into another wine book.

British Columbia Wine Country, with an initial print run of 7,500 copies and a second printing of 4,000, was a great success, no doubt because Kevin's photography was so good. It spent several weeks as number one on the BC Bestsellers List and many more weeks on that list between May and December 2003. A second edition had to be done within two years to add the new wineries that were opening. These books led me to write two new editions of *The Wineries of British Columbia*, also best-sellers.

CedarCreek: A Wine Journal was commissioned by Senator Ross Fitzpatrick in 2002 and published in 2004. I have a receipt on file for $4,000 from the winery. I considered that fair compensation for writing an eighteen-thousand-word manuscript based largely on several interviews with the senator.

In particular, there was one poignant day with him that included a visit to the graves of his parents in Oliver and inspired this passage: "The neatly-groomed cemetery at Oliver, with its shady arbour for peaceful reflection, stirs a well-spring of memory in Senator Ross Fitzpatrick.

The steep hill on the cemetery's northern border was where, as teenager, he joined other Oliver residents in stopping a raging wild grass fire from razing the town. From the arbour named in honour of his parents, he can view the headstones of his father (Raymond Ernest 1892–1955, whom everyone called Bud) and his mother (Alice Frances 1902–1986). Not far from the cemetery is Oliver's museum, a former local police headquarters that included two jail cells. Fitzpatrick once was threatened with an overnight stay in one cell after winning an impetuous altercation with another youth at a Saturday night dance. The museum has other reminders of his Oliver roots, including labels from McLean & Fitzpatrick Ltd., the packing house managed by his father."

The attractively produced book was briefly available in the CedarCreek wineshop—until it had to be withdrawn when Gordon Fitzpatrick, Ross's son, divorced his first wife, Mairead. The book had been packed with family photographs, several of which included Mairead. That was an unfortunate fate for the book, which included a lot of worthwhile history of the Okanagan. For example, CedarCreek had planted a vineyard just north of Oliver (called Desert Ridge) that the senator told me had been a zucca melon farm in the 1940s. "This forgotten vegetable, a giant bottle gourd, was a major crop in both the south Okanagan and the Similkameen Valleys for perhaps twenty years before being displaced by orchards and vineyards," I discovered with a bit of research. "The zucca melon belongs to the same vegetable family as cucumbers, squash, and zucchini. The seeds, it is believed, came to North America from Sicily, brought by immigrants whose families had cultivated the zucca for years. It arrived in southern British Columbia about 1938, to be embraced with a passion because the fruit grows as prodigiously as the zucchini but with a big difference: mature zuccas are giants averaging sixty to one hundred pounds each. Neutral in taste, the melon's flesh is a chameleon assuming whatever flavour is added in the processing. During World War II, the zucca served as the base for simulated strawberry jams and other faux confections. The melon disappeared from cultivation so quickly after 1950 that the Grist Mill at Keremeos could find seeds only in California when it added zucca to its heritage garden in 1990."

After the CedarCreek book, I began producing my tour guides. Between 2006 and 2020, I wrote six editions of *John Schreiner's Okanagan Wine Tour Guide*. The title reflected my view that I had established my brand in writing about British Columbia wines. Each book had the same format: snappy profiles (350–400 words) of wineries and their principals in the Okanagan, the Similkameen, and elsewhere in the interior. I believe the profiles enriched a wine tourist's visit. The really enthusiastic tourists got someone at each winery to autograph their page in the book. Each edition was fatter than the previous one. The first edition had 248 pages while the fifth edition had 429 pages. That reflected the explosion in the number of wineries over a decade. The books generally did well, selling between three to four thousand copies each until the fifth edition. By that time, Whitecap had been taken over by Fitzhenry and Whiteside, which was undercapitalized. The release of the fifth edition was delayed from April to August, clearly costing sales. It was the slowest seller of the five.

An even slower seller was *John Schreiner's BC Coastal Wine Tour Guide*, a companion to the Okanagan Tour Guide that was released in 2011. Less than half the print run was sold. There were several reasons why the book was a dismal commercial failure. First, a competing guide to Vancouver Island wineries was published at the same time. Secondly, not many wineries stocked the book in their wine shops (unlike those in the Okanagan). Thirdly, there was far less wine touring on the island at the time. By the end of the decade, the publisher still had more than two thousand unsold copies, or half the print run.

The other unsatisfactory experience with a publisher involved Mitchell Beazley of Britain which, in 2004, commissioned a book for their Classic Wine Library series. Books in that series involved various national wine industries (Chile, New Zealand, and so on). They seemed to want a book on Canadian icewine and I persuaded them it should be a book on all Canadian wine. *The Wines of Canada* was published in 2005 with a modest print run. Whitecap collaborated with McArthur & Co., the Canadian distributor for Mitchell Beazley, on a softcover edition in 2006 with a larger print run. The sales of both were dismal.

The Mitchell Beazley edition was a $40 hardcover that looked like a homely textbook. The cover photograph was of icewine harvesting in Ontario (the British could not get over their icewine fixation when it came to Canada). A friend remarked that the black and white cover photo reminded him of a concentration camp: the tangle of vines looked like barbed wire from which several pickers were trying to escape. The $25 Whitecap edition had a more colourful cover. I do not know what the publishers were thinking, but I suspect the cheaper paperback killed further sales of the hardcover. According to a letter in July 2007 from David Lamb, the Mitchell Beazley publisher, total sales of *The Wines of Canada* to that point were 6,683 copies. It appears that my revenues from the book totalled $8,838.14. That may have covered the expenses I incurred in travelling to Ontario, Quebec, and the Atlantic provinces to research the wineries. The paperback did not generate significant royalties.

One of my most ambitious books was *Icon: Flagship Wines from British Columbia's Best Wineries,* published in 2017 by TouchWood Editions, a small but excellent Victoria publisher. Whitecap had actually accepted the book and sent a very modest advance but, when their publisher said *Icon* would be delayed a year, I concluded I did not need them to screw up another of my books. I sent the advance back and took the manuscript to TouchWood. The title describes the concept: I selected what I believed to be the most collectible wines from about one hundred different wineries, with tasting notes and cellaring recommendations for most back vintages. The book made the statement that the wines of British Columbia now could take their place on the world stage. TouchWood produced a handsome $40 hardcover with full colour photographs. The book was well received, winning the Gourmand World Cookbook Award as the "national winner for Canada" in the New World Wine Book category. It was also a finalist in the Taste Canada 2018 awards for best wine and cookbooks.

I had not intended to write a sixth edition of *Tour Guide.* But as the new wineries continued to proliferate, I was asked again and again when I was going to update the fifth edition. What the public did not know is that Fitzhenry & Whiteside (which had taken over Whitecap

Books) had about 1,500 unsold copies in a warehouse in Ontario and no strategy to sell them. However, TouchWood's parent company has a province-wide distribution network. We purchased the unsold copies and got the remaining copies of the fifth edition on the market while I was writing the new one. And I was firm that this was my last wine book.

On the chance that TouchWood might want to continue the franchise, I enlisted Luke Whittall to write some of the profiles. At the time, Luke was working on a history of British Columbia wine and working in the tasting rooms of various wineries. The sixth edition, called *The Okanagan Wine Tour Guide,* ended up as a 510-page book with 240 profiles. Book launch events were planned for the first week of May 2020, just after the book's official release. Those never happened because all winery tasting rooms had closed in mid-March as the province rolled out efforts to contain the spread of the COVID-19 virus. Wine tours did not resume until June. As a result, there was almost no opportunity to sell the book when it was fresh. The sixth edition's sales were not as robust as we would have liked, but at least it is not a publisher's fault this time.

Twenty-three:
The photography hobby

The return mail after Christmas 2013 brought the card that I had sent to Ralph Scane with "deceased" written on the unopened envelope. A quick internet search produced his obituary: he had died in April. Ralph was a lawyer and a long-time professor and associate dean at the University of Toronto's law school. Ralph also was the person who had sold me my Leica camera many decades earlier.

Ralph and Joyce Scane lived just down the block on Old Orchard Grove when we returned from Montreal in 1969. We became friends when Marlene and Joyce began playing tennis. One evening, we were invited there for dinner. At some point, the conversation turned to photography, a growing passion of mine. I think it was Ralph—but it may have been Joyce—who asked if I would like to try a Leica. They had a camera that formerly belonged to Joyce's late father, stored simply in a brown grocery bag in their basement. The bag included two additional lenses, a light meter, and assorted other camera paraphernalia. I jumped at their offer and, after putting a few rolls of film through it, I asked if I could buy it since they were clearly uninterested in using the camera. Ralph agreed to sell it, asking only for the estate valuation of $210. It was worth far more than that, and I told Ralph he was not asking enough, but he would not take more. Subsequently, the value of Leica M2 cameras rose at least to $2,000. Now, in the digital age, the value may have retreated but not to what I paid Ralph. (Leica manufactured 88,000 M2 cameras between 1958 and 1967.)

My first camera was a Japanese-made Ricoh twin-lens reflex that I bought for $25 (in two payments) when I was still at university in Saskatoon. Unfortunately, I did not have the money for a light meter and relied on the exposure instructions that came with each roll of film. Because of that and the camera's limitations (the top shutter speed was only 1/200th of a second), I did not make much progress in photography.

My serious interest in photography began after our daughter, Maureen, was born in 1962, providing me with a subject that I wanted to document. I bought a 35-mm Canon RM single lens reflex with a built-in light meter and got deep enough into the hobby that I joined the North York Photography Club in 1964. I don't think I was a very active club member. The only reason I even remember it is that I still have one mimeographed copy of the December 1964 issue of *Cable Release*, as the club newsletter was called, with a list of the members.

The price of that first Canon was quite reasonable because, as I discovered later, it was a discontinued model and additional lenses were no longer available by the time I could afford to buy some. The succeeding Canon SLR models, the FT and then the AE, had different lens mounts. Over the years, I upgraded to those models, ending up with three AE models and various lenses. Most of my photography was done with those cameras rather than with the Leica because I preferred the flexibility of the zoom lenses. My Leica came with three lenses: the standard 55-mm lens, an ancient 90-mm lens, and a Minolta wide-angle lens, my favourite with that camera.

I did take the Leica with me to Japan on one trip. The camera was in a rather beaten-up leather case. A Japanese companion suggested I should buy a new camera while I was there. When I told him my camera was a Leica, both I and the camera were accorded much more respect. I also took the Leica on business trips but, after almost losing it twice, I learned to travel with my Canon. On one occasion when I was flying on a plane in California, I had the Leica under my seat and was almost out of the plane at my destination when I remembered it. On another occasion, I was covering a conference in Edmonton and left the camera under a seat in an auditorium. Once again, I remembered in time to go back and retrieve it. After that, I usually left the camera locked up at home, depriving myself of the pleasure of using one of the world's iconic cameras regularly.

Of the thousands of photographs I have taken, one of my favourites is of two Italian tradesmen seated under two shutters and beside two large terracotta pots. The reproduction, in a surprising large size for a 35-mm image, has been hanging in our home for several decades. It has the depth and richness of a carefully composed work of art. However, the shot was entirely opportunistic. I was on a wine tour in Northern Italy in 1991. We were on a bus one day driving from the Veneto region toward Milan. The driver pulled into a village piazza for directions, stopping just long enough for most of his passengers to leave the bus momentarily. As I walked around the back of the bus and looked across the plaza, I spotted the two tradesmen resting in what was an ideally composed pose. I had time for just two exposures—and got a perfect photograph.

Since the *Financial Post* did not have a staff photographer during the 1960s and 1970s, I began taking a camera with me on assignments as soon as I learned to use one properly. Most of the people I interviewed happily posed for a few quick shots if I needed some. Perhaps they were not always expecting me to produce a camera at the end of the interview, but there was seldom any reluctance on their part.

I moved onto digital photography in 2006 when I purchased a Panasonic Lumix camera—the first of three increasingly more sophisticated Lumix cameras I have owned. The appeal of these models is they all have Leica zoom lenses. I no longer needed to carry telephoto lenses in my camera bag. The quality of the photographs is very high. Most of the photographs in my *Wine Tour Guides* were taken with the Lumix cameras.

Since 2008, I have used my own photographs to produce an annual calendar just for our family. A small portrait appears on each person's birthdate. The subject matter each year usually has been a selection of images from wherever Marlene and I had travelled to that year: Sicily one year; Russia, Germany, Argentina, or the Okanagan wine country in other years. The pandemic stopped us from travelling. In 2020, I used images reflecting the year of being semi-locked down, including the colourful murals covering windows of closed stores in central Vancouver. In 2021, I used the superb camera on my iPhone to take images of the wild flowers along the routes of my daily walks in North Vancouver. I had Maureen lay out the images in a format that was sent to a professional printer.

The idea of doing a family calendar emerged from a gift exchange I had been doing each Christmas with Joe, my brother. We were both challenged to find gifts that the other needed until we started exchanging commercial calendars. Eventually, I concluded I could produce more original calendars by using my own photographs.

Twenty-four:
Why the Bishop got my parka

I have had numerous opportunities to travel north of latitude 60° in Canada, an interesting region of this vast country that most Canadians never see.

My Arctic adventures began in March 1975, when the *Financial Post* sent me to Yellowknife to cover the start of Thomas Berger's Mackenzie Valley Pipeline Commission. A group of energy companies had applied to build a natural gas pipeline down the Mackenzie Valley. The controversy sparked by the application led the federal government to fund a public hearing presided over by Berger. He was a curious choice (unless the government wanted to kill the project). He was a Vancouver lawyer and later a judge who once been leader of the New Democrats in British Columbia.[89] He spent two years travelling around the North and listening to anyone who wanted to be heard. In the end, he recommended a ten-year delay in the project. I was back in Yellowknife in May 1977, when the Berger Commission reported. "Berger came down hard on the Arctic Gas proposal, as expected," I wrote in my diary. Not everyone in the North agreed with him. "One chap on TV, an indigenous person from Inuvik, said he was the father of 21 children—and where would they work if there is no pipeline?" I was in Whitehorse earlier in 1977 when Kenneth Lysyk began his inquiry on an application for

89 *Financial Post*, March 15, 1975: "Sorting out the claims of pipeline and people."

a gas pipeline along the Alaska Highway.[90] This was approved in 1982. But neither pipeline was ever built; the projected capital costs would have funded a mission to Mars. The projects made even less sense when significant reserves of gas were discovered south of latitude 60°.

Perhaps my briefest trip to the north was early in 1977. I was assigned to do an article for our Defence Report on how the Canadian Forces were defending the North. It required an interview with Brigadier General Kenneth Thorneycroft, who was based in Yellowknife and commanded a force whose air power was a fleet of Twin Otters. I flew from Edmonton to Yellowknife in the morning, arrived in the dark, did my interview, and left about 4:00 p.m., again in the dark. It was a bleak day—but I got an entertaining feature that included a history of northern defence starting with the Yukon Field Force in 1898.[91]

In June 1977, I spent several days visiting Dome Petroleum's drilling camp near Herschel Island in the high Arctic, the first of several trips to energy or mineral projects in the far north. There was always an exotic appeal to trips like these, especially in the twenty-four-hour midsummer sunshine. I had earlier been in Alaska in the fall of 1974, visiting British Petroleum's operations and the oil pipeline then under construction across Alaska from the North Slope.[92] The landscape invariably was bleak, made more so by restrictions on drinking and on fraternization with the local population. In compensation, the personnel on the Dome drill ships got extraordinary food, considering where they were. The menus on one drill ship included steak, roast beef, cold salmon, cold cuts, and abundant fresh fruit. At the time, Dome operated three drill ships supported by seven supply ships, three helicopters, and a fleet of aircraft including two Hercules. However, no hydrocarbons were ever produced from the Canadian High Arctic in spite of the enormous investments made in exploration.

In September 1981, I was on a trip to the Polaris mine on Little Cornwallis Island, sponsored by Cominco Ltd., operators of the mine.

90 Kenneth Lysyk was then Dean of Law at the University of British Columbia.

91 *Financial Post*, February 19, 1977: "Forces spread thin in North."

92 *Financial Post*, November 23, 1974: "Alaska's anxious ambivalence: the pipeline changes a way of life."

The bright red, orange, blue, and black mine buildings contrasted dramatically against a landscape that is monochrome much of the year except for the brief but vivid appearance of wild flowers in summer. The almost luxurious furnished quarters for the mine workers—including satellite television and a swimming pool—was in stark contrast to the Narwhal Hotel in Resolute where our group stayed. That was a large Quonset hut with windowless rooms and a dining room with no menu (we were served veal cutlets and vegetables). The only bar was five miles (eight kilometres) away at the airport hotel. With a population of less than two hundred—mostly Inuit—Resolute is one of Canada's most northerly villages. It has been an occasional base for mineral exploration and for the military. We passed the evening in conversation with a garrulous Canadian, Major Pierre Lachapelle from Winnipeg, who had a fund of tales about the colourful characters that had passed through the village. Among them was a French journalist in a wheelchair who had come to write about wildlife but instead wrote a piece for a French trade magazine on the military's four-wheel drive vehicles. My souvenir of the trip was an Inuit soapstone carving I bought for Marlene's birthday.

Sometime in the mid-1980s, perhaps 1984, I had a fly-in visit to a gold mine about 400 kilometres (248.5 miles) northeast of Yellowknife that was operated by Echo Bay Mines Ltd. of Edmonton. The Lupin Mine, as it was called, was a shallow underground mine. I still recall walking down into the mine; but I don't recall much else about the place. After all, it was not the most scenic place either. In my article, I quoted Echo Bay president John Zigarlick Jr.: "It's a great country if you like the colour of white."

In June 1990, I was on a trip, along with some mining analysts, to what was then the Eskay Creek gold and silver deposit, located remotely in northwestern British Columbia. The property had been explored intermittently since 1932, but the substantial mineral resource was not discovered until 1986 by geologists funded by Prime Resources, a junior controlled by Vancouver promoter Murray Pezim.

The Eskay Creek discovery provided reams of good stories. One of my favourites was a column I wrote in July 1990 about a woman named

Marguerite Mackay.[93] She was president of Stikine Resources Ltd., one of the juniors involved with Eskay Creek. She was the widow of Thomas Mackay, the prospector who staked the Eskay Creek property in 1932 and still owned it when he died in 1982. He had also had a remarkable career, including being an RCAF wing commander during World War II. Around 1950, he joined a Vancouver brokerage firm where Marguerite, who became his second wife, was already a partner. She and Tom soon were devoting themselves to managing their portfolio of juniors. "I think every con artist in Vancouver was in to see me," she told me, reflecting the treatment then afforded a woman running junior mining companies. Sharing her husband's faith in the Eskay Creek property, she still controlled Stikine when gold was finally discovered in 1989. When I interviewed her, she was a feisty sixty-nine-year-old with $14 million of Stikine shares.

In 1991, *Canadian Geographic Magazine* accepted my proposal to write an article celebrating the fiftieth anniversary of the Alaska Highway in 1992. For the research, Marlene and I flew to Whitehorse in mid-May to do some interviews; then we drove from there to Fairbanks, Alaska, and returned to Whitehorse by way of the Top of the World Highway and Dawson City.

Ideally, I would have driven the highway from Mile Zero at Dawson Creek. That would have involved a two-day drive from Vancouver just to get to Mile Zero, and another three or four days to get to Whitehorse. I did not have the time, and I certainly did want to not risk my car on those roads. So in Whitehorse, we arranged a Ford Tempo rental car through my friend Rolf Hougen. The leading businessman in the Yukon, he owned two car rental franchises. We got a favourable rate—and we also had dinner with Rolf and his wife, Marg. He was the honorary French consul in the Yukon and used his consular privileges to stock his wine cellar and his extensive personal collection of spirits, which he displayed on bookshelves in their living room. On his many business trips, he had collected almost every potable spirit known to man. There was, for example, a bottle of a clear spirit in which an eviscerated snake

93 *Financial Post*, Standing tough pays off for Stikine's gritty grande dame, July 2, 1990.

254

was floating. It was from China. Rolf and perhaps another guest had consumed some because a few ounces were missing. I passed on the opportunity to taste it, much preferring the Meursault and the Sancerre wines he opened for us.

The Alaska Highway was built initially as a military supply route against the threat of Japanese invasion of Alaska. The original highway was about 1,700 miles long (2,736 kilometres). Significant improvements, including straightening a road that was pushed hurriedly through muskeg, has reduced it to about 1,400 miles (2,253 kilometres). I got a lot of detail on the current highway from a civil servant, and I also interviewed an old-timer, Orval Couch. A mechanic, he had come north from Timmins to work on the road in 1942. He was eighty when I met him, and his anecdotes tended to drift in different directions but added colour. I knew from my BC Sugar experience that the memories of old-timers are not always reliable. We also spent a day in the Yukon Archives before proceeding with our drive west.

We had chosen exactly the right time in the season, experiencing good weather and days so long that we could still read by natural light at 11:00 p.m. Traffic was comparatively light and finding accommodation was easy. We generally chose bed and breakfast stays for our entire trip. Perhaps the best was in Fairbanks because the guests, who all gathered for Sunday breakfast together, were interesting and well-travelled companions. There were stunning views along the highway, which parallels the St. Elias Mountains to the south. Again and again, I would stop to take photographs and just to marvel at the wonder of it all.

The Top of the World Highway runs roughly two hundred miles (321 kilometres) from Tok, Alaska, north to Chicken, Alaska. The highway, which was gravel, is so named because it runs along an almost endless ridge, with breathtaking views in all directions. The landscape was barren. There was little traffic and little habitation. Fortunately, our rental Ford Tempo held together. At Chicken, the border community, we took the ferry across the Yukon River from which the ice had just broken. An important tourist destination, Dawson City has worked hard to retain the flavour of its Gold Rush glory, including Diamond Tooth Gertie's gambling house and vaudeville hall. After a few days taking in the character of Dawson City, we drove back to Whitehorse, this time five hundred kilometres (311 miles) on pavement. We stayed there a few more days before flying home. On one of those days, I was browsing a display of well-crafted and colourful paintings in a local gallery. An older gentleman nattily dressed in a tweed suit came in. When he left, the clerk told me that had been Ted Harrison, the artist, who was on his way to a Rotary meeting. The idea of an artist in Rotary seemed an oxymoron to me—but this was the Yukon, after all. My big regret was not buying one of his paintings, which were still affordable then.

One of my last trips to the North was a visit in about 1998 to the Snap Lake diamond discovery in the Northwest Territories. I had been covering the diamond discoveries because Dia Met Minerals, the company that made the first discovery, was listed on the Vancouver Stock Exchange and was run by Charles Fipke. I interviewed him over dinner once, and I may have spoken to him other times. Initially, his story seemed improbable: he was a geologist from Kelowna who had spent years pursuing his theory of how to find diamond pipes. Dia Met Minerals, which he listed on the VSE in 1984, announced the discovery of Canada's first diamond pipe in May 1991. Dia Met may have been the most successful mineral exploration company ever listed on the VSE.

The Snap Lake discovery occurred in 1997. Winspear Diamonds Inc., which controlled the property, was taken over for $305 million in the summer of 2000 by DeBeers; in late 2000, DeBeers also took over Aber Resources, which also had a stake in the Dia Met property. In the summer of 2000, I wrote a profile of DeBeers and its burgeoning diamond exploration projects in Canada.[94] My visit to Snap Lake lasted less than a day and left no vivid memory, perhaps because there is nothing much for a layman to see at such an exploration site other than a big hole in the earth. But it was exciting to report on the beginning of Canada's diamond industry.

Coincidentally, my interest in Aber intersected with my interest in British Columbia wineries. The president of Aber was Grenville

94 *Financial Post*, August 7, 2000: "Merchant of Diamonds."

Thomas, a Welsh-born mining engineer who, with his geologist daughter, Eira Thomas, specialized in exploring mineral properties in the Northwest Territories. The Thomases and their partners staked property around the Dia Met property and also discovered diamond-bearing pipes. Some years later, I found a reason to interview Eira, who now was running a mineral exploration company of her own. At the time, she was, or had been, in a relationship with Vancouver broker Eric Savics, the owner of Tantalus Vineyards in East Kelowna. Eric had acquired Tantalus in 2004. There was a rumour, which turned out to be untrue, that Eira's sister, Lyndsay, was to become the Tantalus winemaker. Lyndsay had studied winemaking at Okanagan College and then at Christchurch in New Zealand. On returning to Canada, Lyndsay and husband Graham O'Rourke in 2007 developed their own winery, Tightrope Winery on the Naramata Bench. Both Tantalus and Tightrope are very fine producers.

In late May 2000, I was invited by Miramar Mining Corp. to join a small group, mostly analysts, to visit its Hope Bay gold deposit in Nunavut, three hours by air north of Yellowknife and right on the shores of the Arctic Ocean.[95] We were each given warm parkas. They were welcome because the weather in late spring that far north still is quite brisk. We spent two nights in fairly basic accommodation at one of Miramar's exploration camps, called Boston Camp. I had time one afternoon to walk out on the tundra to take photographs of a majestic Inukshuk on a hilltop about a mile from the camp. That photograph, framed, has hung for years on a wall in our living room.

After I retired, Miramar thought I might be able to do some public relations work for them and paid me to do a report with some recommendations. Nothing came of it. Miramar and the Hope Bay deposit were acquired in 2007 by Newmont Mining Corp. and then in 2013, by TMAC Minerals, a Toronto gold producer which started producing gold there in 2017.

The Miramar parka remained in storage in our basement almost as long as it took TMAC to finish developing the deposit. It was too warm

....

95   *Financial Post*, June 21, 200o: "Hope in that there tundra."

to wear in Vancouver; I wore it once, on a winter trip to Saskatchewan. I had the opportunity to give it a home in 2013 when a priest named Mark Hagemoen was named bishop of the Diocese of Mackenzie-Fort Smith. He had grown up in North Vancouver, and he and his parents were parishioners at Holy Trinity, our parish. I heard a radio interview with Mark after his appointment, in which he remarked he would need a warm parka for his new posting. So I arranged to get my Miramar parka to him. Subsequently, he became bishop of Saskatoon, where the parka still would have been useful.

Twenty-five:
Father MacMahon and friends

Without doubt, the Roman Catholic faith influenced me strongly. My journey in the faith has gone from the naïveté of an altar boy to a skeptical, but still involved, adult. I was born into the religion: the region in Austria where both my parents had their roots had been populated in the eighteenth century by Catholics from Southern Germany. There must have been some Lutherans in the mix, since my maternal grandmother was Lutheran. In general, the Reformation had resulted in Northern Europe being Lutheran and Southern Europe being Catholic.

My parents were not militant about their Catholicism. It was part of their social fabric, and they handed it to their children. Later, after my brother, Joe, divorced Carol, his first wife, he became a Lutheran because that was the religion of Sandra, his second wife. In any event, the Church would not have allowed him to remarry if he had remained a Catholic even if he had sought an annulment from a marriage tribunal.[96]

---

96 When Alison married Rodney, who was divorced, they applied to the Diocesan Marriage Tribunal. The process was totally unhelpful. The application lingered for months, grinding to a halt when the Tribunal asked for a statement from Rodney's former wife. He did not even know where she was living. Rodney, who has no interest in religion whatsoever, and Alison had a civil marriage and Alison stopped attending Church. The Marriage Tribunal also would have driven my brother from the Church. He just saved them the trouble.

I became an altar boy as soon as I was old enough. I attended catechism classes at St. Joseph's Church in Indian Head. In effect, this was a two-week camp every summer taught by nuns sent in especially for the purpose. The parish priest, Father Missere, also was involved, mostly playing sports with the boys. We had Mass every morning and Benediction every afternoon, in a church hazy with incense and the summer heat.

St. Joseph's was a small, sleepy parish until the bishop sent in Father Charles McMahon, an energetic and strapping Australian, in 1949. Unlike the previous priest, Father McMahon was not reluctant to ask for money often from the pulpit, even though some parishioners gave reluctantly. One Sunday, he railed against those who only put twenty-five cents into the collection plate, saying that quarters "stink". Later, one parishioner said he had kept his quarter in his pocket and spent it on a brick of ice cream after church. "The ice cream didn't stink," he was quoted as saying.

Father McMahon's sermons, which he delivered with his eyes closed, were long and repetitious, often revolving around three famous converts to the Church, including John Henry Cardinal Newman. I never understood what relevance they had to a congregation of Saskatchewan farm folk, none of whom were converts unless they did so to marry.

Still, Father McMahon's ability to preach led me to ask him to coach me in public speaking. In the 1950s, oratorical competitions were held in many of Saskatchewan's high schools. The first time I competed, I was so nervous that I grasped the back of a chair in a death grip. Father's coaching gave me the confidence to stand up without that crutch and to recite a memorized speech. I believe I won $100.

Father spent the first ten years after his 1916 ordination in Australia. He spent the next six years in the United States, including Los Angeles where he made friends in Hollywood. In 1932, he came to the Archdiocese of Regina. The obituary that his sister sent me does not explain the circumstances of that move—but he remained in Saskatchewan until he retired. He was posted to St. Joseph's Parish at Indian Head in 1949, where he soon set about raising money for a new church. The church was built in 1960 by volunteers, including my father, and opened in 1961. The old church was sold to the much smaller Lutheran congregation.

When he retired in 1966, Father went back to Australia to live with his sister in Sydney. His was a peripatetic retirement, spent visiting his favourite altar boys around the world. On various occasions, we would be surprised by a phone call from the airport: Father was in town and needed a place to stay for several days. On occasions, the call came in the middle of the day, and Marlene drove to the airport to fetch him. He was a voluble dinner guest for the next few days, with our house as a base from which he visited other acquaintances. He died in 1980, age ninety-three.

When I went to the University of Saskatchewan, I enrolled in St. Thomas More College (STM), the liberal arts school on campus run by Basilian priests. The Congregation of St. Basil had been founded in 1822 in France, dedicated to education. The priests at STM also were qualified academics who taught university courses, including history, philosophy, psychology, and French. Father O'Donnell, the principal of STM, also taught English. My favourite was Father Montague, the chaplain. He was a gentle person, easy to take one's troubles to, as I did once when the pressures of university were wearing me down. The Basilian approach to Catholicism was in tune with the liberalism introduced by John XXIII, who became pope in October 1958, a few months after I graduated from university.

Swept along perhaps by the excitement of Vatican II, I became a member of the Regina chapter of the Third Order of St. Francis early in 1959. Joe Gattinger, my deeply religious brother-in-law, may have recruited Marlene and me. A lay branch of the Franciscans, it was run from the modest Franciscan monastery that then existed in Regina. At one point, I edited the newsletter for the Third Order. I still have warm memories of cranking it out on a Gestetner machine in the monastery while listening to the brothers chant the orders.

In 1984, I volunteered to work in the media room in Vancouver during Pope John Paul II's visit to Canada. My role was minor, but I wanted to participate in the visit by a pope who was then at the height of his celebrity. There was an event at BC Place; Alison and John both attended. I did not because no tickets were allocated to my group of volunteers. Like so many others, I was wowed by his charisma and did not appreciate until much later how aggressively he undid some of the liberal reforms of John XXIII. I thought it was cynical of Pope Benedict to canonize both of these popes at the same time. While John XXIII was, and still is, widely beloved, John Paul II was a contentious choice for sainthood. But the critics appeared to have swallowed their bile, not wanting to diminish John XXIII's elevation.

The spiritual inspiration from the Basilians and the Franciscans has sustained an interest in the faith, even when it flagged somewhat in later years. Vatican II taught Catholics not to accept everything by rote. When I was a child in catechism, I was taught that there was only One True Church, and we belonged to it. In time, the arrogance of that became self-evident. One is now inclined to ask whether any religion is true, given the example set by some of the adherents.

None of our children remained active in organized religion even when all took Sunday School lessons; John even took his high school at Vancouver College, a school run by the Christian Brothers. One Saturday early in October 1973, I took John on what was surely our first hike; it lasted four hours. We went up the side of Grouse Mountain and came across a rock on which someone had written: "Prepare to meet thy God." John asked me to read it and then remarked that: "God doesn't live on a mountain." I asked where God does live. "In the city," John said. I should have known that he would grow up a skeptic.

Twenty-six:
The business beat

What made my journalism career engaging were the interesting business stories and business people that I reported on.

Without doubt, few compared with Edgar F. Kaiser Jr., who died in 2012, aged sixty-nine, after a life filled with drama—some of which I reported. He was the grandson of Henry Kaiser and son of Edgar Kaiser Sr., who had made their first fortune building ships for the American navy during World War II. Kaiser Resources Ltd., the family company, had invested in a major coal mine in southeastern British Columbia to supply steel-making coal to Japanese and Korean steel mills. When an unexpected collapse in coal prices in the early 1970s almost bankrupted the business, the family sent young Edgar to Vancouver in 1973 to turn it around. I chronicled his brilliant turnaround in several *Financial Post* articles, starting with a lengthy piece published November 16, 1974. It detailed some of the technical and operational issues that were being overcome. As well, depressed coal prices had begun to recover.[97] Edgar, who was then 32, was easy to write about because he was so charismatic. Henry Volkmann, one of the coal mine executives told me, with some sincerity, "If Kaiser Resources found coal or oil on the moon, and Edgar asked for volunteers, we'd all go."[98]

....

97 *Financial Post*, November 16, 1974: "Japan ups coal prices and Kaiser lifts off."

98 *Financial Post*, September 8, 1979: "Edgar Kaiser gets the job done his way."

In January 1980, I did a profile of Edgar for *Kanata*, the inflight magazine for CP Air. Before that decade was over, he had built the business into the largest coal producer in Canada (coal prices having recovered). After he diversified into oil by buying the Canadian assets of Ashland Oil, he sold nearly all the assets to the British Columbia Resource Investment Corp. (BCRIC) in a negotiation where he persuaded the chief executive of BCRIC to pay a big premium. BCRIC was a public company created by the British Columbia government. It had raised at least $500 million in a wildly oversubscribed public offering. The shareholders pressed BCRIC to invest the funds, and Kaiser took advantage of that atmosphere to cash in on Kaiser Resources. BCRIC later took big write-downs when oil prices collapsed.

Kaiser had kept some oil exploration assets in the United States. When that business went sour, he walked away from debts owed to the Bank of Montreal. That backfired on him when he was running the Bank of British Columbia, where he had become chief executive in 1984. Then eighteen years old, the bank almost went under due to inept lending to offshore clients, and to the failure of some of its major clients in British Columbia. Kaiser rescued the bank by raising $200 million, including $8 million of his own resources. I did a rather glowing profile of him at the time. The article also delved into another of his turnarounds: in 1981, he bought the ailing Denver Broncos professional football team for US$33 million and revived the team by acquiring star quarterback John Elway from the Baltimore Colts. That team was owned by a friend of Kaiser's father, and Kaiser charmed him into making the trade. In our interview, Kaiser left no doubt he had taken advantage of his father's friend. He also admitted to being bored with football, after having doubled his money when he sold the team in 1984.

Two years after Edgar took charge, the Bank of British Columbia was in trouble again. The failure of two small banks in Alberta had made depositors nervous about regional banks, including the Bank of British Columbia. Edgar's strategy of growing the bank out of trouble by expanding with branches on the Prairies was not succeeding. He needed capital from the other Canadian chartered banks to protect the Bank of British Columbia's liquidity. Because he had walked away earlier from the Bank of Montreal, the Canadian banks refused to keep him afloat. Finally in 1986, the Hong Kong and Shanghai Bank took over the Bank of British Columbia's operations. Because the bank's liabilities were greater than its assets, the Canadian Deposit Insurance Corp. had to inject $200 million into the bank before the Hong Kong bank would take it over. Kaiser was disgraced within the business community. Several shared negative stories with me. Edwin Philips, then a recently retired chief executive of a pipeline company, said Kaiser was the "most devious" businessman he had ever dealt with.

The final episode in his career on which I reported was his investment in a potato chip vending machine company in the early 1990s. At the time, I was writing about junior companies on the Vancouver Stock Exchange. These included companies operating or proposing to operate such vending machines. Yukon Spirit Mines Ltd., as one example, set up a vending machine in the summer of 1993 in the Arbutus Room of Vancouver's Four Seasons Hotel and invited stock brokers to a reception. The pervasive aroma of deep frying and French fries wafted through the hotel even as the machine kept breaking down. That was not unusual for these vending machines. I profiled the industry in a magazine article that summer.[99] Patents had first been filed in 1980 for the concept. Mr. Crispy's Corp of Downsview, Ontario claimed to have deployed five hundred or so operating units in Asia and Europe. Caltec Investments Ltd. of Calgary was trying to develop a machine. H.J. Heinz Co. had spent $20 million developing two designs. The investor behind Yukon Spirit was a Miami investor trying to salvage the money he had put into the project. He complained to me it was taking longer to develop a working unit than the three years it took the Manhattan project to build the atom bomb.

Another company working on a vending machine for fries was Sedona Industries Ltd. A predecessor vending company, called Tub O' Spuds, had been developed about 1980 by a food technologist in Delta. When he ran out of money, he sold the technology to Sedona. It began manufacturing its vending machines in Minneapolis, having raised money with a Toronto Stock Exchange listing. I first wrote about

99   *Financial Post Magazine*, July/August 1993, p. 41: "This spud's for you."

it in December 1991. It was then trading over the counter, having run out of money in 1989. It attracted my attention when it did a $945,000 private placement with Harvard Capital Corp, described as a Vancouver merchant bank. The individuals contributing to the placement included Sam Belzberg, investment dealer Peter Brown, and Edgar Kaiser. Sedona was folded into Harvard International Technologies, with Kaiser sinking $2.6 million into the company. The vending machine, now called Spud Stop, was the size of a large refrigerator. Kaiser demonstrated one unit in his Vancouver office by having it make a tasty serving of fries for me. Kaiser was convinced there was big money to be made. "Our [business plan] forecast looks like Disney World, it makes so much money," he told me. He convinced Pohang Iron & Steel Co. of South Korea to build the plant to manufacture the Spud Stop. He brought high-profile investment bankers into the business. John Turner, who was briefly Canada's prime minister in 1984, agreed to be Harvard's chairman. Even with all that engineering and business talent behind it, the Spud Spot was a flop, and Harvard failed in 1994.

There were other sides of Kaiser that I just got to read about, including a messy divorce from his second wife. He was so hard-nosed that a judge had to order him to release her snow tires to her. He was a bottomless pit of good copy.

In the late 1970s, the *Financial Post* did a series on leading families in Canadian business. I worked on two: the Mannix family in Alberta and the Woodwards in Vancouver. The famously private Mannix family had built a major group of companies throughout the twentieth century, but they were not in the habit of giving interviews to the press.[100] I did talk to some of their staff, and there was information on the public record. As well, I had enough contacts in the Calgary business community that, with diligent work, I put together a profile. The family, of course, knew I was working on the article. The girlfriend of a friend of mine in Calgary was a public relations staffer for Loram Corp., the major Mannix company, and she told me how the family reacted when the *Financial Post's* article was published.

100 *Financial Post*, November 26, 1977, page 40: "The Mannixes: rich, private, dynastic, and inaccessible."

I recounted it in my diary on November 30, 1977: "When FP hit the street in Toronto, Mannix lawyers there phoned Calgary with the news. In Calgary, there was an unsuccessful scramble to find copies. So the people at Loram set up *two* tape recorders (should one fail) and had the story read from Toronto. The tape was flown down to Palm Springs where Fred [Mannix Sr.] listened to it—and approved." It must have been a stressful time for the Mannix family: the *Edmonton Journal* a few weeks later ran a three-part series on the Mannix family, once again without interviews.

The Woodward family was much more accessible. Previously, they had sponsored a rather good history written by a long-time employee.[101] In late January 1978, I interviewed Chunky Woodward, who was then running the company. His executive offices were on the fifth floor of the company's department store in Gastown. That meant walking through various merchandise departments to get there. The company had been started by Chunky's father, Charles, in 1882, and at one time was the leading, and widely beloved, department store in Western Canada. Chunky seemed more interested in the Douglas Lake Cattle Company, his ranch in the British Columbia interior, leaving much of the retail management to Woody McLaren, his brother-in-law, and presumed heir apparent. Chunky also had two sons involved, and Woody was forced out in 1985. My article in May 1988 implied that the sons might not have what it took to keep the company going. The lede read: "The hard question facing department store heirs John and Kip Woodward is whether there will be a company for them to take over." John, with advice from a New York consultant, had adopted a merchandizing strategy that was too radical for traditional customers of the department store. In 1993, Woodward's Ltd. went bankrupt.[102]

101 *The Woodwards: A family story of ventures and traditions* by Douglas E. Harker; Mitchell Press, 1976.

102 Some years later, Marlene and I were at a Vancouver Symphony Orchestra reception when another attendee struck up a conversation. He introduced himself as Tony Antonias, a former copywriter for CKNW radio. It seems the crowning achievement of his career was authoring the popular jingle that Woodward's used to promote its $1.49 bargain days. The Hollywood Advertising Club named it one of the world's best broadcasting advertisements.

I wrote about a number of western-based retailers over the years. Joseph Segal generated a lot of copy when he was president of Fields Stores, which he sold to Zellers. Subsequently, he started a retailer called Mr. Jax. I recall once interviewing him and discovering his interest in wine. I actually gave him a bottle of a Cabernet Sauvignon I had made and received a complimentary note from him. I assume he was just being generous; I am sure he routinely drank better wines because he lunched almost daily at the Four Seasons Hotel. In 1979, I wrote a profile of Army & Navy Department Stores Ltd.[103] It was then headquartered in Regina, and the president was G.C. Kennedy, a good interview. It was one of Canada's original discount stores. I quoted an unnamed competitor who said Army & Navy "tends to cater right at the babushka trade." When the chain finally closed in 2020 after 101 years, the president now was Vancouver socialite Jacquie Cohen, the granddaughter of the founder. The company had outlasted most of its tonier competitors.

Arthur Child, who was the chief executive of Burns Foods in Calgary when I first interviewed him in April 1974, was a renaissance man. Born in Britain, he was an ardent monarchist and kept a portrait of the Queen in his office. He was a military history enthusiast who admired Field Marshall Erwin Rommel and knew his widow. He once vacationed by following Alexander the Great's route march. He was an art lover; when he had earlier been president of Intercontinental Packers in Saskatoon, he had helped the family of Fred Mendel (which owned the meat packing house) to develop the Mendel Art Gallery. Mendel had begun sponsoring young artists after World War II. In the mid-1950s, he was hanging the paintings on the second floor of the meat packing plant. I knew that because, in my second year at university, I took an art appreciation course that included a field trip to see Mendel's collection. The aromas of sausage making from the floor below added nothing to the appreciation of the paintings. That explained why Mendel relocated his collection to a proper gallery.

103 *Financial Post*, April 28, 1979: "The bargain hunters keep Army & Navy stores going strong."

Art Child was ticked off because he got no credit for his role in developing it. In his own collection, Child owned forty watercolours by Robert Hurley, then a well-known Saskatchewan artist. On the weekend after our interview, he flew Hurley—then in his nineties—to a Saskatoon retrospective showing scheduled deliberately to clash with a Mendel gallery event.[104] I learned subsequently from a posting in Wikipedia that Child, who died in 1996, had been a board member of the Canadian South African Society, a front group that supported apartheid. My interview with him, however, never strayed into politics.

He was vain about his bald head. Published photographs of him always had him wearing a hat. But at the end of our interview, I produced my camera and asked him to stand behind his desk. The photograph I snapped was one of very few in which he was hatless. Perhaps, as happened to Karsh, the photographer, when he whipped the cigar from Winston Churchill's mouth to take a portrait, my subject did not have time to object. Of course, my portrait was nothing near as fine as the Karsh image of Churchill. (In March 1978, Marlene and I attended a lecture by Karsh at the University of British Columbia; that was near the end of his illustrious career.)

The public relations executive representing Burns at the time, Jack Robbins, was equally larger than life. He once drove me to Lethbridge to visit a Burns subsidiary, entertaining me with stories from his life. He had been in the Royal Air Force during the war, achieving the rank of Air Commodore by 1945. He was then seconded to the British occupation force in Berlin for five years. When a British military policeman found him living in a cheap hotel, he arranged to move Jack to a comfortable rent-free apartment that the policeman had commandeered. "*We* won the war, didn't we?" Jack was told.

Funeral home operator Ray Loewen enabled me to earn a Jack Webster award for business journalism in 1999. The Webster awards, named for a legendary Vancouver broadcaster, are administered by the Jack Webster Foundation, which was set up in 1986 on his retirement. The awards are the most prestigious in British Columbia journalism.

---

104 This is based on an extensive entry in my personal diary.

My *Financial Post* article, "In the palm of Ray's hand," published June 2, 1999, was my only entry in the Websters. As a footnote, I wrote much of it while I was at home with influenza (the last time I remember having the flu).

I had written about his Loewen Group often during its spectacular rise and equally spectacular fall. Ray was a compelling character, a graduate in theology who started Loewen Group board meetings with a prayer. Born in 1940, Ray grew up in Steinbach, Manitoba, a Mennonite community where his father ran a funeral home. He took over the business when his father died in 1961. He owned fourteen funeral homes in Western Canada by 1975 and then, after forays into politics (as a Social Credit member of the British Columbia Legislature) and into real estate development, began acquiring funeral homes in earnest in the early 1980s. He soon had the largest funeral home company in Canada. In 1990, Loewen bought a group of funeral homes in Mississippi. One of the sellers kept a funeral insurance business, and he sued when Ray moved into the same business. A Mississippi jury awarded damages of US$500 million. The award was ludicrous; the suit had only asked US$5 million in damages, but the jury did not like the brash Canadian.[105]

Ray Loewen could not raise the bond that would have allowed him to appeal, so he settled for US$165 million. That depressed the Loewen Group's stock price, which attracted a takeover bid from Service Corp. International, the world's largest funeral home operator. Loewen and Service Corp. had competed for a number of years to take over funeral homes and cemeteries; Loewen eventually owned almost nine hundred funeral homes. Loewen successfully defeated Service Corp.'s takeover bid in 1997.[106] Because Loewen over-expanded and overpaid for assets, the company could not service its debts. The board deposed Ray Loewen in April 1999, and the company filed for bankruptcy protection later that year. The restructured Loewen Group emerged in 2002 as Alderwoods Group and was ultimately taken over by Service Corp. When Marlene and I were planning our funerals in 2018, we took

---

105 I did a major profile on the Mississippi fiasco. Published in the *Financial Post* on November 11, 1995, it had the cheeky headline "Stiffed!".

106 *Financial Post*, January 11, 1997: "Ray Loewen busts his ghost."

pains to find an independent, family-owned company not controlled by the Service Corp.

Vancouver never was short of improbably colourful individuals. Nelson Skalbania, for example, was one who enabled me to get one of my better scoops as a journalist. Born in 1938, he had success as a consulting engineer before he took up a career as a wheeler/dealer, both in sports and in real estate. When he owned the Indianapolis Racers franchise in the World Hockey Federation, he managed to sign a young Wayne Gretzky and then flipped him to the Edmonton Oilers. Long after the Racers franchise evaporated, the season ticket holders sued Skalbania for $20 million because they had lost the chance to watch Gretzky play.

I heard about that suit in 1983, when I attended a creditors' meeting, representing *Financial Post* when Skalbania filed for personal bankruptcy over $30 million in debts. Journalists seldom get into meetings like that. However, the receiver had sent a big binder to all of the creditors, detailing what was owed to them. One binder arrived on my desk at the *Financial Post* because Skalbania owed us for an unpaid subscription. I managed to sign into two creditors' meetings before the receiver cut me off. At the end of the first, I came out of the meeting at the Hotel Vancouver to find the foyer full of other journalists. I turned around and left the hotel by a back door, went back to my office, and filed the inside story from the meeting. I did much the same a month later. I heard of the Gretzky suit when a representative of the receiver was explaining to creditors that outstanding litigation over Gretzky was one reason why they had yet to get a nickel from Skalbania. It was so absurd that the room dissolved in laughter. He never did repay that group of creditors but, somehow, bounced back to more wheeling and dealing and to live in a mansion on Point Grey Road.

Robert Friedland perplexed me. He is now in the Canadian Mining Hall of Fame, but when I first wrote about him, I thought he was just another promoter, perhaps flakier than most, who had taken over in about 1980 a shell company on the Vancouver Stock Exchange called Galactic Resources.[107] His back story made him seem dubious: born

107 I wrote a major profile of Robert Friedland, "Robert Friedland's Galactic Quest," in the *Financial Post*, July 23. 1990.

in 1950, he had been at college in Oregon in the 1970s where Steve Jobs, the founder of Apple, was said to have been a friend. "He is my role model," Friedland told me in an interview in March, 1984. "I have determined to form a major mining company." At the time, Galactic was a VSE junior that went public in 1983 and then acquired the Summitville gold project in Colorado. There had been a small mine in the area that closed in 1942. Two majors had explored there in the 1970s but gave up on the property. Friedland had no background in mineral exploration (he had graduated with a degree in political science and had owned some timber properties in Oregon), but he maintained that Summitville could become one of the largest gold producers in the United States. Galactic spent millions on developing the unsuccessful mine, which became one of Colorado's biggest environmental disasters. The company took a US$40 million write-down in 1988. The following year, when Friedland was getting the company involved in a South Carolina gold project, he actually said to me: "Galactic was born in what I would describe as a well-crafted puff of smoke and mirrors."[108] Galactic went bankrupt in 1993 after Friedland had cashed out. He next launched a gold project in Venezuela; it also was unsuccessful, but Friedland again made millions selling his shares.

His luck finally changed with a junior called Diamond Fields Resources. After the discovery of diamonds in the Northwest Territories, Canadian diamonds had become the flavour of the day among promoters like Friedland. He backed two prospectors to explore for diamond pipes in Newfoundland. They stumbled on a major nickel deposit instead. Friedland orchestrated a bidding war among majors for Diamond Fields, ending with a fortune in cash and shares of International Nickel Co., the winning bidder. That established Friedland's credibility.

In the 1990s, he had his head office in the penthouse of the Marine Building. That remains one of the most attractive office towers in Vancouver. It had been built about 1929 by the Guinness family. A member of the family lived for years in that penthouse suite, a cramped

108 *Financial Post,* May 8, 1989, page 36: "New U.S. mine restores some of Galactic's shine."

suite with terraces and fine views of the harbour. After the nickel win, Friedland's ambitions went international, and he moved his headquarters from Vancouver to Singapore. On one of the last occasions that I wrote about him, I suggested that his real headquarters was seat 1A on Singapore Airlines.

He turned out to be much more substantial than I had believed initially. In 1994, he founded Indochina Goldfields to do deals in Asia. The name was changed in 1999 to Ivanhoe Mines, borrowing the identity of Ivanhoe Capital Corp., the investment firm he started in 1987. Among other deals, Ivanhoe fostered the development of a rich copper/gold mine in Mongolia. Rio Tinto took it over in 2012. His companies also were active in such exotic places as Kazakhstan and the Democratic Republic of Congo. The flaky promoter I wrote about became wealthy enough to buy a $26 million mansion in Los Angeles in 2020, complimenting his villa in Thailand and his luxury suite in Singapore.

Margaret Witte, a rare female mining executive, provided a great deal of copy. A Nevada-born metallurgist, she had come to Canada in 1979 and set up a consulting company. Her major public company was Royal Oak Resources Inc., which she ran from 1990 to 1999. Among other assets, it owned the Giant Yellowknife Gold Mines in Yellowknife. It was a decrepit mine when Royal Oak took it over in 1991 and was then hit by a strike. Royal Oak brought in replacement workers and a hot-headed striker set off an explosion in the mine that killed nine workers. Royal Oak also had a difficult project in the Northwest Territories, the Colomac Mine, which did not succeed. She took over Geddes Resources in 1992 and tried to get its Windy Craggy copper project approved by the BC government. She did not succeed, although the province agreed in 1995 to award compensation to Royal Oak.[109] I wrote a lot about her in the summer of 1994 when Royal Oak launched an audacious takeover bid for a much larger Toronto company called Lac Minerals. She did not succeed, but she had a high profile in those years: Mining Person of the Year 1991 and Woman of

109 Royal Oak was to get $29 million in cash and another $20 million supporting mineral exploration elsewhere in BC. As well, the province said it would spend $118 million on infrastructure to help Royal Oak develop a different mine.

the Year 1995 in *Chatelaine* magazine. Royal Oak went bankrupt, but she rebounded to run other mines.

Rakesh Saxena was one of the more charming scoundrels associated with the VSE. Born in India, he was a banker in Thailand when he was attracted to the VSE in 1992 by a consultant the exchange had retained to get listings from Asia. Several problematic companies associated with Saxena were on the VSE until the VSE delisted them in 1999 to get rid of the promoter. By that time, he was three years into fighting extradition to Thailand over the failure of a Thai bank he was accused of defrauding for $80 million. When I last wrote a long feature on him in July 1999, I interviewed him by telephone because he was under house arrest in his condominium at False Creek in Vancouver. Thai police had come to Vancouver in 1996 to arrest him, finding him in Whistler with a suitcase full of Swiss francs. He had also tried to get a false Yugoslavian passport. The suits and countersuits swirling around him were rich in salacious detail—he was a plaintiff in 36 different lawsuits filed in BC. During his years in house arrest, he continued to wheel and deal in worthless penny stocks. He even was involved in plotting a military coup in Sierra Leone while under arrest.[110] I was long retired by the time the Thais succeeded in extraditing him in 2009. He received a ten-year jail sentence in 2012 in Bangkok.

Bre-X Minerals Ltd., once a listing on the VSE, became notorious for salting cores in a mineral property in Indonesia. The consultant who looked at the core samples after the fraud was exposed said that it "is without precedent in the history of mining anywhere in the world." I first wrote about the company in September, 1993. I interviewed its president, David Walsh, who was based in Calgary. He told me that he had met John Felderhof, a geologist, in Indonesia in 1983. Walsh originally set up Bre-X in 1989 to get into the Northwest Territories diamond play. When I wrote about him, he was re-focussing the company on the so-called "Ring of Fire" and had several exploration properties in Indonesia. Over the next several years, the reported drilling results from one of those properties got better and better. In June

---

110 David Baines in the *Vancouver Sun*, August 6, 2012.

1995, Bre-X announced an estimated reserve of 2.4 million ounces from just one zone. By late July, with the release of more drill holes, analysts were talking of eight million ounces.[111] By August 1996, there was suggestions that Bre-X had a fifty-million-ounce resource. In a final conference call to analysts that I listened to, it was suggested the reserve might be two hundred million ounces. One analyst told me that this could be the largest undeveloped gold reserve in the world. Bre-X had a market value of $6 billion. In January, 1997, Placer Dome proposed taking over Bre-X. Then Freeport-McMoRan, a major, became involved. A review of the core samples showed no significant gold. Michael de Guzman, the project manager, was said to have jumped from, or was pushed from, a helicopter over the Indonesian jungle in 1997. Bre-X imploded. Death from a brain aneurysm in 1998 spared Walsh from court. Felderhof faced a series of fraud and insider trading charges in Ontario but, with the help of a very good lawyer, was exonerated. He died in 2019 in the Philippines where he had settled.

C. Calvert Knudsen was one of my favourite executives, and not just because he was a major figure in the Oregon wine industry. Cal came to Vancouver from Tacoma in the fall of 1976 after he had been recruited from Weyerhaeuser to be the chief executive at MacMillan-Bloedel Ltd. I did my first article on him on August 21, 1976, commenting on his "informal manner" and on the fact that "he is an investor in three West-Coast vineyards."[112] MacMillan-Bloedel was then the largest forest products company in British Columbia. It was a corporate icon, headquartered in a tower on Georgia Street designed by Arthur Erickson, then the major architect in Vancouver. The company had been run from 1957 to 1972, and with a firm hand, by the legendary former judge, J.V. Clyne. In 1975, when I did a profile of him, he still had an expansive office on the twenty-sixth floor of the MacMillan-Bloedel building.[113] At the end of the interview, I had him in my viewfinder for

111 *Financial Post*, July 28, 1995: "Hot Stock—Bre-X Minerals soars on Indonesia gold play."

112 *Financial Post*, August 21, 1976: "MB's new chief expects U.S. market recovery."

113 The building was renamed the Arthur Erickson Building in 2021 since the MacMillan Bloedel name has disappeared from corporate usage.

a photograph when I noticed greenery in the background. Stupidly, I asked if the trees were real. His reply was a snort of exasperation that I should even think the former chief of the province's largest forest company would have artificial trees in his office.[114]

It was said a few years later that, from his perch on the twenty-sixth floor, Clyne interfered with the executives then running the company. Cal came on the scene five months after the MacMillan-Bloedel board had fired both chief executive Dennis Timmis and chairman George Currie, who were no longer on speaking terms with each other after the company suffered a major loss due to a ship chartering fiasco. To turn the company around, Cal was forced to terminate one hundred management staff. The *Vancouver Sun* savaged him as "King Kut." It was cheap journalism. Curiously, he did not get a similar treatment in 1982 when he terminated 1,400 to dig out MacMillan-Bloedel from under major losses caused by a recession. He left MacMillan-Bloedel in 1983 and returned to the United States.

I had discovered soon after he arrived that Cal was in the wine business. He had a vineyard in Oregon and was the co-owner from 1975 to 1988 of the Knudsen-Erath winery. The challenge was that we both preferred talking about wine rather than about the forest industry. After he returned to United States, he dissolved his partnership with Dick Erath and, in 1988, took over Argyle Winery. Weyerhaeuser took over MacMillan-Bloedel in 1999.

Ross Fitzpatrick was another executive about whom I wrote extensively, both because of his ownership of CedarCreek Estate Winery and his mining activities. In the early 2000s, he even commissioned me to write a book about the winery. I had already included a short biography of him in my 1996 book, *The British Columbia Wine Companion:*

> **Fitzpatrick, Ross (1933-):** The proprietor of *CedarCreek Estate Winery*, Fitzpatrick is the Renaissance Man of British Columbia wine, given his many other interests. He was born in Kelowna, the son of a fruit-packing house executive and

---

114 *Financial Post,* July 12, 1975: "He may have mellowed, but those strong views remain."

the grandson of farmers who had settled in the Okanagan in 1913.

Fresh from the University of British Columbia with a commerce degree, Fitzpatrick worked for a royal commission on the fruit industry, then enrolled at Columbia University in New York for a master of business administration degree and in 1963, before having time to write a thesis, he went to Ottawa as an executive assistant to Liberal cabinet minister John Nicholson. Fitzpatrick's three years in Ottawa left him with a lifelong interest in politics and a close friendship with Jean Chretien, then an ambitious young politician from Quebec who became the prime minister of Canada, with Fitzpatrick managing Liberal party affairs in British Columbia for Chretien.

The business career that Fitzpatrick took up after returning to the West from Ottawa in 1966 included a successful aircraft parts brokerage firm in Seattle, a successful Calgary oil company, and a successful Vancouver company, Viceroy Resource Corp., with a gold mine in California.

Fitzpatrick's entry into the wine business was a matter of chance. He sought an Okanagan orchard as a weekend hobby farm and found an attractive lakeside property on the Okanagan Lake south of Kelowna, just across the road from struggling Uniacke Estate Winery [one of the early estate wineries]. The owners of Uniacke sold the winery to Fitzpatrick who renamed it after CedarCreek, which flows through the property, and soon found winemaking more compelling than apple growing. A demanding taskmaster and a perfectionist, Fitzpatrick changed the winemaker at CedarCreek three times in the first decade under his ownership, in a quest to produce both red and white table wines of award-winning finesse.

I always looked forward to interviewing Ross in the Viceroy offices in Vancouver and subsequently in Kelowna. As happened with Cal Knudsen, we spent as much time talking about wine as about the affairs of Viceroy. And there was a bonus: his offices always served excellent coffee.[115] By 1996, he had left Viceroy and moved his office to Kelowna to manage a junior called Channel Resources Ltd., which was exploring in Burkina Faso. I don't believe anything came of it. In 1998, he was appointed a senator and had his plate full with Liberal politics again. He had long since given his son Gordon responsibility for running CedarCreek and the sister winery, Greata Ranch, which had opened near Peachland in 2003. CedarCreek was sold in 2013 to Anthony von Mandl while Greata Ranch was transformed into Fitzpatrick Family Vineyards, a sparkling wine producer managed by Gordon.

Sam Belzberg, who died in 2018 at age eighty-nine, generated a great deal of copy in the 1980s as a "greenmailer." That was jargon for a certain type of corporate raider. Greenmailers accumulated undervalued shares in public companies prior to launching takeover bids. I first wrote about Sam in April 1971, when he was forty-three and putting together First City Financial Corp., his major company over the next decade or so. By coincidence, the *Financial Post* Vancouver office at the time was in the First City building at 777 Hornby Street. In May 1985, I did a cover story on Sam in *BC Business Magazine*.[116] On reading it today, I cannot tell whether Sam gave me an interview—but there was so much about him on record that the story almost wrote itself.

Sam's First City Financial Corp., as an example, accumulated a position in 1979 in Bache, then a major American brokerage firm. To ward him off, Bache negotiated a merger with another big financial company, and Sam's company pocketed a big capital gain after it tendered its Bache shares.

In February 1992, I shared a byline with Susan Gittins, a colleague in Toronto who did most of the reporting, for a major piece on the surprising unravelling of First City.[117] The company failed because it had taken on too much debt and because several takeovers had backfired. The final greenmail attempt was thwarted by anti-takeover legislation

115 On another occasion, I was interviewing Gerald Hobbes, the president of Cominco Ltd., who was a cold fish. He poured himself a cup of coffee but never offered one to me.

116 *BC Business Magazine*, May, 1985, pp. 23–29: "Move over, Bay Street."

117 *Financial Post*, February 24, 1992: "Rise and fall of Belzberg Empire."

in the state of Pennsylvania, leaving First City with shares that tanked and had to be sold at a huge loss. By early 1992, Sam was not giving interviews. The message on his office answering machine was whimsical: "I might be here; I might be there. Who knows? I might be anywhere." Sam later became a major philanthropist, but I never had an occasion to write about him again.

Jim Pattison was always good for a story, if only to recount his rags to riches journey. That he was born in Luseland, Saskatchewan (in 1928), meant we had Prairie roots in common, slim as that is. He started as a used-car salesman. By the time I starting writing about him, his Jim Pattison Group was one of Canada's largest private business conglomerates. His public profile emerged in 1985 when Bill Bennett talked him into becoming the chair of the floundering Expo 86 world's fair. Pattison imposed much needed discipline on the organization, delivering a fair that was very successful and that transformed Vancouver into a world city. Pattison accepted $1 a year for his services. A few months after the fair, I did a post-Expo interview with him. Among other topics, we discussed various pavilions. The Cuban pavilion, he told me, was the biggest disappointment. (I also thought it was poor.) Pattison said that the Cubans sent flowers to his secretary, to his wife, and even to his mother. If the Cubans had spent as much on the pavilion as they spent on flowers, he told me, the pavilion would have been far better. Fidel Castro, the Cuban leader, had agreed to come to Vancouver and pitch at a Vancouver Canadians baseball game. Unfortunately for Expo '86, the Canadian government vetoed the idea because it would be hard to guarantee Castro's safety.

In a short piece in the *Financial Post* magazine in the summer of 1988, I noted that Pattison's company had revenues of $1.6 billion in 1987. The article discussed Pattison's views on free trade. "We've got a chance to access the biggest and most prosperous market in the world," he told me, referring to the United States. "We couldn't ask for anything better." Over the next thirty years, revenues of the Jim Pattison Group rose to $10 billion.

Pattison's deals were often in the news after he emerged from Expo. In 1987, he owned the Vancouver Blazers, a team in the unsuccessful

World Hockey Association. In 1988, he proposed buying the struggling BC Lions football team for $6 million, something I noted in an article in December. He never did buy the team.

His lifestyle has never seemed flashy, although his net worth, according to *Forbes* magazine, had reached US$12 billion in 2022. I interviewed him one December afternoon in 1996.[118] Our appointment was at 3:00 p.m. He had not had lunch. He asked Enzo Centrone, the personal assistant who had been with him since 1961, what he might have. "Anything you want," he was told. He asked for a peanut butter sandwich—and offered me one. The subsequent interview was pleasant, with Pattison evasive about details as always, but disclosing just enough detail so I could do an article. At the end of the interview, he accompanied me to the foyer while I retrieved my coat. Then in an afterthought, he took me to the window to show me the Christmas lights newly installed on his yacht, tied up sixteen floors below in the harbour. The lights were not on, so he had the receptionist call the yacht to have them turned on. We chatted amiably for another ten minutes until the lights warmed up. That yacht, and a larger one purchased subsequently, were one of his few ostentatious luxuries in Vancouver.[119] Marlene and I were among the guests invited on one occasion for a dinner cruise into Howe Sound on a Friday evening in summer. After dinner, someone sat down at the piano; Pattison joined on his trumpet for an informal singalong.

Pattison has had a practice of taking over public companies starting with a modest block of shares and building his position until he can acquire all the shares. On one occasion, the final annual meeting that took Great Pacific Enterprises Ltd. private in May 1997 was at 4:00 p.m. on a Friday afternoon before a long weekend. As a bit of a tease, I

---

118 *Financial Post*, December 27, 1996: "Private progress."

119 He also bought Frank Sinatra's house in Palm Springs in the mid-1990s, to be used for corporate retreats. In the hyper early years of *National Post*, I was asked to chase down a rumour that Pattison had sold it. While I was trying to reach him—he was travelling—I had to write an article based on the rumour. Fortunately, Pattison returned my phone calls just before the newspaper went to press. The rumour had been incorrect.

showed up to cover the meeting. There was not a single minority share-holder there. While the lawyers and the accountants went through the formalities, I chatted with Pattison about a recent business book both of us had read (it may have been *Barbarians at the Gate*).

I did not encounter Pattison during my subsequent wine writing career. Someone recounted a rumour that I question. Pattison had been a lifelong teetotaler. The rumour had it that he asked his doctor what to include in his diet to live to one hundred. The doctor advised two glass of Malbec every evening, and Pattison is said to have complied. He did emerge as a major player in the wine business when his Save-On-Foods supermarket chain began buying the private wine stores marketing VQA wines under licenses controlled by the British Columbia Wine Institute. Pattison became the biggest retailer of BC VQA wines by far.

Jack Poole's meteoric business career provided a good deal of copy. My first lengthy piece on him was published in mid-1975 when his company, Daon Development Corp., had just extracted itself from a liquidity squeeze.[120] The company then had commercial buildings in Vancouver and Calgary and a land bank near Calgary. In 1978, I did a lengthy profile of him in *Kanata*, the inflight magazine of CP Air. He had formed Daon (with Graham Dawson) in 1964. By the late 1970s, the company was Canada's sixth largest property developer. Jack was a magnetic personality with a great story. He told me that he was so bored as a management trainee with Gulf Oil that he took a part-time job with the Fuller Brush Company. "It introduced me to selling," he told me. "I didn't know I was interested in selling."[121]

At its collapse in the early 1980s, Daon was the second-largest development company in North America. The company was overextended at a time of recession and very high interest rates. He had expanded into California in 1976. Accompanied by George Macfarlane, his publicist, I travelled to San Francisco and Los Angeles twice to look at the projects and interview the executives on the ground. George was a baseball fan, so we went to a game at Candlestick Park one evening in 1978.

120 *Financial Post*, July 19, 1975: "Daon Development has built a sturdy house."

121 *Kanata*, Volume 1, Number 1, 1978: "Jack Poole: In business as in sports there are the naturals."

On another occasion, when baseball players were on strike, I arranged a trip one Saturday to taste wine in the Napa Valley. I was no longer writing about business when Jack was appointed head of the organizing committee for the Vancouver 2010 Olympics. Sadly, he died of cancer in 2009 and did not get to see what a great success those games were.

One of the most delicate pieces of my reporting involved a junior mining company called Sutton Resources Ltd., which became involved in a nasty proxy battle. One of its senior executives was Roman Shklanka. He and his wife Pat (a contemporary of mine at the University of Saskatchewan) had been our friends since we both lived in Toronto in the 1960s. Roman had become a senior executive with Placer Dome Inc. where, among other things, he evaluated both a gold property and a nickel property in Tanzania. Placer decided not to develop them. After Roman left Placer, he brought the properties to the attention of Sutton, a junior mining company in Vancouver. Roman joined Sutton's management, eventually becoming the second-largest shareholder and vice-chairman.

The chairman of Sutton was James Sinclair, whose wife, Barbara, was the largest shareholder with 18%. The Sinclairs had been investing in Sutton since 1986. They became unhappy with the Sutton board after the shares, which had hit $55 in 1994, plunged to $8. They also criticized a financing proposed by Sutton because it would be dilutive. When they tried to fire Sutton directors and management in late 1995, Sutton dumped Sinclair as chair, replacing him with Roman. The proxy fight that ensued became quite bitter. I covered the financial brawl without blowing up a friendship. Roman and his fellow managers won. Sutton then sold the Tanzanian gold project to Barrick, and Roman netted one of his several fortunes. Barrick developed the gold mine.[122]

122 *Financial Post*, March 23, 1996: "No stone unturned."

Twenty-seven:
Politicians I have known

In early 1989, British Columbia sent a delegation of business people and politicians, including Premier Bill Vander Zalm, to the World Economic Forum in the Swiss town of Davos. Because Neville Nankivell was keen to rub shoulders with the powerful, he generally attended the Davos conferences. I was included in the *Financial Post* contingent to Davos that year to cover Vander Zalm. Aside from an afternoon of cross-country skiing in the Alps, I managed to file two stories. I stopped in Frankfurt to interview the incoming president of Metallgesellschaft AG; the hook was that he was a director of Teck Corp. and Cominco Ltd. I also stopped in Munich to spend a day with Victor Sabal, my friend from his Löwenbrau days. Because he was a keen political observer, I gathered enough material to write a column on the perceived popularity of the Soviet Union's leader, Mikhail Gorbachev. That was typical of my wide-ranging interests.

Vander Zalm had been premier since 1986, and I had concluded he was a charming lightweight. His Davos presentation did nothing to change my mind. One point in his favour: he created the farmgate winery licences in 1989 that enabled growers with less than the twenty-acre (ten-hectare) minimum vineyard required for estate wineries to open their own wineries and stay in the business. Some of the Okanagan's best wineries, notably Wild Goose Vineyards, Quails' Gate Estate Winery, and Hillside Winery, opened with the farmgate licence.

I covered the Social Credit leadership convention in the fall of 1986 that chose Vander Zalm, a flamboyant populist, from a large field of more substantial candidates, including Kim Campbell, later the last Progressive Conservative prime minister. She nailed it when she characterized Vander Zalm as "charisma without substance." He flailed about so much as premier that I once wrote a column proposing the construction of a British Columbia version of Mount Rushmore. I suggested it have the image of four premiers: Amor de Cosmos (meaning lover of the universe); Sir Richard McBride (he bought two submarines for the Canadian Navy in World War I); W.A.C. Bennett (a great builder); and Vander Zalm. "Why?" I wrote. "So that people would look up and ask, 'What the hell is he doing there?'"

Here I was beside him at a dinner in Davos. While the oyster soup was being served, he recited a litany of his food phobias. He was soon to travel to China and dreaded all the strange foods he would face. I thought to myself that if the food sustained a billion Chinese, it would not kill a transplanted Dutchman. Later, at a BC dinner in Davos, he lauded a Hong Kong tailor who had made him an $18 shirt—this in front of an audience that included some of the world's richest men. Vander Zalm resigned in 1991 over a scandal involving the marketing of his Fantasy Gardens, a faux Dutch village he had built in Richmond. In a May 1991, column, I lampooned his and the Social Credit administration with a string of quotes from Shakespeare's *Macbeth*. Such as this: "I would not be the villain that thou thinkst." Writing about him was shooting ducks in a barrel.

He was one of many political leaders I came to know. The one I most admired was Tommy Douglas, who was premier of Saskatchewan when I joined *Regina Leader-Post*. In an era of accessible politicians, he was one of the most accessible. His home number was listed in the Regina phone book. He often walked to work, usually arriving about 8:30 a.m. He would take my phone call, and he often lunched with civil servants and journalists in the legislative cafeteria. On more than one occasion, we were side by side in the cafeteria lineup. It seemed he always had poached eggs on toast with a dish of prunes, apparently because he had a stomach problem.[123] His speeches in the legislature could be inspirational, reflecting his background as a Baptist clergyman. His final speech at the end of each session invariably ended with reference to the New Jerusalem his government aimed to create. It was not an idle boast. He came to power in 1944 as Saskatchewan was recovering from the Depression. He brought in public hospital insurance in his first year; his successor, Woodrow Lloyd, completed the suite of services in 1962 with North America's first public medical insurance.

The Douglas government also brought in public power. Once when Douglas was flying across Saskatchewan in a small aircraft, he was asked what he regarded as his finest achievement. He pointed out of the window to the twinkling farm lights and said: "rural electrification." I had experienced that. I came home at Christmas during my first year at university to discover that our farm had been hooked up to the power grid. My parents had quickly purchased a freezer, a refrigerator—and a television set. Their favourite program, I discovered, was wrestling. I had just taken six weeks of wrestling at university, enough to be able to comment on the phony moves of TV wrestlers. My wet blanket commentary was not appreciated.

During my career, I interviewed several other Saskatchewan's premiers. I remember Ross Thatcher as bombastic and occasionally irresponsible. Once, when he was Opposition leader, and I was writing for *The Regina Leader-Post*, I dropped into his office to get a comment on something the CCF government had just announced. He asked me for a summary and, based on that, launched into his criticism of the measure. I learned years later from Ed Whelan, a veteran NDP politician, that Thatcher was a diabetic who did not take care of himself. On several occasions, he went into diabetic comas in the premier's office and was rushed to Grey Nun's Hospital where, for security reasons, he

---

123 This was not unusual. Historian Bill Waiser, in his 2005 book, *Saskatchewan: A New History*, wrote: "There was also nothing fancy about [Douglas]. If he was working in the legislature, he invariably took his lunch in the basement cafeteria and always had the same standing order: poached eggs, tomato juice, and prunes. Official visitors sometimes joined him in line and dined on trays at the arborite tables."

was put in the maternity ward for treatment. The hospital had a code for when he was there: "Ross is having a baby." His government was roundly defeated in June 1971, and Thatcher died of a heart attack a month later. Allan Blakeney and Roy Romanow ran successive NDP governments with general competence, with the exception of nationalizing the potash industry, which Blakeney announced in November 1975. I was in Regina to cover the Throne Speech in which the plans to get into the potash business were announced. This move emanated from the province's desire to tax the industry more aggressively. There was something called the potash reserves tax, which the mining companies challenged in court. The move also was triggered by another fact: potash prices were soaring, but no new mines were under development in Saskatchewan.[124] The Minister of Mines, who later became a good friend, was Ed Whelan. Before he got into politics, he was selling home insurance in Regina. I bought my first policy from him.

When Romanow took over from Blakeney in 1987, I interviewed him during a campaign rally in Yorkton, a small city with a significant Ukrainian flavour. I led the article with an anecdote about his Ukrainian roots; his father had been among the many Ukrainians who had immigrated to Saskatchewan earlier in the century. I wrote: "The roots are deep enough that earlier, during a brief meal break, Romanow settles for a Denver sandwich after expressing surprise that the Corona [Hotel] coffee shop menu has no Ukrainian specialities."

Grant Devine came into power in 1982 as a Conservative, defeating Blakeney; his model was Britain's Margaret Thatcher, and he returned a number of public enterprises, including potash, back to private hands. I interviewed him several times and did not think he was very substantial. In August 1985, I spent some time following him on a pre-election tour. I remember it mostly for the lead I wrote on one article about his stop in the hamlet of Big Beaver: "This hamlet in Southern Saskatchewan is so small that there is one block to the main street and only one name on the war memorial."[125] At the end, his government

124 *Financial Post*, November 22, 1975: "The potash portfolio."
125 *Financial Post*, August 5, 1985: "Liberal revival threatens Devine."

collapsed in scandal, and Romanow easily won the election. He was premier until 1991 and then had a distinguished career in public life and academia.[126]

I wrote about Ralph Goodale in 1983 when, at the age of thirty-three, he took over leadership of the Saskatchewan Liberal party. He had entered politics at the age of twenty-four when he was elected a Member of Parliament in 1974. It was the beginning of his long career, mostly in federal politics. He was not defeated until 2019—and then he was given an assignment by the prime minister during the COVID-19 crisis. He was a likeable politician and one who seemed capable to take on anything that came along. In 2021, he was appointed the Canadian High Commissioner in London, capping his long and effective years in public service.

My admiration for Tommy Douglas created a long residue of sympathy for centre-left politicians, including Lester B. Pearson, the Nobel Peace Prize winner who became prime minister in the early 1960s. I remember him during the 1956 or 1957 campaign speaking from the stage of Convocation Hall at the University of Saskatchewan. The campus Progressive Conservatives had placed a coffin in the stage with "Liberal Party" on the outside. Pearson put a foot on the coffin and remained in that position to deliver his speech. I voted for his party.

A few years later, I was on the other side. After we moved to Toronto, I joined the New Democratic party in the York South constituency and eventually became the riding president. I do not recall being terribly effective because I worried about the repercussions if the *Financial Post* managers took notice. Our candidate was David Lewis, who later succeeded Tommy Douglas as national NDP leader. I knocked on doors for him in three election campaigns (he won two of them). David was one of the finest political orators I ever heard; better than Tommy and certainly better than Lester. In the final campaign in which I was involved, David went across the country inveighing against "corporate welfare bums." He was criticizing corporations taking quite legal advantage

---

126 I did a major profile of Roy Romanow in the *Financial Post* on December 3, 1990: "Romanow: A premier in waiting."

of tax write-offs allowed under federal rules. In my view, David was setting up straw men and that was dishonest.

I did not support the NDP again until 1975, when I voted for Dave Barrett, the one-term NDP premier. He had been elected in 1972 and promptly shook up a province that had been run very conservatively for twenty years by the Social Credit under W.A.C. Bennett. Among other things: no one remembers it, but he outlawed pay toilets. Much of his legislation was very contentious and occasionally ill-conceived. In a broadcast I did for the CBC in October 1975, I said: "Dave Barrett in politics reminds me of George Patton in war: constantly in hot water but always ready with a bold, tactical move." The Barrett government established a public car insurance company—and the employees promptly went on strike for a first collective agreement. Eventually, Barrett had to legislate an end to a number of strikes in 1975. The government set up a petroleum corporation and tried, without success, to get an oil refinery started. There was also a feasibility study in establishing a steel mill in the province, among other grand gestures. Mining companies left the province in droves when the NDP brought in a super-royalty to capture windfall profits after there was a huge spike in copper and other mineral prices.

In March 1975, I did a short profile of Frederick Higgs, who was then taking over as manager of the BC & Yukon Chamber of Mines. He told me that he had just helped an exploration geologist from British Columbia find a job in Zambia.[127] Heavy taxes and regulatory measures devastated the mining industry, while also bleeding into other parts of the economy. For example, in September 1975, I reported that the Vancouver Stock Exchange was suffering a major erosion of trading volumes and revenues. Half of the VSE's 650 listings were junior mining companies. Cyril White, the VSE president at the time, told me: "If we continue to lose money as we have, there will come a time when the governors would have to give serious consideration to whether we should remain as an exchange."[128]

127 *Financial Post*, March 22, 1975: "B.C., Yukon mining fear exodus of funds and to professionals."

128 *Financial Post*, September 20, 1975: "One by one, VSE had its trading options trimmed."

Barrett's government was undermined not just by its own efforts but by the militant labour movement. In November 1975, he had called an election, only to be defeated by Bill Bennett. It was a feisty campaign and one I enjoyed covering, judging from the tone of articles I wrote. Barrett's campaign rhetoric was colourful; Bill Bennett campaigned so hard that he lost his voice.[129] Barrett lost two successive elections to Bennett and was a bitter man when he retired.

Bill Bennett grew into the premiership. I first interviewed him when he was a raw politician during the 1975 campaign. We met for lunch in Hy's Steakhouse. As taut as a fiddle string, he drank copious cups of coffee while he railed about the damage the NDP were doing to the province. But when he took power, he did not unwind all of Barrett's policies. Critically, he kept the professional civil service struc-ture Barrett had put in place to succeed the ossified civil service from the W.A.C. Bennett era. Unlike his father, Bill was not a teetotaler; in fact, it was widely, if inaccurately, rumoured he had a drinking problem. While some controversy surrounded his resignation in 1986, he had run an effective government, which is more than could be said for Bill Vander Zalm.

Bill Bennett's administration was tough—he wrestled down the deficit Barrett had left, and he also took on the militant unions, very nearly causing a general strike. My view is that he ran a generally good administration, perhaps with the exception of his one excursion into capitalism for the people. In January 1979, the province announced that it would distribute to every citizen five free shares of British Columbia Resources Investment Corp. BCRIC had been set up the year before; its assets included 81% ownership of a Prince Rupert pulp mill and 2.3 million acres (930,777 hectares) of oil and gas rights. Giving away free shares primed the public for a public offering later in 1979. The share offering raised $425 million. Over the next decade, BCRIC pro-vided a great deal of copy and was ultimately a failure. David Helliwell, BCRIC's under-qualified chairman, found himself under enormous pressure to invest the cash—and overpaid for Edgar Kaiser's oil and

---

129 *Financial Post,* October 25, 1975: "Old-time politics and shrewd policies."

coal assets. By December 1980, Helliwell was elevated to chairman, and Bruce Howe, a brash young executive, was recruited from MacMillan Bloedel.[130] The business spent a decade going sour until there was not much value left in BCRIC. The debacle, however, never stuck to Bill Bennett.

Bennett's toughness showed early in 1979 when Canadian Pacific Investments tried to take over MacMillan Bloedel. Bennett shut that down firmly. "We don't want to have a branch-plant in British Columbia," he said in interviews with me and my colleague, Jim Lyon.[131] And he declared in a speech that: "BC is not for sale."

On retirement, Bill returned to Kelowna and joined his older brother, Russell, in various businesses. That culminated into reputation-destroying charges of insider trading against the brothers for which the BC Securities Commission gave them ten-year trading bans in 1996. I always believed that Bill took the fall for his brother who had gotten him involved in buying the shares of Doman Industries, a major Vancouver Island lumber company. Russell was a close friend of, and owned race horses with, Herb Doman, the chief executive of the company. In 1987, Louisiana Pacific Industries of Oregon began negotiating the takeover of Doman Industries. The subsequent suspicion was that Herb told Russell who, in turn, told his brother they could profit handsomely by buying Doman shares before the Louisiana Pacific offer became public. The brothers bought almost $6 million worth of shares. Then in October 1988, Louisiana Pacific told Herb it was dropping its bid. Herb immediately told Russell, and the Bennett brothers unloaded their position before Doman Industries disclosed that the takeover was not proceeding. After the Bennetts were acquitted in provincial court of insider trading, the Securities Commission came after them. The hearing lasted sixty-seven days over twenty months. I spent many of those days covering it, filling numerous notebooks. This was an unfortunate end of Bill's public profile. He died in 2015 after a struggle with Alzheimer's disease.

130 *Financial Post*, November 8, 1980: "BCRIC gets a fast-track comer."

131 *Financial Post*, January 20, 1979: "Bennett blocks CPI's bid."

The Social Credit party was decimated, and never recovered, in the election following Vander Zalm's resignation. The New Democrats took over in 1991 under Mike Harcourt, the avuncular former mayor of Vancouver. His administration often came down on the side of environmentalists, and the 1990s had become a decade when the various environmental groups gained momentum. Some major resource projects died, among them the Windy Craggy copper project on the BC-Alaskan border. It was, and remains, the largest undeveloped copper project in North America, with the misfortune of being in a spectacular wilderness area. I wrote a column in spring of 1992 suggesting that the province tax grizzly bears because it would not collect any other revenue from the resource.[132] In June 1993, Premier Mike Harcourt announced the area would be protected permanently as a park. Mineral exploration declined sharply in British Columbia, as had happened during the Barrett administration. Major mining companies relocated exploration offices to South America. I reported that the consequences included even the permanent closure of the Engineers Club, one of Vancouver's oldest men's clubs. The manager, Horst Plaster, was a member of the Commanderie de Bordeaux, and the Commanderie had had at least one dinner there.

In another column that spring, I wrote: "The premier is dedicated to process and consultation, perhaps to a fault. There are gender-balanced committees seeking public input on everything but the premier's taste in ties." The column criticized the political patronage that Harcourt used to appoint his sundry committees. Harcourt was an idealist, and perhaps a bit naïve. Harcourt was embarrassed by some of his appointments. For example, an economist named Robyn Allan was named president of the Insurance Corporation of British Columbia, the underwriter of car insurance. Then the newspapers discovered she had a number of penalty points on her driver's licence and had been under probation. Glen Clark, Harcourt's finance minister, stirred up major opposition with new taxes. A sales tax on legal fees was struck down when a judge ruled it unconstitutional (a ruling I called a "long bow"). An attempt to

132 *Financial Post*, April 14, 1992: "Windy Craggy battle may prove costly."

put a surcharge on houses worth more than $500,000 was withdrawn after six days of protests; I covered one of those stormy protest rallies. Clark still got a lot of tax increases through in his budget, but he had become so unpopular that Harcourt moved him to another portfolio. The protests benefitted the career of Gordon Campbell, another former Vancouver mayor who became Liberal leader and ultimately premier.

Harcourt's administration was undermined by environmentalists as well as by his own party adherents, notably by Dave Stupich who had been Dave Barrett's finance minister. Stupich also ran a charitable society in Nanaimo whose financial mismanagement damaged the Harcourt government. Harcourt resigned even though he had nothing to do with the Nanaimo scandal. Ultimately, Clark became party leader, served a controversial term as premier, and also resigned over another scandal that he had little to do with. The surprise later was that Jimmy Pattison, British Columbia's leading capitalist, then hired Clark, who was quite successful as Pattison's senior executive.

To my mind, the way Harcourt killed the expansion of Alcan's Kitimat power project in 1995 was illustrative of his inability to stand up to environmental lobbyists. He had long opposed the project, but his government nevertheless had the BC Utilities Commission review it. He released the report at the same time as announcing the project would not go ahead. The report was given to reporters at the press conference; the subsequent news stories echoed the spin in his comments and in the government's executive summary. When I read the report, I was astounded to find the BCUC believed the expansion of the dam could go ahead while still protecting the fish in the rivers. I reported Harcourt's press conference, but I also wrote a strongly critical opinion piece.[133] Harcourt surprised the province by announcing his resignation in mid-November 1995, in the wake of very bad polls. He said the party needed someone "free of some of the baggage I have been harnessed with since I have undertaken to clean up some of the problems of the past."

---

133 *Financial Post*, January 26, 1995: "Killing Kemano II is unfair to Alcan."

He was one of the last politicians I wrote about before retiring in 2001. However, I never lost an interest in public affairs. Some years later, I joined the Liberal Party of British Columbia in order to vote in a party leadership contest. The candidate I supported, George Abbott, lost to Christie Clark, who then became premier. I still believe Abbott was far more substantial.

Twenty-eight:
The prodigious freelancer

There was never a time in my writing life when I was not doing free-lance writing and broadcasting, both to supplement my income and to stretch my abilities. In the 1980s and 1990s, my freelance earnings often were 10% of my total income, The royalties from the twenty-two books I wrote accounted for some of this income but seldom a major part (excluding the years when the BC Sugar contract ballooned my earnings). Looking back on it, I wonder how my family put up with me spending so many evenings and weekends working in my den and not working around the house. It might have been hard to rein me in because I was also writing all the time for the pure love of writing.

In my years at the *Regina Leader-Post* in Regina, the initial impulse to freelance was a need to bolster my modest income. *Regina Leader-Post* salary started about $200 or $250 a month. It had risen to $325 a month by the time I was hired by the *Financial Post* in 1961.

In 1964, CBC Radio asked me to do a series of "How to Invest" broadcasts on *Trans-Canada Matinee*, a popular national afternoon program hosted by Pat Patterson. I wrote and broadcast a dozen scripts, each running seven minutes in length. The CBC offered free transcripts to listeners. We were all dumbfounded when close to two thousand were requested. Looking back on it, I was pretty audacious to take the project, considering how little I knew about the topic. But I did a great deal of home work and read some key books on the markets. And

I also had Paul Deacon, the editor of the *Financial Post,* look at and make suggestions on the scripts. He was as surprised as I was that I had pulled it off. Had I been sufficiently interested in the subject, I might have levered this into a popular book on managing money.

The file of copies of my broadcasts between 1973 and 1982 is as thick as a phone book. I probably stopped keeping hard copies when I began writing on computers and saving to disks. A number were written for a CBC segment called "Shoptalk" and dealt with trade unions and labour relations. Others dealt with economic or political issues. For example, I did a commentary in June 1973, on the impact of rising gold prices on mineral exploration in British Columbia. But my interests were extensive. In September 1976, I did a script for CBC's international service on ombudsmen, focussed on the ombudsman that New Zealand appointed in 1962—the first in the English-speaking world. I cannot tell from the script what triggered it; likely an ombudsmen's conference in Vancouver. But it was an interesting script. I also did a five-part series of broadcasts on wine in 1977.

The CBC at the time paid $45—$50 for each three-minute script. A number of my scripts were broadcast on the international service that the CBC once operated. Those scripts often were longer and paid slightly better. I seem to have milked the CBC at every opportunity. In 1973, I sometimes did scripts every two weeks.

That year, I was signing off as Jack Schreiner. In 1974, I began signing off occasionally as John, initially on the CBC International scripts and eventually on all scripts. That merits a digression to explain my name. My parents had not even settled on a name when I was born prematurely. According to Roman Catholic doctrine, I could not remain unbaptized when my survival was uncertain. It had to be done promptly in the hospital. Apparently at the suggestion of the doctor, I was baptized as Adam, my father's name. A few months later, at a second baptism in church, I was christened John Adam—although the name on my birth certificate remained Adam. I was not aware of that until, years later, I needed a birth certificate to apply for a passport. For my first two passports, I needed to have someone swear an affidavit that Adam Schreiner was also known as John Adam Schreiner. I changed my name legally to John Adam so that my birth certificate lined up with my second christening name. The legal name change eliminated the hassle of getting sworn affidavits.

My parents called me Jack to distinguish me from a cousin named John Schreiner. I grew up calling myself Jack, and writing and broadcasting as Jack. Marlene met me as Jack and continues to call me by that name. However, my byline in the newspaper had been changed from Jack to John when Paul Deacon, the editor at the time, decided *Financial Post* bylines needed to be formal. He did not ask my concurrence when the byline was changed to J.A. Schreiner. I was so incensed at not being consulted that I insisted on John for the byline. Soon after coming to Vancouver, I discovered that I was causing confusion when people called up to speak to John and I was answering the telephone as Jack. Eventually, I learned to call myself John—and came to prefer it.

Tucked away with the file of scripts is an article I did in the fall of 1973 for an American management consulting company called George S. May International. They had a newsletter or magazine called *May Trends*. The editor paid me $250 for a lengthy piece on the Canadian economy. I must have had a lot of self-confidence to take on such an assignment, but the article reads well. The Canadian economy was then running at full capacity, and the Toronto-Dominion Bank was projecting double-digit growth in business investment (except for one year) over the next eight. Canada was on the threshold of an inflationary decade that led to wage and price controls. Such a policy was already being discussed. I did not forecast it, although I hinted at the coming "energy crisis." I have no idea how May International found me. I believe this was the only article I wrote for them.

Shortly after we moved to Vancouver in 1973, I was able to start writing about wine in *Vancouver Magazine*. A note in my diary in October 1982, says I took over the *Vancouver Magazine* column that month. I cannot explain the discrepancy. In my files, I found copies of columns on Port that I did for the magazine in October 1984 and March 1986. The *Vancouver Magazine* columns, which lasted almost ten years, established my credibility as a wine writer in Vancouver. It also led to numerous hosted invitations to many wine regions, allowing me to educate myself at someone else's expense.

There were not a lot of active wine writers in Vancouver at the time. Jarvis Whitney wrote about wine for many years in *The Province*. Jurgen Gothe, who had started hosting a popular classical music program on CBC radio in 1985, had emerged as a very fine wine writer as well. Jarvis, Jurgen, and I were frequently invited to judge at the wine competitions that started in the Okanagan in 1982. Because the radio program had given him a much higher profile that I had at the time, I asked Jurgen write the introduction to *The Wineries of British Columbia* in 1994. He was generous enough to do it without a fee. "I'm a wine writer, after all," he wrote. Jurgen began writing an excellent wine column in the *Georgia Straight* in 1997 and continued to do so until 2014, the year before he died from cancer.

In the 1970s and 1980s, I wrote for various inflight magazines. *Kanata*, an inflight magazine for CP Air, published my lengthy profile of Ed Phillips, then the chief executive of Westcoast Transmission Co. He became one of my favourite executives and a source of inside gossip about other business people. He had a low-key manner and such an ability to get along with others that, as I wrote, the bureaucrats in Victoria had nicknamed him "Easy Ed."[134] This was one of several profiles I did for *Kanata*, including one at the beginning of 1978 on Jack Poole and another in the fall of 1978 on Ronald Southern, the president of Atco Industries Ltd. in Calgary.

I did regular columns for *Skyword*, the in-flight magazine for Pacific Western Airlines, beginning in about 1978. After PWA merged with Canadian Pacific Airlines to form Canadian Airlines in 1987, I also wrote for the succeeding in-flight magazine, called *Canadian*. I cannot recall how this connection came about. However, I dealt with a woman in Vernon whose marketing company edited the magazines. Apparently, I had extensive discretion when it came to choosing topics. In June 1980, I wrote about the impact of rising interest rates on mortgages, using the example of a friend renewing for one year at 16.5%.

----

134 *Kanata*, May-June 1979: "Ed Phillips."

I predicted that interest rates were close to peaking. I was not too far off. I seem to have moved from doing financial columns for *Skyword* to doing wine pieces. In March 1986, I wrote about liqueurs; in July 1986, about wine appreciation clubs; in December 1986, about Spanish wines. For *Canadian*, I did columns on the wines of Australia, New Zealand, and Champagne.

I also wrote profiles for *Skyword* as well. In September 1984, I profiled Eugene Nesmith, president of the Hongkong Bank of Canada and the man who engineered the takeover of the Bank of British Columbia from Edgar Kaiser Jr. A thorough gentleman, Eugene had joined the Bank of Montreal after high school and worked his way up until, in 1976, he was the bank's senior vice-president in Western Canada. The Hong Kong bank had recruited him in 1980. In November 1984, I wrote a profile of another banker, Jacques Seigneuret, who was running The Western and Pacific Bank. This bank had been chartered in 1982 and was taken over in 1993 by the Canadian Western Bank. I did a lot of banking stories in the 1980s because there were two banking failures and one near-failure in Western Canada, the first since the 1920s.

In June 1985, I profiled John Murchie who was then running the tea and coffee retailer that his grandfather had founded in 1894. The retail stores—several in Vancouver and one in Victoria—were eventually taken over by his wife, Gwen, after they divorced. The business subsequently was taken over by owners unrelated to the Murchies.

During the 1980s, I wrote occasional articles for *BC Business Magazine*. At the time, the editor was Joe Martin, who was incredibly slow in paying freelancers. He founded BC Business in 1973 and sold it in 1984 before setting up Cambridge House, a company that ran investment conferences. I got along well with Joe, a fellow University of Saskatchewan alumnus, but would have preferred it if the magazine had had a better cash flow.

A letter in my files indicated that I did an article in early 1987 on "Cabernet" for a Winnipeg-based magazine called *Canadian Spirit*. This was my second article, I believe. The magazine was published by Public Press, a division of United Grain Growers Ltd. (as unlikely as that seems) and the editor was Ida Osler. She had me do an article on Gray Monk Winery for the inaugural issue in the fall of 1986.

I have clippings for wine columns I wrote in 1997 and 1998 for community papers, including one called *The Vancouver Echo* and another called *West End Times*. I started writing those columns in May 1996 and was paid $30 a column from each newspaper. Tony Whitney, a former Maclean-Hunter colleague, was my editor. (I believe the publications were merged and then closed.) The long-forgotten publications were related but circulated in different parts of the city; the same columns ran in both. The headlines were usually different and sometimes a column would be edited for space. In that era, I wrote more often on international wines (Germany, California), usually based on tastings I had attended or trips to wine country. A September 1997 article on the J. Lohr Winery in San Jose clearly emerged from a trip there. A January 1998 column referred to a visit I had made (with other writers) to Cloudy Bay Winery in New Zealand. The spin in that piece was that I had insulted the winemaker, Kevin Judd, by not buying his Sauvignon Blanc at the Cloudy Bay wine shop but rather a Zinfandel from Cape Mentelle, Cloudy Bay's sister Australian winery. Apparently, I told him I could buy Cloudy Bay in Vancouver but not the Cape Mentelle wines. That anecdote was the hook for an account of how Zinfandel vines got to Australia in 1963.

In 1998 and 1999, I had a column called Wine Cellar in *Hospitality Today*, a magazine that Canada Wide Magazines & Communications published, primarily for the restaurant trade in Alberta. I assume I was recruited because the editor worked from Vancouver and knew who I was.

My best-paying wine assignments came from Peter Collum, an editor at the *Edmonton Journal*, who did annual supplements on the British Columbia wine industry in 2007 and 2008. He paid $1 a word and asked for a lot of words. For example, I was able to invoice him for $11,269.00 in 2007. I was obviously sad when those supplements ended.

The Deep Cove Crier was one of my longest but lowest paying gigs ($25 a column). I started writing the wine column from at least 2002 until 2007 as a favour to the editor, Bruce Coney. It proclaimed a

monthly circulation of 8,400 "east of the Seymour River" by free distribution. Occasionally, I would hear from a reader, but not often. I wrote
for the pleasure of writing and the love of wine. *The Crier* continued
for some years as an adjunct to the *North Shore News* but without a
wine column.

Overlapping the last few years of my *Crier* columns (called Bacchus'
Notes), I wrote columns for *The Daily Courier* in Kelowna. That opportunity came about because David Bond, a former chief economist at
the Hongkong Bank of Canada and briefly one of Mission's Hill's
presidents, complained to the editor of the newspaper that they needed
a good wine column. A rather forceful personality, David persuaded
the editor to retain me. I have clippings of columns from 2003 through
2005. The readership was good but the column was dropped after the
ownership of the newspaper changed and the editor left.

From 2003 to 2006, I wrote for a magazine published in Vancouver
called *Simply Gourmet California Style*. It was sponsored by the
California Wine Institute. I was paid $250 a column, hardly a princely
sum considering the sponsor. After that ended, I began doing a wine
column for *More Living*, a bi-monthly magazine that originated in
Nanaimo and was aimed at a Vancouver Island audience. That lasted
just a year or two, but it was not as short-lived as *Shore Things*, a glossy
and well-edited magazine launched for North and West Vancouver by
Jeff Pierce, an ex-Maclean Hunter advertising salesman. Unusual for
wine columns, he paid well—about $500 a column. I got to write six
columns, titled *First Rackings*, before the magazine folded in 2007.

Rather than freelance writing, the work I did for Bob Williams in
2004 and 2005 was consulting on wine and the fee was fair. At the time,
Williams owned The Railway Club, a well-known Vancouver night
club. As well, he and his son-in-law had opened a wine retail store, and
they decided they need some informed recommendations on stocking
it. I had known Williams and interviewed him when he was the smart-
est and most powerful minister in Dave Barrett's cabinet. It surprised
me to be asked to give him advice. He probably had forgotten (as had
I) that I took quite a shot at him in 1988 when I was writing periodic
commentaries in the *Financial Post* called Dateline Vancouver. On

this occasion, I took issue with Williams, then still in the Opposition, for criticizing Premier Bill Vander Zalm's including an executive from Krupp AG on an advisory economic council. Williams railed about Krupp's unsavoury role in supporting Nazi Germany during the war. I reminded Williams in my column that the war had ended long ago and the executive in question was just nine years old in 1933. "… What Krupp did in the past is history and nothing else," I wrote. I suppose what I wrote about Williams in 1988 (it was a lively column!) had also become history.

Between 2008 and 2015, I wrote for a magazine called *Indulge*. It was a magazine owned by Black Press and was edited by a woman named Melissa Smalley. I seem to have had a free hand with the topics. One of my first columns was about racing car drivers, such as Jarno Trulli, who were involved in vineyards and wine. One of the last columns discussed dining in Okanagan winery restaurants.

In 2001, I wrote a number of pieces for *Winetidings*[135] and earned $1,450 for my efforts. I wrote a number of articles for the magazine throughout the 1990s. Perhaps there was a change in editors at the magazine after 2001 because the assignments went to other wine writers in Vancouver. I wrote occasionally for *Wine Access, enRoute, Western Living* (which turned me down as a wine columnist), and *NUVO*. The latter is, or was, a vanity magazine published by the owner of a Vancouver jewelry business. It paid well but kept most of the wine assignments in house. However, one of my best business articles was published there in 2004: a profile of a Vancouver scientist, Julia Levy, who had developed a drug to treat macular degeneration. She gave me an extraordinary interview, so compelling that I listened to the tape again in the car on the way to the Okanagan. In 2005, I conceived of, and wrote, a profile of Blasted Church owner Evelyn Campbell, who is a certified general accountant, for the *CGA Magazine*, her profession's publication.

135 That included an article called *Courting Peter Draper*, for the March 1999 edition of Winetidings. He was an Australian winemaker with excellent credentials, who was recruited by Quails' Gate Estate Winery in 1999. Sadly, he died suddenly midway through that vintage. Rumour suggested it was a drug overdose. Later that year, I sent $50 to the Peter Draper Educational Trust.

The most miserable outlet I wrote for was CKNW, a major Vancouver radio station which aired my weekly broadcasts for three years but never paid me. This started in 2011, when I was asked for a one-off broadcast on a now-forgotten wine subject. The response was good, and the producer asked for more. From time to time, I asked to be paid at least an honorarium. I was told that would happen if an advertiser came on board to sponsor the broadcast. I doubt the CKNW marketing department even made a serious effort. My only remuneration was a lunch with the producer once at an Italian restaurant; and he had to rush back to the station after lunch. I finally quit in the fall of 2014. The producer apologized that he had "failed" me. A bit of an understatement!

My final wine column began in 2014 in a magazine called *Westcoast Homes and Design*. It circulates about four to six times a year with the *Vancouver Sun* and *The Province*. The relationship came about in a strange way. The magazine's advertising manager at the time was Peter Reisner, who had been a university classmate and friend with my son, John. The magazine, whose content was driven by the advertising, was planning a feature on a chocolatier and the editor wanted a piece pairing the chocolates with wine. Peter remembered that I was a wine writer and suggested my name. At this writing, I am into my sixth year writing for the magazine.

In addition to all that writing for other publications, I started my own wine blog in 2008 (the link is johnschreiner.blogspot.com) and so far, have posted more than 1,400 blogs. It generates no revenue because I chose to set it up, perhaps naïvely, without advertisements. At the time, I had been contributing wine items to a friend's website as a favour to support her. However, she was often slow to post my items, which annoyed me when I had newsworthy material. So I decided to take my fate in my own hands. The blog has served as a useful vehicle for posting reviews of the many wines that I am sent each season. My running joke is that I supplement my retirement income by taking the empty bottles to the recycling depot and collecting the ten-cent refund on each bottle.

Twenty-nine:
The pandemic

The world became aware of the COVID-19 outbreak late in 2019 when the Chinese government revealed that a virus had jumped from animals to humans in the city of Wuhan. Travellers soon took the virus around the world. By February 2020, communities in Northern Italy were in the news because outbreaks there began overwhelming hospitals. I was aware of that during the Vancouver International Wine Festival in the last week of February, but was not overly concerned. I attended a seminar involving a number of Italian winemakers. I even approached one participant with a question after the seminar. None of us were wearing masks or making any effort to be socially distant.

That may have been a close call. One week later, in the same convention centre in which the wine festival was held, there was a major dental conference with 40,000 delegates. This time, there was a virus outbreak and it led to the death of Dr. Denis Vincent, a dentist from North Vancouver who had been a delegate. Shortly after that, the virus got into a seniors' care home in Lynn Valley and seniors began dying. By the time that outbreak was contained in early May, twenty seniors had died at the home from COVID. Seniors were dying in care homes across the country. I became quite alarmed, noting in my diary: "Seniors of my age, especially males, are at the highest risk of dying."

By March 9, 2020, there were seventy COVID cases in Canada. By March 16, there were one hundred cases in British Columbia alone. By

March 18, the public health officer in British Columbia, Dr. Bonnie Henry, began taking measures to stop the spread of the virus, such as suspending school attendance and shutting down public events like concerts and hockey games. She began holding daily press conferences (with the health minister) to advise the public on how to deal with what was now recognized as an international pandemic comparable to the so-called Spanish flu pandemic in 1918 and 1919. By the spring of 2020, many offices, retail outlets, and churches had closed, with people working from home if they could. Seniors like Marlene and me, because seniors were especially vulnerable to the virus, kept to ourselves except for weekly visits to the grocery stores, which had begun opening for a seniors' shopping hour at 7:00 a.m. *Tuesdays At Doug's,* the informal discussion group I had joined a few years earlier, suspended in-person meetings in March. A few months later, we reconvened on Zoom.

It was during that time that I occupied myself with finishing this memoir. I was grateful to have a major project to work on, distracting me somewhat from all the negative news about the virus.

It was a very tense time. COVID-19 took over the media. The flagship morning program on CBC Radio One was expanded from ninety minutes to three hours, largely devoted to covering the pandemic for the next several months. I found myself listening to much of it, in part because the topic was as compelling as reports from the frontlines during a war. At times, that inspired fear. However, I wanted to be well-informed so that Marlene and I could take measures to avoid the disease, as we did.

I seldom missed Bonnie Henry's press conferences, which were livestreamed on the CBC, if only because her attractive good looks and her sweet personality made the information much more palatable. I had been introduced to her a few years earlier at one Vancouver International Wine Festival by Spencer Massie, who was then her husband. He and Bonnie led the four couples who founded the Clos du Soleil Winery near Keremeos. I interviewed Spencer extensively in the early days of the winery, which opened in 2008, but I had no reason to interview her because she was not active in the winery. However, the winery connection was an extra reason drawing me to her press conferences.

And I was so impressed with them that I nominated her, successfully, to be honoured with the Meyer Vineyards Tribute Chardonnay 2019. (Meyer has released a tribute Chardonnay every year since the 2006 vintage. I had refused an offer of a John Schreiner Tribute wine because of what I perceived as a conflict of interest, since I reviewed Meyer wines each year.)

In the spring of 2020, Dr. Henry was counselling self-isolation for British Columbians as a way to contain the spread of the virus. We took her advice. We stopped attending church physically (as did most people) in favour of finding Mass online. We did not limit ourselves to churches in the Vancouver diocese. Twice, we even took in Mass celebrated by the Archbishop of Singapore. At Easter 2020, I decided to get Mass from Dublin. I only realized I had the wrong country when the celebrant had a Canadian accent. It seems there is a small community near Windsor in Ontario also called Dublin. Eventually, we stumbled on Mass from St. Joseph's Basilica in Edmonton where the celebrant usually was Archbishop Richard Smith, who gave interesting and concise homilies. He was so good that, when we were able to attend Mass again in our own church in North Vancouver early in 2022, we did so with some reluctance.

Self-isolation put an end to family dinners in 2020; the last one had been a celebration of my birthday that February. At Easter, Marlene and I had dinner at home and then had a glass of wine with family members over Facetime. For Father's Day, our daughters brought take-out food from the Indian Fusion restaurant, which we ate in safety on our well-ventilated back deck. Over the summer, we had several family dinners there, confident that it was a safe place for social events when our "bubble" was limited to the family. At Thanksgiving that October, we went for a walk to Cleveland Dam with Maureen, Alison, and their families, coming back to our house where we enjoyed coffee and muffins while seated in the carport. Christmas 2020 was equally sere: we did not even decorate a tree in our living room because no one could come for Christmas dinner.

In mid-April 2020, I began to take photographs for my annual family calendar, producing a montage of COVID-19 images. Most of the previous calendars, done every year since 2008, had used photographs from our travels as the theme. There was no travel in 2020 or 2021. Instead, I took pictures of empty Vancouver streets, closed playgrounds, window displays of flowers or, in one window, a sign reading "Hope". I had images of nearly empty grocery store shelves; people bizarrely had begun to hoard toilet paper and eggs in the mistaken belief there was a shortage. I took the bus downtown one day to photograph the murals painted on closed storefronts. Downtown Vancouver was a ghost town. There were very few people around and so few cars that the city stopped collecting at parking meters for several months. My calendar turned out to be a useful record of what we endured during a year of semi-lockdowns.

In 2020 and again in 2021, for the first time in forty-five years, I did not travel to the Okanagan to visit wineries when they began reopening their tasting rooms in June 2020. That meant cancelling several signings in late April and May to launch the latest *The Okanagan Wine Tour Guide*, written with Luke Whittall. As I wrote in my diary on April 30: "My [book] was released this week. Not that anyone will notice, given that bookstores and wine shops are generally closed. I don't expect anyone will review it, since it does not deal with the coronavirus, the all-consuming media obsession."

Fortunately Luke lives in the Okanagan and was able to do a few signings. As it happened, one of the planned launch events did not go ahead for a reason unconnected with the pandemic. The book had been dedicated to Harry McWatters, who had died in 2019 after a fifty-one-year career in the wine industry. I had arranged with his daughter, Christa-Lee, to do a signing and a reception in May at the Time Winery, which Harry had opened in 2018 in a renovated movie theatre in downtown Penticton. On May 7, 2020, the week of the event, the winery filed a bankruptcy proposal. Time and a sister winery had liabilities of $17,953,699.22 against assets of $3,366,005.46. Time was closed for several months while new owners recapitalized the business. By then, it was too late to reschedule the book launch. As well, I thought the risk of getting the virus was too high to justify travelling to wineries and signing books.

There have been at least six waves of coronavirus infection throughout the pandemic, because the virus kept mutating. Donald Trump, the American president at the time, initially suggested the virus was no worse than influenza. By late August, the death toll in the United States was 180,000—more than the American death toll in the Vietnam war. (It eventually reached one million deaths by mid-2022.) Trump continued holding election rallies and refused to wear a mask. Finally, he got COVID-19 in early October and was briefly hospitalized. As irresponsible as his behaviour was during the pandemic, he deserves some credit for directing billions toward the development of vaccines. By November 2020, two American and one British vaccine were ready for release. Healthcare workers and first responders in British Columbia got the first vaccinations in this province in December. Marlene and I had our first vaccinations (with the Pfizer vaccine) on March 24, 2021, followed by the second one in June and booster shots (with Moderna) in late November.

With all those vaccines in our bodies, we were able to shake off the concern for our safety that had marked the first year of COVID-19. We had more family dinners in 2021, including a big one in September at Fishworks to celebrate our sixty-first wedding anniversary. We resumed attending Mass at Holy Trinity and we went to several concerts.

However, the waves of virus outbreaks created something of a revolving door of closings and re-openings on economic activity, including restaurants. Dr. Henry outraged restaurateurs when she ordered an early closing on New Year's Eve 2020 to prevent the celebrations from becoming super-spreading events. The restaurants had just hours of notice and thus no opportunity to make sensible arrangements for the use of the food and wine ordered for the evening. New Year's Eve in 2021 was more organized because the high number of vaccinated British Columbians made it much safer for restaurants and other public venues to operate.

By the end of April 2022, 83% of British Columbians had received two doses of vaccine against COVID-19; 52% had received a third dose. Because variants of the virus keep triggering new waves, a fourth booster dose of vaccine had begun to be administered. Marlene and I had that booster in late May 2022 and a fifth booster in November 2022.

The efforts of Dr. Henry and her colleagues to keep the majority of people alive have been remarkably contentious. Many people initially opposed vaccines, either because some thought the vaccines had been developed too quickly, or because some opposed vaccines in general. Those of us who got vaccinated each got a so-called vaccine passport, typically a bar code downloaded to a smart phone. For a year and a half, until the end of March 2022, one had to display the passport to get into restaurants and many other public venues. The need to do that impelled many vaccine-hesitant people to get vaccinated.

Then there were widespread objections when it became mandatory to wear masks in public places, like grocery stores and public transit. Early in the pandemic, Dr. Henry and some other public health officials had downplayed the use of masks as a protection against COVID-19. The recommended defence was frequent hand-washing and maintaining a distance of one meter from strangers on the street. The advice against masks proved to be wrong. When the health officials realized that, mask wearing was mandated widely and was not lifted until April 2022.

Marlene and I never hesitated to wear masks. In fact, in the summer of 2020, I decided to order a mask from the McLaren Formula 1 team. While watching the races on television, I saw that all Formula 1 drivers and officials wore masks at the races. I thought the papaya-coloured McLaren mask was especially handsome, so I ordered one from the team's website. That turned out to be ridiculously expensive. The masks were couriered from Amsterdam. By the time I paid for the masks, the courier charges, the Canadian duties, and the exchange rate, that single mask cost about $90! Ironically, I seldom wore it. Both Burrowing Owl Estate Winery and Roger Wong's Intrigue Winery produced branded masks for their tasting room. Both wineries sent samples, which we were happy to wear.

I began to take some modest risks by the spring of 2022. COVID-19 was still putting some people into the hospital and causing some deaths but that was primarily limited to the unvaccinated or to those with other health conditions. The first public tasting I attended in two years was one that Hillside Winery had to show the new label for its flagship wine, Mosaic. A group of thirty or forty wine trade people gathered in a private room at the Georgia Hotel, a well-ventilated room with a high ceiling. It seemed to me to be a safe event. A few days later, I got this startling email from the winery: "I am sorry to have to inform you that we have a confirmed case of COVID-19 amongst the people who were at our Mosaic tasting on Thursday, March 31. We wanted everyone to know in order for you to self-monitor for symptoms. This was not an invited guest, rather one of the organizers, so this is not someone who would have been seated next to you. They were in the room, however." I did not become ill after that tasting, nor after spending two afternoons in mid-May at the first Vancouver International Wine Festival in two years.

COVID-19 did touch members of our family. When John was still living in Moscow, he had two bouts of the disease. He had not been vaccinated because Russia's Sputnik vaccine was not believed to be very effective. John arranged two business trips with stopovers in London, where his British citizenship gave him access to the National Health Service's supply of Pfizer vaccines. In September, 2022, both Alison and Rodney, who were fully vaccinated, had mild cases of the disease. David and Maureen both had Covid in October, presumably having been infected during a trip to Ontario that fall.

While the virus is still around, the high level of vaccination in British Columbia allowed a return to normal business and recreational activities after two of the most risk-fraught years I have ever lived through.

Thirty:
The future

I have been fortunate to have enjoyed a long life in surprising good health, given my premature birth. Undoubtedly, my success in journalism and in wine writing owed a great deal to the support I had from Marlene during a very happy marriage. She managed the household finances, many of the household chores, and our three children, allowing me to spend a great deal of time researching, travelling, and writing.

It is largely to her credit that our children have been successful. Maureen retired in 2022 after a career in advertising and marketing. David Romanick, her husband, also retired after a series of careers that included ironworker, geoduck diver, and latterly Canada Post letter carrier. They have two children. Adam became a recreational administrator after getting a degree at Langara College. Sylvie has done travel industry studies at Capilano University.

Alison earned a bachelor's degree in psychology at the University of British Columbia but ended up with a career in the financial industry—with several brokerage houses, a money management firm, and latterly, doing research and technical support at Blue Shore Financial in North Vancouver. Her husband, Rodney Cameron, an immigrant to Canada from Britain, has pursued a career in the printing industry, primarily as an estimator. Alison paused her financial industry career to raise three boys. James, the oldest, has studied at the University of Ottawa and aspires to get into sports management. Alison's twins,

Rob and Joey, who are not identical, entered Simon Fraser University and University of Victoria respectively in 2022 after graduating from Handsworth High School in North Vancouver. They were among the top students in their graduating class, where Rob won the most outstanding student award.

While both daughters live with their families in North Vancouver, John, our son, has not lived in Canada since graduating in Asian studies from the University of British Columbia and moving to Taiwan in 1992. He worked and studied there for two years, then worked in Hong Kong for five years before moving to London in 1999. The following year, he joined IMAX Corp., the Canadian company that has theatres around the world. After selling IMAX franchises from London for five years, he moved to Moscow. A natural salesman, he turned Russia, now with more than fifty IMAX theatres, into the world's third largest IMAX territory after the United States and China. However, Russia's invasion of Ukraine in early 2022 resulted in a wide range of sanctions against Russia that devastated the IMAX business there because the theatres no longer got major Hollywood films. That forced John to move back to London in mid-2022 and then on to Dublin as an officer at the IMAX subsidiary there. His sales territory now is Europe.

The international isolation of Russia, which is justified in my view, caused serious difficulties with John's family. He had three children with his second wife, Olga, who is Russian and lives in Moscow. They divorced in 2020 and have shared custody of the children: twins Michael and Alexandra and their younger sister, Eva. Since he is no longer working in Russia, John needs a visa to visit his children in Moscow, where he still owns a dacha, or to bring the children to Britain or Ireland. The children, who also have British and Canadian citizenships as well as Russian citizenship, need various valid passports to travel. The ban on flights between Russia and Western Europe, put in place early in 2022, forces travel to and from Moscow to transit through Dubai or Istanbul. It is all complex and expensive, reducing John's contacts with his children (and ours, too) largely to Facetime, Zoom, and similar internet apps.

Russia's Orwellian politics have reinforced how fortunate my family and I are to have been born Canadian. This is a prosperous and peaceful country that has become better and better throughout my life. My account in this memoir of how Canadian wines went from mediocre to world class in a generation is just one example. Our grandchildren, even the ones now in Russia, should be able to achieve so much more in their generation.

John Schreiner in November 2019

Index

A

B

British Columbia Resource Investment Corp. 264,
British Museum 185
Brno 181
Brouwer, Ted 209, 217
Buenos Aires 178, 179
Bukowina 1, 2, 3, 4, 5
Burns Foods 268
Burrowing Owl Winery 202, 203, 206, 230, 308
Busnardo, Joe 191, 196, 218

C

Calgary Herald 53
Calendars 58, 250, 306
California Wine Institute 300
Calona Winery 99, 155, 158, 192, 197, 198, 204, 205, 206
Cameras 58, 105, 110, 121, 247-250, 269
Cameron, Rodney 78, 310
Campbell, Evelyn 192, 301
Canada Department of Labour job offers 55
Canadian Chamber of Commerce meetings 54
Canadian Pacific Airlines, flight attendant uniforms 138-139
Canadian Pacific Railroad 1, 10, 19, 63, 84, 222,
Canadian Trade Office in Taipei 124
Capozzi family 204, 205, 206
Carménère grape 177
Casabello Winery 155, 198, 199, 232, 233
Casa del Bosque winery 177
CBC Radio 52, 294, 295
CedarCreek Estate Winery 208, 231, 242, 243, 276
Champagne 167, 298
Chardonnay and Friends 234, 235
Chateau Gai winery 233
Château Lafite Rothschild invests in Chile 175
Château Mouton Rothschild 153, 170

E

F

Fargo truck 36
Farmgate wineries 210, 230, 283
Financial Post 52-62, 90-95
Fipke, Charles 256
First City Financial Corp. 278-279
Fitzpatrick, Gordon 243
Fitzpatrick Family Vineyards 278
Fitzpatrick, Ross 208, 242, 276-277
Flanagan, Glen 94
Fordham Johnson, J.W. X, 221, 222
Formula 1 motor racing 42, 308
Francis, Diane 92, 145
French fry vending machines 265
French lessons 84
Friedland, Robert 271-273
Front de Libération du Québec 87
Fujita, Tak 114

G

Gallo brothers 205
Gattinger, Joe 146, 261
Gattinger, Oly 146
Gehringer, Walter and Gordon 236, 241
Geisenheim Research Institute 190, 238
George S. May International 296
German Wine Academy 160
Ghezzi, Carlo 205
Ghezzi, Guiseppe 204
Ginter, Ben 212-213
Gismondi, Anthony 168
Givton, Albert 190
Globe & Mail newspaper 90, 93, 94, 118, 143, 144, 171
Godfrey, John 91

Liquor Control Board of Ontario 150, 229
Liquor Distribution Branch 152, 188
Little Mosque on the Prairie 19
Little Straw Vineyards 193
Lodge Road residence 77
Lodi 172
Loewen Group 93, 269-270
Loewen, Ray 269-270
Long, Zelma 151-152
Lougheed, Evans 198, 217, 232-233
Lovell, Sir Bernard 106
Löwenbrau brewery 107, 283
Lungarotti winery 157
Lupin Mine 253
Lysyk, Kenneth 251
Lyon, Jim 141, 220, 290

M

Mabel (pony) 12
Mackay, Marguerite 254
Maclean-Hunter 54, 55, 56, 91, 92
Mair, Rafe 97
Malaysia 131-132
Mannix family 266-267
Marlene, courtship 26-32
Marcos, Ferdinand 127, 134
Maréchal Foch grapes 158, 201, 204
Marsala 169
Martin, Jeff 204
Masks 308
Mason & Risch piano 75
Massie, Spencer 304
Mathias, Philip 138
Matkin, James 99, 101

S

U